T0305393

The Political Economy of International Finance in an Age of Inequality

To Bob Pollin: my great friend and PERI "comrade in arms"

The Political Economy of International Finance in an Age of Inequality

Soft Currencies, Hard Landings

Edited by

Gerald A. Epstein

Professor of Economics and Co-Director, Political Economy Research Institute (PERI), University of Massachusetts-Amherst, USA

 Edward Elgar
PUBLISHING

Cheltenham, UK • Northampton, MA, USA

Published by
Edward Elgar Publishing Limited
The Lypiatts
15 Lansdown Road
Cheltenham
Glos GL50 2JA
UK

Edward Elgar Publishing, Inc.
William Pratt House
9 Dewey Court
Northampton
Massachusetts 01060
USA

A catalogue record for this book
is available from the British Library

Library of Congress Control Number: 2018954369

This book is available electronically in the **Elgar**online
Economics subject collection
DOI 10.4337/9781788972635

ISBN 978 1 78897 262 8 (cased)
ISBN 978 1 78897 263 5 (eBook)

Typeset by Servis Filmsetting Ltd, Stockport, Cheshire
Printed and bound by CPI Group (UK) Ltd, Croydon CR0 4YY

Contents

Contributors

Mohit Arora is a doctoral candidate in the Department of Economics at the University of Massachusetts-Amherst, USA. His research interests are international finance and development economics (particularly issues concerning industrialization in developing countries). Prior to joining the doctoral program at the University of Massachusetts, he received an MPhil in Economics from the Centre for Economic Studies and Planning, Jawaharlal Nehru University, New Delhi, India and an MA in Economics from the School of Economics, University of Hyderabad, India.

Elissa Braunstein is a professor in the Department of Economics at Colorado State University in Fort Collins, USA, as well as editor of *Feminist Economics*. She previously served as a senior economist in the Division of Globalization and Development Strategies at the United Nations Conference on Trade and Development (UNCTAD).

Hasan Cömert is Assistant Professor of Economics at Trinity College, Connecticut, USA and Research Associate at the Political Economy Research Institute, University of Massachusetts-Amherst, USA.

Devika Dutt is a PhD candidate, Department of Economics, and Research Assistant, Political Economy Research Institute, University of Massachusetts-Amherst, USA.

Nina Eichacker is Assistant Professor in the Economics Department at the University of Rhode Island, USA.

Gerald A. Epstein is Professor of Economics and Co-Director of the Political Economy Research Institute (PERI) at the University of Massachusetts-Amherst, USA.

Ilene Grabel is Professor of International Finance at the Josef Korbel School of International Studies at the University of Denver, USA. She is the author of *When Things Don't Fall Apart: Global Financial Governance and Developmental Finance in an Age of Productive Incoherence* (MIT Press, 2017). Her earlier book (co-authored with Ha-Joon Chang), *Reclaiming Development: An Alternative Economic Policy Manual* (Zed Books) was republished in 2014.

Sana Khalil is a PhD student in Economics at the University of Massachusetts-Amherst, USA.

Mariam Majd is an Instructor of Economics at Stockton University, New Jersey, USA.

Francisco Perez is a PhD student in Economics at the University of Massachusetts-Amherst, USA.

Luis D. Rosero is Associate Professor of Economics and Co-Director of the MetroWest Economic Research Center (MERC) at Framingham State University, USA.

Zhandos Ybrayev is a PhD candidate in Economics at the University of Massachusetts-Amherst, USA.

Preface

This is my second volume of edited essays on international finance written primarily by my current and former graduate students from the University of Massachusetts-Amherst. I would first like to thank Alan Sturmer, Edward Elgar Publishing's acquisition editor, for his and Edward Elgar's support of both of these projects.

The first of these two edited volumes was *Capital Flight and Capital Controls in Developing Countries*, published by Elgar in 2004. That book was inspired by the path-breaking work of my colleagues James Boyce and Léonce Ndikumana. That book is also the key to this one as well. In the fall of 2017, I taught my PhD class in International Finance to a particularly lively and precocious group of graduate students. They saw the earlier book, which had also stemmed from my class in international finance and they said: "Hey: we want to do that too!" So the idea for *The Political Economy of International Finance in an Age of Inequality: Soft Currencies, Hard Landings* was born. Unlike the *Capital Flight* book, whose main chapters were country applications on one particular topic – capital flight – the current book contains chapters on a variety of topics on the general themes of power, instability and inequality in the international financial arena.

I am lucky to have such talented and enthusiastic current graduate students. I am also grateful to those of my former graduate students, all of whom have now launched very successful careers, who have agreed to join my current students in publishing chapters in this book. All these authors – both new and "more mature" – have in common an interest in "international finance" and in exploring the power and political dimensions involved in structuring international financial relations. They also share a concern about the inequalities that are often generated or reinforced in the process.

Many thanks to Mariam Majd and Devika Dutt, contributors to this book and my research assistants for the project, for doing a marvelous job of keeping the project moving forward, from beginning to end. Thanks also to Political Economy Research Institute (PERI) Administrative Manager Nicole Dunham and Communications Director Kim Weinstein for important assistance along the way. I also thank the production staff at Elgar for their excellent work on the manuscript.

Finally, I thank my comrade and PERI co-director, Robert Pollin, whose unstinting intellectual and comradely support of this and all my PERI research projects has been fundamental to whatever success they have achieved. In another respect, Bob is represented in this volume because the book is inspired by a key goal Bob and I had in creating and continuing PERI: helping to create the next generation of rigorous and engaged progressive economists. I dedicate this volume to Bob in recognition and gratitude for his support of my work and of our joint project.

Gerald A. Epstein

1. Introduction

Gerald A. Epstein

BACKGROUND TO THE VOLUME

Many observers thought that the financial crisis of 2007–08 would be a watershed moment in global finance. They believed the crisis would demonstrate, once and for all, the instability and inefficiency of this hyper-speculative global financial system, and finally bring an end to the destructive "neoliberal moment" and its "Washington Consensus" dictates in domestic and global economic policy (see, for example, Blanchard, Dell'Ariccia and Mauro, 2010). But, something surprising happened to "neoliberal financialization" on the way to the "dustbin of history": it escaped. Financial deregulation and "neoliberal" populism in finance are in the ascendant in the United States and elsewhere, and the bankers are laughing, well. . .all the way to the bank.[1]

To be sure, there are important cracks in the old free market consensus on international financial issues. These cracks are leading to what Ilene Grabel (Chapter 5, in this volume) calls "productive incoherence" in theory and practice, which is leading to important opportunities for policy change in some areas. But, in many other areas, the old theories and practices are being resurrected after near-death experiences in the period following the crisis.

This raises a number of important questions in the political economy of international finance. What are the important cautionary lessons from the crisis of 2007–08 that we must remember if we are to push back against a repeat of this unfortunate history? At a deeper level, what are the underlying economic and power structures that allow these destructive practices to survive and thrive in the aftermath of such a catastrophic meltdown? How do these underlying structures affect different nations differently, and why? Moreover, if the underlying forces of instability and inequality are continuing, how can countries manage these destructive forces and not be drawn into the whirlpool of instability, as afflicted many countries during the Global Financial Crisis?

In this volume, the authors address these questions mostly from the perspective of the so-called "emerging market countries" and other countries at the "periphery" of the developed capitalist economies. In doing so, they study these countries with lenses not often utilized by economists: they analyze institutions and power relations – in addition to economic forces – to understand the experiences, constraints, and opportunities facing countries as they try to navigate the riptides of global finance.

The title of this volume – *The Political Economy of International Finance in an Age of Inequality: Soft Currencies, Hard Landings* – reflects two key, related aspects of the "political economy" of international finance: the structures of inequality that both undergird and result from the relations of international finance; and the important distinction between soft and hard currencies that is a central aspect of these structures of inequality. "Hard currencies," in contrast to "soft currencies," can easily be used to buy goods, services and assets from virtually anyone in the world. Soft currencies can be used primarily only in the country of issue, and must usually be exchanged for hard currencies for buying foreign-owned goods, services and assets. It turns out that this distinction puts people and institutions from developing and emerging countries at a significant disadvantage in the global economic and political arenas. *Soft Currencies, Hard Landings* explores numerous examples of this disadvantage.

With respect to inequality, it is well known that income and wealth inequality have been dramatically on the rise in the last several decades, even as poverty levels in some key developing countries have dramatically fallen (Milanovic, 2016; Saez et al., 2018). The causes of this rise of inequality are diverse, though not completely understood. Still, it is safe to say that they partly result from deep underlying structures of inequality embedded in the global architecture of international economics, including international financial relations (Akyüz, 2017). In this volume, we identify a number of those key structures and show how these can lead to inequality as well as instability.

This inequality stems from four aspects of current-day international finance: the scale and complexity of international financial transactions; their concentration in a relatively small number of banks and other financial institutions; the prominence of a handful of international currencies – primarily the US dollar – at the center of these transactions; and inequalities in military and underlying economic power that, in many ways, lie at the very foundation of this edifice. A key implication is that this structural architecture gives oversized economic and political power to a relatively small group of international banks and financial institutions and to institutions and policymakers that control the supply of and access to hard currencies (primarily US dollar assets).[2] And it means that those soft currency countries without easy access to these hard currencies are at a profound structural disadvantage in the global financial system: they must rely on a handful of countries and financial institutions for credit that they can use internationally, for reserves that they can use to manage their exchange rates, and for access to currencies for international transactions of all kinds (Ocampo, 2017; D'Arista, 2018).

Scale and Complexity

Estimates of the size of international financial markets are so large they are either dumbfounding or mind-numbing. The Bank for International Settlement's most recent estimates for the amount of trading in foreign exchange indicates that in 2016, an average of $5.1 trillion dollars in foreign exchange traded hands *daily*, and this figure is actually *down* from $5.3 trillion three years before. To take another huge number: the Bank for International Settlements (BIS) estimates that that amount of credit given by US banks alone to borrowers outside the United States has exploded from $2 trillion in 2000 to over $10 trillion in 2017 (BIS, 2017). By comparison, US gross domestic product (GDP) in 2016 was about $18 trillion.

But even this huge number is likely to be an *underestimate* of the total credit lent by creditors in general and US financial institutions in particular across borders in recent years. As with evolving estimates of the number of planets and moons in the universe, estimates of the size of the international financial system keep growing as researchers generate measures of massive numbers of "missing" transactions that had not been accurately seen or measured before. As a recent study by researchers at the BIS explains:

> Every day, trillions of dollars are borrowed and lent in various currencies. Many deals take place in the cash market, through loans and securities. But foreign exchange (FX) derivatives, mainly FX swaps, currency swaps and the closely related forwards, also create debt-like obligations. For the US dollar alone, contracts worth tens of trillions of dollars stand open and trillions change hands daily. And yet one cannot find these amounts on balance sheets. This debt is, in effect, missing. (Borio, McCauley and McGuire, 2017, p. 37)

Borio and colleagues estimate that the credit generated in these "hidden" markets add more than $10 trillion to balance sheet debt of institutions in the global economy, much of this denominated in US dollars. Of this, lending to so-called emerging market countries has grown significantly since the Global Financial Crisis (BIS, 2017). The size and complexity of this arena has a number of important implications, including the difficulties in monitoring and managing these markets, and the large impacts they can have.

Concentration and Market Power of a Small Number of Large Financial Institutions

This last point about hidden credit in the forms of swaps and other derivatives stems from the complexity and opacity of many international financial transactions. Complexity and opacity, in turn, facilitate both the accumulation of power and profits by institutions that can profit from this complexity and opacity (Crotty, 2017). The sale of complex financial instruments such as credit default swaps, are highly concentrated among a few large international banks who are able to make substantial profits by controlling these markets. Only huge banks with large amounts of assets on their balance sheets can manage and finance these complex and opaque debts. Moreover, in a dynamic feedback loop, the opacity and complexity of these markets feed the profits of these few massive financial institutions.

Dominant Role of a Few Hard Currencies and the Power of their Central Banks

The size and power of these private financial institutions, mostly head-quartered in the center countries, is greatly facilitated by the government institutions – and especially the central banks – that have the capacity to create an extremely large – some say an unlimited – supply of hard currency, to undergird the operations of these financial institutions and their supply of hard currency credit.[3] Among these hard currencies, there is one – the US dollar (and its central bank, the Federal Reserve) – that stands supreme. As the most recent BIS triennial survey of foreign exchange trading shows:

> [t]he US dollar held its place as the dominant currency – it was on one side of 88% of all trades in April 2016. The euro remained the second most actively traded currency, but its share fell to 31% in April 2016, well below its peak of 39% in April 2010. Many emerging market currencies saw an increase in their share of global trading. The renminbi's share doubled to 4% as it became the world's eighth most actively traded currency. (BIS, 2016a, citing BIS, 2016b)

This dominant role of a handful of hard currencies, and especially the US dollar, is the third component of this underlying structure of inequality that profoundly affects the workings of the international financial system. For one thing, as recent research has shown, the interest rate policies of the Federal Reserve have an outsized impact on international economic trends (Rey, 2015; Avdjiev et al., 2018). In addition, as mentioned earlier, soft currency countries must gain access to these hard currencies to import needed goods, to manage their exchange rates, to finance key investments, to diversify their financial portfolios. This dependence on hard currencies places these countries' governments, households and businesses in a subordinate economic and political position in the international financial system. And they provide privileges to hard currency country banks and financial institutions. This privileged connection was made clear, for example, in the Global Financial Crisis when the Federal Reserve used its ability to create dollar credit out of "thin air" to bail out the large US financial institutions that had got themselves – and the world economy – into severe straits with their toxic behavior. This dollar-based bailout allowed these banks and bankers to maintain their central role in the global financial system.

Importantly, the Federal Reserve not only bailed out US banks; it also lent dollars freely to foreign central banks so that the large European banks that had made terrible dollar-denominated bets on the US housing bubble, could also be bailed out. In other words, the US Federal Reserve acted as an "international lender of last resort" (ILOLR) (D'Arista, 2018; Dutt, Chapter 7, in this volume).

Political and Military Power and the Structure of International Finance

This point about the role of the Federal Reserve as an ILOLR introduces the fourth aspect of the underlying international financial structure: inequality in military and political power in the global economy. This fourth aspect both underpins and results from global inequality. Asymmetries in underlying military, economic and political power in the world system and how the dominant country/countries choose to exercise their superior power are crucial. Mainstream economists mostly ignore these issues. There is, however, one "entry point" that the famous economic historian Charles Kindleberger introduced to the profession. In his important study of the causes of the Great Depression of the 1930s, Charles Kindleberger introduced the economics profession to the concept of "hegemony."[4] His thesis, now hotly debated, argued that the international financial system needs a hegemonic country to remain stable, because these systems are fundamentally, inherently unstable. According to Kindleberger's (1973) argument, the Great Depression was caused by an interregnum between hegemons – when the British were no longer powerful enough to manage the international financial system, and before the United States became politically willing to take over from the British. From this perspective, it matters greatly how the "hegemonic" government and central bank behave.[5]

International finance economists have not sufficiently generalized Kindleberger's argument, which is fundamentally about the role of power in the structuring of the international financial system. That is, underlying the international financial system is a structure of power that has profound impacts: for example, it can increase inequality, or it can reduce it. It can contribute to international financial stability or to instability. As Francisco Perez argues in Chapter 11 in this volume, hegemons can be "good" in the sense of contributing to equality and stability of the system, or they can be "bad" hegemons, doing just the opposite.

The role of military and political power in the structure of international finance is pervasive and is explored by a number of the authors in this volume. Even the existence and certainly the pervasiveness of international financial markets, operating across national borders with no international courts to adjudicate contracts or global military force to enforce property rights, illustrates the tenuous underlying structure of international lending and borrowing (Epstein and Gintis, 1992). In this world, international lending and borrowing depend on other mechanisms to enforce contracts and ensure repayment. In older times, gunboats from the dominant creditors were an important enforcer. These days, subtler, but no less effective means, emanating from economic and political threats from the leading financial and governmental institutions, take the place, for the most part, of gunboats. But, as Majd and Arora show in Chapters 9 and 10 respectively, military and political power of creditors to protect property and contract are never that far from sight.

OVERVIEW OF THE BOOK

Part I: Capital Flows and Financial Crises

In the previous section, we have seen the mindboggling size and discussed the complexity of current day financial markets. This size and complexity were reflected in the highly destructive Great Financial Crisis of 2007–08. (Wolfson and Epstein, 2013; Akyüz, 2017; Ocampo, 2017; D'Arista, 2018; Tokunaga and Epstein, 2018).

As Elissa Braunstein shows in Chapter 2, "Financial crises among emerging and developing economies in the modern era," these large and highly speculative markets can create large problems for "emerging and developing economies" (EDEs). Braunstein sets the stage for the *Soft Currencies, Hard Landings* with an overview of the nature of capital flows and their impacts on financial instability and crises in developing countries in the last several decades. Braunstein shows that these capital flow "bonanzas" as she calls them, are much more likely to have caused financial crises than other culprits often identified by neoliberal economists and policymakers – such as government regulations or budget deficits. Though not all countries receiving capital inflow bonanzas experience financial crises, they make having such a crisis much more likely.

Nina Eichacker, in Chapter 3 "Too good to be true: What the Icelandic crisis revealed about global finance," details a particularly devastating example of global finance gone wild. As Eichacker shows, some of the standard suspects such as corrupt bankers and politicians played important roles in the drama, but there were also fundamental political economy forces driving excessively risky and unsustainable capital flows into Iceland. Neoliberal ideology was also to blame, with exceptionally "rosy scenarios" being drawn by key mainstream economists.

In Chapter 4, Khalil reminds us that financial crises, such as the Great Financial Crisis, can have very different effects on different groups. Contributing research to a hugely understudied subject, Khalil analyzes "the gender-specific effects of the Great Recession" on the OECD countries. This is an example that relates clearly to the subject of our volume: *The Political Economy of International Finance in an Age of Inequality*. Khalil's study raises key questions about a common interpretation of the recession following the financial crisis as a "mancession," that is, that it affected men more than women. Khalil shows that the negative impact of the recession on women was in fact much more severe than most analysts have realized. Her chapter makes a significant contribution to this important but woefully understudied area in international finance.

Part II: Managing International Capital Flows: Costs and Dilemmas

The chapters in Part I detailed some of the large problems and costs experienced by countries as a result of financial instability and financial crises stemming from international financial flows. Naturally, as a defensive measure, governments try to manage and protect themselves from the negative consequences of these flows. The tricky part, however, is that many of these governments want also to try to *benefit* from these capital inflows. Finding the balance that works and the tools to achieve this balance is difficult as the authors of the chapters in this part of the book show.

Ilene Grabel, in "Capital controls in a time of crisis" (Chapter 5) describes an important tool that countries can use – capital controls. As Grabel describes, developing and emerging market countries have not had complete freedom to choose whether they use this valuable tool to manage flows. Because of their historical dependence on hard currencies and their desire to attract loans and investments from abroad, they have depended on the approval of international investors to attract credit (Epstein and Gintis, 1992; Akyüz, 2017; Grabel, 2018). Typically, getting this approval depended on the "blessings" of the International Monetary Fund (IMF). The focus of Grabel's chapter is the evolving view of the IMF toward capital controls. In a fascinating analysis, Grabel shows that, while for years the IMF was adamantly opposed to the adoption of controls by developing countries, with the financial crisis came a re-evaluation of the role of controls and a complex, grudging acceptance of them. Grabel describes this important evolution and calls it an example of the "productive incoherence" of current policy views at the IMF in particular and among mainstream economists in general.

A more common tool that developing countries have adopted to help them manage the massive flows of global finance is the accumulation of hard currency reserves. The idea is that governments can use these reserves – usually controlled by their central banks – to manage their exchange rates, and to make it less likely that will they have to turn to foreign institutions, including the IMF, for help in a period of crisis. Two chapters in Part II address the possible benefits and costs of holding on to such large amounts of foreign exchange reserves.

In "Easing the trilemma through reserve accumulation? The Latin American case" (Chapter 6), Luis D. Rosero takes a new look at the impact of reserve accumulation by emerging market countries in Latin America on exchange rate stability and crisis vulnerability. As Rosero details, economists and policymakers have claimed that foreign exchange reserve accumulation has significant stabilizing benefits for emerging market economies. But with a series of statistical exercises, Rosero casts significant doubt on the existence of these benefits, at least in the case of Latin America. Importantly, he shows that the one exception to this negative verdict is for countries that accumulate an extremely large trove of reserves.

But, as Devika Dutt shows in Chapter 7, "The costs of foreign exchange intervention" (Chapter 7), the holding and utilizing of reserves to stabilize exchange rates can be very costly for developing countries. Together, Rosero's and Dutt's chapters demonstrate that hard currency (foreign exchange) reserve holding is no panacea for soft currency countries.

Interestingly, Dutt's chapter also links up with the issues of the political economy of access to support from the center countries. She shows evidence that suggests that countries that have access to ILOLR help from the Federal Reserve face fewer costs in terms of managing reserves. This implies an asymmetric power relationship between the key central banks and these developing countries relative to countries that do not have access.

In the final chapter of Part II ("Monetary policy under financial dollarization: The case of Eurasian Economic Union," Chapter 8), Zhandos Ybrayev discusses another way in which countries deal with the hard currency/soft currency dilemma: their countries become "dollarized," that is, the hard currency is used domestically as money. He shows that a high degree of financial dollarization can create difficulties for these countries. In his chapter, Ybrayev studies the case of the Eurasian Economic Union countries and specifically looks at the impact of dollarization on the ability of these countries to conduct monetary policy. He also looks at whether inflation targeting monetary policy is a useful tool to manage dollarization.

As these chapters show, there are various policy tools that developing and emerging market countries can utilize to help them deal with the massive and destabilizing financial forces emanating from the global financial markets. But none of these policies come without significant costs and none is fail-safe. As long as countries want to try to attract financial flows, they might have to make significant sacrifices (see also, Epstein and Gintis, 1992; Akyüz, 2017; Ocampo, 2017).

Part III: Power Relations in the International Financial System: Global and Regional Dimensions

This final part of *Soft Currencies, Hard Landings* explores the underlying inequalities in political and economic power that structure the financial relationships examined in the previous two parts of the book.

In "The cost of a SWIFT kick: Estimating the cost of financial sanctions on Iran" (Chapter 9), Mariam Majd analyzes the costs of raw economic and political power as can only be exercised by a hegemon. In a very original study, Majd examines the unprecedented US financial sanctions imposed on Iran in 2012. They required that Iran be blocked from using the Society for Interbank Financial Telecommunication (SWIFT) payments platform which is a crucial infrastructure for making and receiving international financial payments. Though touted by the United States as a form of "smart sanction" designed to hurt elites without harming the general population, Majd finds that these sanctions had very large economic costs to the whole country. This raw and asymmetric power through which financial transactions are structured can be utilized for political ends by the dominant countries, and also helps to further these countries' economic and political dominance. However, populations in less developed countries can suffer under these circumstances.

In the second chapter of Part III, Mohit Arora pursues a similar theme. In "Changing rules of the game of global finance: Glimpses from Argentina's sovereign debt restructuring" (Chapter 10), Arora explores the political economy of international debt contract enforcement and its recent evolution, using Argentina as an example. Arora describes the problems of debt enforcement in the international arena. Because of the general absence of an international court of law with enforcement powers (so-called "exogenous enforcement"), the international financial markets have resorted to other mechanisms of enforcement, which have involved the exercise or threat of exercise of power by powerful financial institutions, or powerful governmental or quasi-governmental entities, like the IMF, or creditor governments. In the nineteenth century and earlier, such force or threat of force was usually backed up by military might – "gunboat diplomacy"; in more recent years, by threats of economic or financial sanctions by creditors, their governments and/or their agents, like the IMF.

Arora then outlines the attempt by powerful creditors to create legal, rather than diplomatic or military, contract enforcement mechanisms, in the recent case of Argentina's debt restructuring. Focusing on the successful action by so-called "vulture funds" to get full repayment through the New York courts, Arora describes the costs that this kind of "exogenous enforcement" can impose on debtor developing countries. Arora notes that, given these costs, it is hard to see how such "exogenous enforcement" could work to the benefit of the debtor countries.

The final two chapters in *Soft Currencies, Hard Landings* look at the underlying power dynamics in currency unions. Currency unions are an attempt by countries to join forces to create a larger economic and political entity to help stabilize financial and monetary relations and exchange rates. These are attempts to create cooperative financial relationships among countries as a possible solution to some of the difficult problems, such as financial instability, that can arise in market-based international financial flows. In "Solidarity vs similarity: The political economy of currency unions" (Chapter 11), Francisco Perez takes a unique and insightful look at three attempts at the creation and sustenance of common currency unions: the Eurozone, the African Currency Union, and the East African shilling. In this original and insightful chapter, Perez examines with fresh eyes the conditions that are likely to enable currency unions to succeed. Perez argues that for currency unions to succeed, "political solidarity" is likely to be more important than economic similarity, which is often stressed by mainstream economists. An additional key characteristic in a situation of unequal power in currency unions – a situation that is almost always the case – the behavior of the hegemonic country is crucial. In particular, a supportive hegemon can be crucial to the success of the currency union. Perez argues that, whereas the French government has been a willing hegemon in West and Central Africa, ensuring the survival of the CFA franc,[6] Germany has not played that role in Europe, contributing to the severe problems facing the euro and many of the countries that adopt it.[7]

The connection between capital flows and political power – a theme emphasized throughout this volume – is the central issue in the final chapter of *Soft Currencies, Hard Landings.* Hasan Cömert in "International financial flows and the future of EU–Turkey relations" (Chapter 12) argues that Turkey's acceptance of large capital flows from the international markets, including from the EU, not only makes it more vulnerable to crises – a point emphasized in Part I of this volume – but also weakens Turkey's bargaining position with respect to political issues such as political integration with Europe. This chapter well illustrates the themes of Part III in that it illustrates the intimate, two-way connections between international financial markets and political and economic power. It also illustrates asymmetries and inequalities inherent in these relationships.

NOTES

1. The term "neoliberal" populism might seem like an oxymoron, but it is meant to convey the juxtaposition of populist rhetoric with neoliberal financial policy so characteristic of neoautocratic regimes, such as those in the United States under Donald Trump and in contemporary Turkey, India and Hungary, among other places.
2. For a pioneering and informative quantitative discussion of the role of these factors in the architecture of the international financial system, see Avdjiev et al. (2016, 2018). However, Avdjiev et al. do not discuss the political economy implications of their analysis, which, by contrast, is on center stage here.
3. There is a debate about the structural limits of hard currency central banks' credit supply, which revolves around the issue of market confidence in the value of the currency, and whether this confidence declines – and even evaporates – if the supply of hard currency credits get too large. The so-called "Modern Money" theorists generally argue that these limits are non-existent or highly exaggerated. Their critics point to many historical examples of limits imposing themselves through rapidly accelerating inflation and exchange rate collapses as in 1920s' Germany and 1980s' Latin America.
4. Hegemony is defined as "leadership or dominance of one country or social group over another."
5. Barry Eichengreen and others have claimed that hegemony is not necessary because cooperation among nations is a good substitute for hegemony (Eichengreen, 1989). Another strand of the debate, initiated by libertarians, claims that the free market is inherently stable and, therefore, neither hegemony nor cooperation among states is necessary. Note that the Great Financial Crisis, the Great Depression and other international crises should have laid the free market claim of stability to rest a long time ago.
6. See Perez, Chapter 11 in this volume, or Wikipedia for the definition and somewhat complex history of the CFA franc.
7. For a vivid description of this point, see Varoufakis (2017). For a fascinating discussion of the financial aspects of Britain as a "bad hegemon" in the days of the British Empire, see De Cecco (1984).

REFERENCES

Akyüz, Y. (2017), *Playing with Fire: Deepened Financial Integration and Changing Vulnerabilities of the Global South*, Oxford: Oxford University Press.
Avdjiev, S., V. Bruno, C. Koch and H.S. Shin (2018), "The dollar exchange rate as

a global risk factor: Evidence from investment," *BIS Working Papers No. 695*, January.

Avdjiev, S., R.N. McCauley and H.S. Shin (2016), "Breaking free of the triple coincidence in international finance," *Economic Policy*, **31**(87), 409–51.

Bank for International Settlements (BIS) (2016a), "Global FX trading averages $5.1 trillion a day in April 2016" [press release], accessed July 15, 2018 at https://www.bis.org/press/p160901a.htm.

Bank for International Settlements (BIS) (2016b), *Triennial Central Bank Survey of Foreign Exchange and OTC Markets*, accessed July 15, 2018 at https://www.bis.org/publ/rpfx16.htm.

Bank for International Settlements (BIS) (2017), "Recent enhancements to the BIS statistics," *Quarterly Review*, September, 25–35.

Blanchard, O., G. Dell'Ariccia and P. Mauro (2010), "Rethinking macroeconomic policy," *IMF Staff Position Note*, Washington, DC: IMF.

Borio, C., R. McCauley and P. McGuire (2017), "FX swaps and forwards: Missing global debt?," *BIS Quarterly Review*, September, 37–54.

Crotty, J. (2017), *Capitalism, Macroeconomics and Reality*, Cheltenham, UK and Northampton, MA, USA: Edward Elgar Publishing.

D'Arista, J. (2018), *All Fall Down: Debt, Deregulation and Financial Crises*, Cheltenham, UK and Northampton, MA, USA: Edward Elgar Publishing.

De Cecco, M. (1984), *The International Gold Standard: Money and Empire*, 2nd edition, London: Pinter.

Eichengreen, B. (1989), "Hegemonic stability theories of the international monetary system," in R. Bryant (ed.), *Can Nations Agree? Essays in International Economic Cooperation*, Washington, DC: Brookings Institution Press, pp. 255–98.

Epstein, G.A. and H. Gintis (1992), "International capital markets and the limits of national economic policy," in T. Banuri and J.B. Schor (eds), *Financial Openness and National Autonomy*, Oxford: Clarendon Press, pp. 167–97.

Grabel, I. (2018). *When Things Don't Fall Apart: Global Financial Governance and Developmental Finance in an Age of Productive Incoherence*, Cambridge, MA: MIT Press.

Kindleberger, C. (1973), *The World in Depression, 1929–1939*, Berkeley, CA: University of California Press.

Milanovic, B. (2016), *Global Inequality: A New Approach for the Age of Globalization*, Cambridge, MA: Harvard University Press.

Ocampo, J.A. (2017), *Resetting the International Monetary (Non)System. WIDER Studies in Development Economics*, Oxford: Oxford University Press.

Rey, H. (2015), "Dilemma not trilemma: The global financial cycle and monetary policy independence," *NBER Working Paper No. 21162*.

Saez, E.F.A., G. Zucman, L. Chancel and T. Piketty (2018), *World Inequality Report 2018*, accessed July 15, 2018 at http://wir2018.wid.world/.

Tokunaga, J. and G.A. Epstein (2018), "The endogenous finance of global-dollar-based financial fragility in the 2000s: A Minskyan approach," *Review of Keynesian Economics*, **6**(1) 62–82.

Varoufakis, Y. (2017), *Adults in the Room: My Battle with the European and American Deep Establishment*, New York: Farrar, Straus & Giroux.

Wolfson, M. and G.A. Epstein (eds) (2013), *The Handbook of the Political Economy of Financial Crises*, New York: Oxford University Press.

PART I

Capital flows and financial crises

2. Financial crises among emerging and developing economies in the modern era: A brief history and some stylized themes

Elissa Braunstein

INTRODUCTION

This chapter develops a thematic overview of financial crises among emerging and developing economies (EDEs) between 1980 and 2007.[1] It covers four major waves of crises, and then identifies a set of stylized themes emergent in all four. The main narrative is that financial liberalization provides an opening for booms in capital inflows and domestic credit markets. The consequent build-up in financial fragility, driven by largely private speculation and risk-taking, is often swiftly unwound by a crisis, with substantial negative real effects and an (often explosive) increase in public debt. How economists and policymakers understand these dynamics is also an important part of the story, as the pathway towards growth and development proffered by financial liberalization is guided by one's underlying confidence in markets. Market fundamentalists – those who believe that market mechanisms are almost always the best way to organize social provisioning – maintain that macro policy should essentially stand aside (albeit in ways advantageous to finance, such as via implementing tight monetary policy regimes) to let global financial markets increase the amount and efficiency of investment available for development. That financialization often brings disappointing or destabilizing results becomes reason to doubt the soundness of an economy's economic fundamentals, rather than evidence of the systemic risks inherent in reigning models of financial globalization. Given that the United Nations Sustainable Development Goals (SDGs) is the largest investment plan in history, it is particularly important to understand the modern historical record of the consequences of looking to global financial markets to underwrite them.[2]

Table 2.1 serves as an empirical background that is referenced through-out, and also foreshadows the stylized themes developed. It lists countries and the dates of their currency, sovereign debt or banking crises, grouped according to the four waves of financial crises identified: the 1980s, the Mexican crisis in 1994–95 and its so-called "Tequila Effect," the Asian financial crisis (AFC) in 1997–98, and the AFC's ripple effects outside the Asian region.[3] It is not a complete list of all of the financial crises that occurred during the period, but rather a representative sample dictated by data availability and principle themes. Almost all of these crisis episodes were accompanied by a capital flow bonanza (31 out of the 33 episodes listed), defined as an unusually large negative surge in the current account balance.[4] Similarly, domestic credit booms precede crisis nearly 75 percent of the time (24 out of the 33 episodes listed). Minimum real per capita GDP growth notes the minimum growth rate within four years of the start of the crisis (including the crisis year, recorded as the earliest year that any of the three types of crises began and referred to as time T). The intent of marking minimum growth rates is to note, however roughly, the real costs of financial crisis.[5]

The last two columns document the costs of financial crises in terms of expanding public debt, both to domestic and external creditors. Comparing public debt as a share of GDP the year before financial crisis begins ($T - 1$) relative to two years after ($T + 2$) for the entire group of crises listed, the median (average) increase in total gross central govern-ment debt is 85.9 (124.3) percent, while the median (average) increase in external government debt is 42.0 (60.5) percent. Interestingly, although fiscal malfeasance is a frequent refrain in mainstream accounts of financial crises, it is typically the public fielding of the bust that inevitably proceeds after the boom, and all the costs associated with it (e.g., nationalizing private debt, recapitalizing banks, and the impact of currency devaluation on the value of foreign currency liabilities) that run up public debt.

THE LESSONS OF THE 1980s

Often set as a cautionary tale on the pitfalls of over-borrowing and fiscal mismanagement, the Latin American debt crises of the 1980s caught many by surprise.[6] The world had not had a major financial crisis since the 1930s, commodity prices were high and real interest rates low (Reinhart and Rogoff, 2009). Bolstered by the flush of petrodollars, advanced economy (AE) banks doled out financing to (mostly private) borrowers in EDEs as an alternative to the lackluster investment opportunities at home (Akyüz, 2014). That loans were overseen by banks (and not based on bonds) was

Table 2.1   Eras of financial crises, capital flows and public debt

Country	Currency Crisis (Year)	Sovereign Debt Crisis (Default Year)	Banking Crisis (Start Year)	Capital Flow Bonanza	Domestic Credit Boom	Minimum Annual Real Per Capita GDP Growth (%)	Change in Total Gross Central Government Debt as a Share of GDP (%)	Change in Gross External Government Debt as a Share of GDP (%)
The debt crises of the 1980s								
Argentina	1981	1982	1980	x		-7.1	417.7	53.4
Chile	1982	1983	1981	x	x	-11.7	161.7	106.9
Mexico	1982	1982	1981	x	x	-6.1	95.7	117.9
Uruguay	1983	1983	1981	x	x	-10.9	378.5	302.9
Colombia	1985		1982	x	x	-1.3	71.1	35.2
Ecuador	1982	1982	1982	x		-2.9	60.5	16.0
Paraguay	1984	1982		x		-5.9	78.7	35.5
Turkey			1982	x	x	1.2	83.1	32.7
Venezuela	1984	1982		x		-6.3	95.2	62.1
Brazil		1983		x		-5.6	12.7	39.7
Peru	1981		1983	x	x	-12.5	127.6	73.4
Philippines	1983	1983	1983	x	x	-9.8	na	34.2
Argentina	1987		1989	x		-8.8	111.4	87.7
Peru	1988			x	x	-14.2	146.8	68.7
Venezuela	1989			x	x	-10.9	43.9	8.8
Brazil			1990		x	-5.9	191.1	32.1
Group median						-6.7	95.7	46.6
The Mexican crisis and the Tequila Effect								
Mexico	1995		1994	x	x	-7.6	26.4	47.0
Argentina	1995		1995	x	x	-4.1	14.5	41.3
Group median						-5.9	20.5	44.2

The Asian financial crisis

Country	Crisis date 1	Crisis date 2	Capital flow bonanza	Domestic credit boom	Minimum real per capita GDP growth	Government debt	Total gross external government debt
Indonesia	1997	1999	x	x	−14.4	246.0	100.9
Korea	1997	1998	x	x	−6.4	278.8	65.3
Malaysia	1997	1998	x	x	−9.6	7.1	38.1
Philippines	1997	1998	x	x	−2.7	10.4	42.5
Thailand	1997	1998	x	x	−11.5	597.7	28.0
Group median					−9.6	246.0	42.5

AFC ripple effects

Country	Crisis date 1	Crisis date 2	Capital flow bonanza	Domestic credit boom	Minimum real per capita GDP growth	Government debt	Total gross external government debt
Colombia	1998	1999	x	x	−5.8	117.5	20.8
Ecuador	1998	1999	x	x	−6.6	49.9	28.9
Russia	1998	1998	x		−5.1	39.5	96.4
Ukraine	1998	1998	x		−1.0	70.0	na
Brazil	1999		x		−1.2	−15.2	46.1
Turkey	2000	2001	x	x	−7.1	144.4	35.1
Argentina	2001	2001	x	x	−11.7	208.1	149.9
Paraguay	2002				−2.0	−3.3	18.5
Uruguay	2002	2002	x	x	−7.8	88.6	60.7
Venezuela	2002	2002	x	x	−10.5	22.5	10.1
Group median					−6.2	60.0	35.1

Sources and notes:

Country and crisis listing: Countries are listed in order of earliest crisis year of the three types of crises listed, referred to as time *T*, and then alphabetically. Dates for currency, debt and banking crises from Laeven and Valencia (2008).

Capital flow bonanza: An "x" indicates that a capital flow bonanza occurred within any one of the three years preceding the earliest crisis date; from Reinhart and Reinhart (2008).

Domestic credit boom: An "x" indicates that a domestic credit boom was identified preceding time *T* in one of three sources: Elekdog and Wu (2011), Takáts and Uper (2013) or Arean, Bouza and Dabla-Norris (2015).

Minimum real per capita GDP growth: This refers to the lowest annual growth rate within four years of the beginning of the crisis (i.e., the range is time *T* to *T* + 3); data from World Development Indicators Database.

Government debt: Total gross central government debt includes both domestic and external debt. Total gross external government debt includes all external debt to both the public and private sectors. Data are from Reinhart and Rogoff (2010), except for data on Ukraine, which is from De Bolle, Rother and Hakobyan (2006); percentage changes are based on author calculations of the change between *T* − 1 and *T* +2.

supposed to enhance information and oversight, adding to the general sense of confidence and optimism that prevailed (Reinhart and Rogoff, 2009). Many emerging economies used these funds to cope with oil price shocks, maintaining growth in the face of mounting balance-of-payments constraints; even oil exporters borrowed heavily, drawn in by international lenders eager to make loans (Palma, 2003). At the policy level, domestic financial and international trade liberalization commenced among a number of Latin American countries in the 1970s, though there were fewer changes to policies governing international capital movements (Morley, Machado and Pettinato, 1999).

The opening of the 1980s ushered in a series of global economic shocks – real interest rate hikes as a consequence of American efforts to tame inflation, intensified recession among AEs and a fall in non-oil commodity prices – that swiftly turned optimism to panic. The cutoff in lending, devaluations and balance-of-payments crises that ensued led to a cascade of defaults (see Table 2.1 for a partial list). In response to the alarming specter of widespread bankruptcies and foreign takeovers of domestic banks, EDE governments nationalized what had been largely private debt, with renegotiation and servicing orchestrated by international financial institutions on the condition of implementing stabilization and structural adjustment programs (Diaz-Alejandro, 1985; Damill, Frenkel and Rapetti, 2013). The consequent explosion in public debt is documented for a number of these crises in Table 2.1, and serves as a preface to what became a decade-long struggle under the weight of structural adjustment and the burden of servicing public debt.

Looking back on this era, there is plenty in the way of domestic policy choices that generated deserved critique. For instance, liberalizing domestic financial markets without implementing adequate oversight, or underestimating the deleterious effects of real exchange rate appreciation in the context of trade liberalization, are fitting fodder for critical post-mortems. But there was more variety in domestic policy and economic structure than is typically emphasized. For instance, some governments exercised very interventionist models of economic governance (Brazil), while others engaged in more free market reforms, including financial liberalization (Argentina, Chile and Uruguay). A third set had open capital accounts but imposed limits on private sector access to external finance (Mexico and Venezuela) (Diaz-Alejandro, 1984). What these countries did share were the same external economic conditions, circumstances that generated capital flow bonanzas in the years leading up to the crisis, a building up of financial fragility as a consequence, and the inevitable crash that followed on the heels of common economic shocks (Stiglitz, 2003).[7] Explicit and implicit public guarantees of private debt then transformed the crises into a sovereign debt problem.

Predictably, given the dominant neoclassical economic paradigm of the era, early economic models that grew out of the experiences of the 1980s' debt crises focused primarily on the challenges of "fiscal sustainability," and how things like fiscal deficits and expansionary policies made economies vulnerable to speculative attack in the context of effectively fixed exchange rate regimes (e.g., Krugman, 1979; Obstfeld, 1994). Thus, government missteps could generate a loss in investor confidence, inducing a self-fulfilling prophecy as investor fears generate the currency depreciation that sparked their unease in the first place (Krugman, 2014). The conventional wisdom that emerged emphasized getting one's fiscal house in order, and letting markets do the rest (Calvo, 2005). This perspective was also reflected in the policy prescriptions associated with structural adjustment, which prioritized servicing debt and required liberalization and privatization.

HIGH NEOLIBERALISM AND THE RETURN OF CAPITAL FLOWS TO LATIN AMERICA

In 1989, Mexico signed on to the US government's Brady Plan, a plan designed to further encourage neoliberal market reforms and ease debt burdens by converting government debt into bonds collateralized by US Treasury bills; a number of other countries swept up in the 1980s' debt crisis soon followed. It also marks the beginning of the era of "high neoliberalism," particularly in Latin America, where the Washington Consensus on development-oriented macroeconomic policy dominated much of the thinking on how to manage global integration and the domestic economy, including strong commitments to financial liberalization and privatization (Damill et al., 2013). These neoliberal reforms and debt restructurings eased concern over the supposed key policy mistake of the 1980s – fiscal debt – and reopened access to international capital for debtor countries.

Attracted by relatively high returns, and reassured by domestic policy reforms and the prospect of North American Free Trade Agreement (NAFTA) negotiations, portfolio investors herded into Mexico, driving booms in domestic credit (helped along by the privatization of commercial banks) and stock prices, with little result in terms of higher real gross domestic product (GDP) growth (Grabel, 1996). However, 1994 brought with it an increase in US interest rates, as well as a series of destabilizing political events in Mexico (including the Zapatista rebellion and the assassination of a leading presidential candidate), ending the capital flow bonanza and necessitating the drawing down of reserves in order to finance the substantial current account deficit (Moreno-Brid and Ros,

2004). International investors rightly worried that Mexico's exchange rate, which was essentially pegged to the US dollar, was headed for a devaluation. As these self-fulfilling crises typically go, the consequent capital outflows induced the currency crisis that investors feared. In the lead-up to the crisis, additional risks were introduced by Mexico's increasing reliance on dollar-denominated debt instruments called *tesobonos*, stoking investors' fears of default and crisis (Lustig, 1995). The Clinton administration helped secure a quick bailout that prioritized bond repayment and furthered neoliberal reforms (Grabel, 1996).

The Mexican crisis created devaluation pressure among a number of other emerging markets as worried investors re-evaluated risk in the context of fixed exchange rates (the so-called "Tequila Effect"). But the strongest impact was felt in Brazil and the Southern Cone countries of Latin America. In early 1991, Argentina had established a currency board, which maintained a fixed peg of the currency to the US dollar (an arrangement that persisted to 2001). While the regime was effective at curbing high inflation, combined with liberalization of trade and finance it led to appreciation of the real exchange rate, increasing current account deficits and external debt (Damill et al., 2013). When the Mexican crisis hit, Argentina also faced sudden capital outflows, including non-resident deposits in domestic banks. The pressure on Argentina's banks proved to be too much, and the government negotiated a bailout agreement with the International Monetary Fund (IMF) in 1995 on the condition that it tighten fiscal policy by increasing taxes (Boughton, 2012). Brazil avoided a similar fate, largely by raising short-term interest rates, which introduced other fragilities (namely, incredibly high interest on public debt) that would render it susceptible to crisis later on in the decade (Palma, 2011).

Though limited in scope and relatively short-lived, these crises challenged some of the economic profession's conventional wisdom on the determining roles of fundamentals and liberalization. Indeed, one of the reasons that Stanley Fischer, then Deputy Managing Director of the IMF, wanted to resolve the Mexican crisis so quickly was to avoid the "contagion of intellectual doubt" that might ensue after the failure of one of its star neoliberal pupils (Boughton, 2012). There were some efforts to identify the lack of domestic savings as an insufficiently recognized vulnerability, but the spectacular savers caught up in the Asian financial crisis a couple of years later quickly quashed that line of reasoning (Calvo, 2005). A longer-lived alternative explanation was given by what would become a common neoliberal exceptionalism story: much of the blame for the crisis was set on the government for economic mismanagement, political overreach and corruption (Grabel, 2006). Echoes of this reasoning would reappear to try to explain the AFC.

THE ASIAN FINANCIAL CRISIS AND BEYOND

If the Mexican crisis was surprising, the AFC must have come as a veritable shock. The region's macroeconomic fundamentals were indisputably sound: growth and savings rates were high, and fiscal policy was generally conservative, so most borrowing was private (Reinhart and Rogoff, 2009). In 1996, the year before the crisis hit, current account deficits in Thailand and Malaysia were on the large side,[8] and the region's growth slightly lower overall, but none of this really substantiates the extreme alarm and consequent dislocation that would soon follow (Krugman, 1999).

As with other crises, the pathway to the AFC began with financial liberalization, both on the capital account and in domestic financial markets (Montes, 1998). These reforms came partly in response to pressure from domestic firms and banks, who were eager to access lower interest loans in global capital markets to make investments at home; large institutional investors in AEs were happy to oblige (Wade, 1998). Perhaps Asian governments were also responding to the tenor of the times, when neoliberal approaches to development macroeconomics held sway at the major international financial institutions. The practical result was a widespread expansion of private lending, much of which was linked to short-term hard currency–denominated debt instruments (Grabel, 1999). At the same time, domestic inflation and dollar appreciation (the region's currencies were pegged to the dollar) resulted in real exchange rate appreciation and a loss in international competitiveness, worsening current accounts and driving even more investors into the real estate and stock market bubbles, especially in Southeast Asia. With growing signs of weakness in Thailand's asset markets by 1995, and global capital starting to shift away from emerging markets as the US Fed raised interest rates in March 1997, investors became increasingly worried that Thailand's pegged exchange rate would not hold (Wade, 1998). The Thai Central Bank, after unsuccessfully using its reserves to defend the baht against speculative attacks, finally let the currency float in July 1997. The currency's consequent depreciation spooked investors, setting off contagion first to Southeast Asia (Malaysia, Indonesia and the Philippines), and then to Taiwan, Hong Kong and Korea.[9] The IMF swiftly moved in to help contain the crises, pushing an agenda that has since been critiqued as probably worsening the contagion and deepening the crises (Radelet and Sachs, 2000), as well as serving as a sort of Trojan horse designed to recast the state-led Asian development model into the Fund's own neoliberal image (Crotty and Lee, 2004).

Outside Asia, Russia was next to get pulled into the crisis. Soon after liberalizing finance and seeing more foreign participation in its stock and public bond markets, Russia faced an increasingly global reversal in capital flows to emerging markets – initially led in Russia's case by the exit of Korean and Brazilian investors responding to the AFC (Pinto and Ulatov, 2010). Declining commodity prices further compromised Russia's ability to defend its fixed exchange rate, resulting in devaluation and default in 1998. The large private sector losses (both domestically and among international investors) generated by the Russian crisis induced a sudden stop of capital flows to Latin America, which manifested as a series of financial crises and low growth that came to be called the "lost half-decade" of 1998–2002 (UNCTAD, 1999; Calvo and Talvi, 2005).

Brazil and Argentina's experiences illustrate these dynamics and their links with vulnerabilities established in prior crises. Brazil's system of public financing was greatly weakened by its efforts to weather the Tequila Effect, where in addition to raising interest rates, a banking sector restructuring loaded the government with lots of additional dollar-linked debt (UNCTAD, 1999). Defending the currency peg rapidly became untenable in light of the sudden stop and insufficient reserves, and currency crisis and devaluation ensued in early 1999. Argentina faced deflationary pressures from the Brazilian devaluation, and given the extensive dollarization of its domestic liabilities and an already stagnant economy, Argentina defaulted on its external debt in 2001 (the largest default in history at the time), finally letting its currency freely float in early 2002 (Calvo and Talvi, 2005; Grabel, 2006; Damill et al., 2013). Real average annual per capita GDP growth in Argentina sank to −4.2 percent during the lost half-decade, while the average for Latin America as a whole was 0.2 percent.[10]

As with other waves of crisis, economists engaged in an ex post search for systematic explanations, generating so-called third generation crisis models. These models linked sudden stops of capital inflows with substantial negative real consequences, largely because of the combination of fixed exchange rate regimes, liability dollarization and the requirements for real exchange rate depreciation (e.g., Krugman, 1999; Calvo, Izquierdo and Mejía, 2004). This was a shift away from identifying domestic fundamentals as the source of the problem and towards focusing on the financial sector. However, for neoliberal policy stalwarts who seemed less concerned with sorting out the technical mechanisms of crises than defending their own approaches to economic management, the AFC illustrated the limits of the Asian development model. According to this view, the "moral hazard" and "crony capitalism" associated with Asian state-led capitalism created the over-indebtedness and rampant speculation that precipitated the crisis (Chang, 2000). IMF demands for neoliberal-style structural reforms in economies suffering only from short-term liquidity problems (e.g., Korea) illustrate this point. Versions of it were also applied to assessing other emerging markets swept up in AFC contagion. For instance, Russia supposedly broke under the weight of corruption, tax evasion and government mismanagement; Brazil was insufficiently committed to neoliberal reforms and overly wed to fixing its currency (Grabel, 2006). Whatever the domestic policy specifics, such perspectives ignore the systemic risks introduced by financial liberalization and massive capital inflows, and how self-fulfilling crises and contagion embroil a wide variety of emerging markets in financial crises with serious and long-lasting real effects.

CONCLUDING DISCUSSION

Financial Liberalization and Systemic Risk

As EDEs have liberalized their capital accounts and domestic financial markets, so too has the likelihood of all sorts of financial crises increased, driven primarily by surges in capital inflows and the sudden stops or reversals that almost always ensue.[11] And though capital flow bonanzas have increased as liberalization has proceeded, these flows are significantly driven by circumstances external to the economies that host them, for example changes in global commodity prices or US interest rates, or the psychological and economic contagion effects of crises elsewhere. These external forces interact with domestic macro policy and structure in ways that raise overall fragility and risk. Capital bonanzas are overwhelmingly procyclical, feeding domestic credit booms and asset price bubbles, while linking them to the sudden shifts in sentiment and herd behavior typical of globalized investors. At the same time, capital inflows are associated with appreciation of the real exchange rate, worsening the current account and most commonly (and quickly) unwinding via nominal depreciation in the form of currency crisis (Goldfajn and Valdes, 1999). The mismatches of currency (borrowing in foreign currency) and maturity (using short-term liabilities to finance long-term investments) typical of the events discussed made economies extremely vulnerable to a cutoff in lending, and the consequences of currency crisis and devaluation very costly. But the domestic particularities are only significant in that they exist within a larger global financial system characterized by too much liquidity and not enough prudential regulation, cycling through states of optimism, excessive risk-taking and over-borrowing that precede the inevitable crash – a dynamic endemic to the financial system itself (Minsky, 1992).

The Role of Public Debt

The largely private risk-taking associated with liberalization and financiali-zation becomes a public debt problem. The most proximate reasons involve the explicit and implicit guarantees that governments provide on private liabilities and the nationalization of bad private debts. But financial crises also systematically compromise public income and wealth via the effects of exchange rate depreciation on public assets and liabilities, increases in real interest rates, declines in real output, and the new borrowing required to deal with the costs of the crisis (De Bolle et al., 2006). Although sovereign defaults are a common feature of EDE financial crises, contrary to the rhetoric around neoliberal development macro policy, public debt is most often consequence, not cause.

Even among countries where public debt has been identified as a key source of the financial fragility that pushed economies into crisis – namely Mexico, Russia and Argentina in the 1990s – there is ample cause for qualification. Table 2.2 takes a closer look at public debt for these three countries in the years that precede and follow their respective crises. Reference level refers to public debt as a share of GDP three years prior to the crisis date ($T - 3$), and pre-crisis growth to the percentage increase in that level over the three years leading up to the crisis. As comparison,

Table 2.2   Financial crisis and public debt in Mexico, Russia and Argentina (%)

Country (Crisis Date)	Total Gross Central Government Debt as a Share of GDP			Total Gross External Government Debt as a Share of GDP		
	Reference level	Pre-crisis growth	Post-crisis growth	Reference level	Pre-crisis growth	Post-crisis growth
Mexico (1994)	42.6	−29.2	26.4	37.3	−10.7	47.0
Russia (1998)	30.2	34.1	39.5	31.0	4.0	96.4
Argentina (2001)	37.6	19.8	208.1	47.9	6.2	149.9

Sources and notes:
Figures based on author's calculations using data from Reinhart and Rogoff (2010); also refer to notes for Table 2.1. Time T refers to the crisis year in parentheses, the columns refer to the following:
Reference level is debt as a share of GDP at $T - 3$.
Pre-crisis growth refers to the percentage change between $T - 3$ and $T - 1$.
Post-crisis growth refers to the percentage change between $T - 1$ and $T + 3$.

the growth in public debt after the crisis presented in Table 2.1 is repeated here. Total and external debt as a share of GDP for Mexico was actually on the decline before the crisis, while both Russia and Argentina's pre-crisis profiles certainly do not bode the disaster of the crises to follow. However, these figures do not capture how the structure of debt makes EDE governments more vulnerable than debt levels reveal (e.g., the extent of foreign exchange–linked liabilities and short-term maturities). Even then there are arguments to be made about the respective roles of fiscal profligacy versus having to bend to the superimposed rules of global financial markets. These lessons are clearly reflected in many of the economic policy choices EDE governments are making in the current era.

Some Policy Changes and Open Questions

One of those choices is a shift away from effectively fixed to more flexible exchange rates, with monetary authorities sometimes intervening in foreign exchange markets to guide the real exchange rate – a sort of managed float (Damill et al., 2013). This helps protect against short-term capital flow volatility and preserves the ability of governments to use the exchange rate as a tool for development (i.e., avoiding real exchange rate appreciation) (Akyüz, 2014). EDE governments and firms have also shifted more of their borrowing from non-residents to domestic currency–denominated debt instruments, avoiding the currency and interest rate risks historically associated with external debt (Akyüz, 2011).[12] But not all EDE governments and firms can attract international investors to domestic securities markets. Even when they can, it means that domestic economies are more exposed to the sudden changes of heart common among internationally mobile investors.

A similar sort of mixed result comes from the tremendous growth of international reserves among EDEs, which went from less than one-quarter of their foreign assets in 2000 to more than 43 percent in 2013; about two-thirds of reserves accumulated since 2000 come from current account surpluses, with the remainder borrowed (Akyüz, 2014, p. 11). The build-up is precautionary in the sense that it guards against a host of ills introduced by international capital flows and the economic consequences of their sometimes sudden or substantial departure. It also hedges against sovereignty risk: the loss of policy autonomy that comes with IMF-type bailouts or having to provide the macro-policy conditions preferred by international investors (Grabel, 2006). Most of these reserves are held in low-yield treasury bonds issued by AEs, and there is an opportunity cost to tying up these funds as they are not being used to invest in development more directly – a central requirement for fulfilling the vision of the SDGs.

Moreover, reserve accumulation has been associated with a decline in domestic investment when it directs domestic savings abroad (Reinhart and Tashiro, 2013).

It may be that these changes have helped EDEs lower their vulnerability to some types of financial crises, as evidenced by the past decade where the only major financial crisis was generated by and largely limited to AEs, but increased their vulnerability in other ways. The widespread response of AE governments to the 2008 Global Financial Crisis, where fiscal expansion was effectively abandoned in favor of unconventional monetary instruments, renewed the flood of financial flows to EDEs, increasing global financial integration and generating new specters of vulnerability (Cornford, 2018). The ongoing tapering of expansionary monetary policy and the prospect of rising interest rates in the United States are certainly foreboding.

In the end, the most important question is whether increasing financial globalization, in its current poorly regulated and systematically risky form, adds to or detracts from development and sustainable, widely shared growth. The empirical evidence for a robust positive connection between financial globalization and growth is simply not there (Kose et al., 2009; Rodrik and Subramanian, 2009). We cannot presume the desirability of external finance, whatever its form, and limit focus and discussion to merely lessening its capacity to wreak economic havoc in one way or another.

NOTES

1. An earlier version of this chapter was written as a background paper for the 2015 *Trade and Development Report* (UNCTAD, 2015).
2. This point about the magnitude of investment required to fulfill the vision of the SDGs is one made by Richard Kozul-Wright, Director of the Division on Globalisation and Development Strategies at UNCTAD.
3. I group these ripple effects separately from the AFC to differentiate between the regional contagion of the AFC and how these costs manifested in other emerging market economies.
4. This data and the term "capital flow bonanza" are from Reinhart and Reinhart (2008), who note that a better measure would be reserve accumulation less the current account balance, but ultimately decide that the longer time series and greater consistency of data on the current account is a satisfactory substitute.
5. A better growth measure would be its cumulative deviation from the long-run trend, but I will do that in the next draft if the work goes that way.
6. In this section we limit our discussion to Latin America. Many other developing countries were swept up in the same cycle of financial crises, but we focus on Latin America as emblematic of the larger economic forces at work.
7. Even Brazil, which had capital controls and did not experience much in capital flight, suffered because of the general cutoff in lending to Latin America (Diaz-Alejandro, 1984).

8. As a share of GDP, the current account deficits for Thailand and Malaysia that year were 28.1 and 24.4 percent respectively (data from the IMF's October 2014 World Economic Outlook Database).
9. Taiwan and Hong Kong successfully fended off speculative attacks, but Korea was much more exposed in terms of short-term debt.
10. Data from the World Bank's World Development Indicators Database.
11. See also Demirgüç-Kunt and Detragiache (1998), Weller (2001) and Reinhart and Reinhart (2008).
12. Data from the World Bank (2013) indicate that at the end of 2012 the share of non-resident holdings of local EDE debt markets was 26.6 percent, and that it was as high as 40 percent in some economies (cited in Akyüz, 2014, p. 20).

REFERENCES

Akyüz, Y. (2011), "Capital flows to developing countries in historical perspective: Will the current boom end with a bust?," *South Centre Research Paper 37.*

Akyüz, Y. (2014), "Internationalization of finance and changing vulnerabilities in emerging and developing economies," *UNCTAD Discussion Paper 217.*

Arean, M., S. Bouza and E. Dabla-Norris et al. (2015), "Credit booms and macroeconomic dynamics: Stylized facts and lessons for low-income countries," *IMF Working Paper WP/15/11.*

Boughton, J.M. (2012), *Tearing Down Walls: The International Monetary Fund 1990–1999*, Washington, DC: International Monetary Fund.

Calvo, G.A. (2005), *Emerging Capital Markets in Turmoil: Bad Luck or Bad Policy?*, Cambridge, MA: MIT Press.

Calvo, G.A. and E. Talvi (2005), "Sudden stop, financial factors and economic collapse in Latin America: Learning from Argentina and Chile," *NBER Working Paper 11153.*

Calvo, G.A., A. Izquierdo and L.-F. Mejía (2004), "On the empirics of sudden stops: The relevance of balance sheet effects," *NBER Working Paper 10520.*

Chang, H.-J. (2000), "The hazard of moral hazard: Untangling the Asian crisis," *World Development*, **28**(4), 775–8.

Cornford, A. (2018), "Playing with financial fire: A South perspective on the international financial system," *South Centre Research Paper 84.*

Crotty, J. and K.-K. Lee (2004), "Was the IMF's imposition of economic regime change in Korea justified? A critique of the IMF's economic and political role before and after the crisis," *Political Economy Research Institute Working Paper 77.*

Damill, M., R. Frenkel and M. Rapetti (2013), "Financial and currency crises in Latin America," in M.H. Wolfson and G.A. Epstein (eds), *The Handbook of the Political Economy of Financial Crises*, Oxford and New York: Oxford University Press, pp. 296–310.

De Bolle, M., B. Rother and I. Hakobyan (2006), "The level and composition of public sector debt in emerging market crises," *International Monetary Fund Working Paper WP/06/186.*

Demirgüç-Kunt, A. and E. Detragiache (1998), "Financial liberalization and financial fragility," *World Bank Policy Research Working Paper 1917.*

Diaz-Alejandro, C.F. (1984), "Latin American debt: I don't think we are in Kansas anymore," *Brookings Papers on Economic Activity*, **2**, 335–403.

Diaz-Alejandro, C.F. (1985), "Good-bye financial repression, hello financial crash," *Journal of Development Economics*, **19**(1–2), 1–24.

Elekdog, S. and Y. Wu (2011), "Rapid credit growth: Boon or boom–bust?," *IMF Working Paper WP/11/241*.

Goldfajn, I. and R.W. Valdes (1999), "The aftermath of appreciations," *The Quarterly Journal of Economics*, **114**(1), 229–62.

Grabel, I. (1996), "Stock markets, rentier interest, and the current Mexican crisis," *Journal of Economic Issues*, **30**(2), 443–9.

Grabel, I. (1999), "Mexico redux? Making sense of the financial crisis of 1997–98," *Journal of Economic Issues*, **33**(2), 375–81.

Grabel, I. (2006), "A post-Keynesian analysis of financial crisis in the developing world and directions for reform," in P. Arestis and M. Sawyer (eds), *A Handbook of Alternative Monetary Macroeconomics*, Cheltenham, UK and Northampton, MA: Edward Elgar Publishing, pp. 403–19.

Kose, M.A., E. Prasad, K. Rogoff and S.-J. Wei (2009), "Financial globalization: A reappraisal," *IMF Staff Papers*, **56**(1), 8–62.

Krugman, P. (1979), "A model of balance-of-payments crises," *Journal of Money, Credit and Banking*, **11**(3), 311–25.

Krugman, P. (1999), "Balance sheets, the transfer problem, and financial crises," *International Tax and Public Finance*, **6**(4), 459–72.

Krugman, P. (2014), "Currency regimes, capital flows, and crises," *IMF Economic Review*, **62**(4), 470–93.

Laeven, L. and F. Valencia (2008), "Systemic banking crises: A new database," *IMF Working Paper WP/08/224*.

Lustig, N. (1995), "The Mexican peso crisis: The foreseeable and the surprise," *Brookings Discussion Papers in International Economics*.

Minsky, H. (1992), "The financial instability hypothesis," *Levy Economics Institute of Bard College Working Paper 74*.

Montes, M. (1998), *The Currency Crisis in Southeast Asia*, Singapore: Institute of Southeast Asian Studies.

Moreno-Brid, J.C. and J. Ros (2004), "Mexico's market reforms in historical perspective," *CEPAL Review*, **84**, 35–56.

Morley, S.A., R. Machado and S. Pettinato (1999), "Indexes of structural reform in Latin America," *Serie Reformas Económicas*, Santiago: Economic Commission for Latin America and the Caribbean.

Obstfeld, M. (1994), "The logic of currency crises," *NBER Working Paper 4640*.

Palma, G.J. (2003), "The Latin American economies during the second half of the twentieth century – from the age of 'ISI' to the age of 'the end of history'," in H.-J. Chang (ed.), *Rethinking Development Economics*, London: Anthem Press, pp. 125–52.

Palma, G.J. (2011), "How the full opening of the capital account to highly liquid financial markets led Latin America to two and half cycles of 'mania, panic and crash'," *Cambridge Working Papers in Economics (CWPE) 1201*.

Pinto, B. and S. Ulatov (2010), "Financial globalization and the Russian crisis," *World Bank Policy Research Working Paper 5312*.

Radelet, S. and J. Sachs (2000), "The onset of the East Asian financial crisis," in P. Krugman (ed.), *Currency Crises*, Chicago, IL: University of Chicago Press, pp. 105–53.

Reinhart, C.M. and V.R. Reinhart (2008), "Capital flow bonanzas: An encompassing view of the past and present," *NBER Working Paper 14321*.

Reinhart, C.M. and K.S. Rogoff (2009), *This Time is Different: Eight Centuries of Financial Folly*, Princeton, NJ and Oxford: Princeton University Press.

Reinhart, C.M. and K.S. Rogoff (2010), "From financial crash to debt crisis," *NBER Working Paper 15795*.

Reinhart, C.M. and T. Tashiro (2013), "Crowding out redefined: The role of reserve accumulation," *NBER Working Paper 19652*.

Rodrik, D. and A. Subramanian (2009), "Why did financial globalization disappoint?," *IMF Staff Papers*, **56**(1), 112–38.

Stiglitz, J. (2003), "Whither reform? Towards a new agenda for Latin America," *CEPAL Review*, **80**, 7–37.

Takáts, E. and C. Uper (2013), "Credit and growth after financial crises," *BIS Working Paper 416*.

UNCTAD (1999), *Trade and Development Report, 1999: Fragile Recovery and Risks Trade, Finance and Growth*, New York and Geneva: United Nations.

UNCTAD (2015), *Trade and Development Report, 2015: Making the International Financial Architecture Work for Development*, New York and Geneva: United Nations.

Wade, R. (1998), "The Asian debt-and-development crisis of 1997–?: Causes and consequences," *World Development*, **26**(8), 1535–53.

Weller, C. (2001), "Financial crises after financial liberalisation: Exceptional circumstances or structural weakness?," *Journal of Development Studies*, **38**(1), 98–127.

World Bank (2013), "Recent developments in local currency bond markets (LCBMs)," Washington, DC: World Bank Group, October, accessed 16 July 2018 at en.g20russia.ru/load/783687600.

3. Too good to be true: What the Icelandic crisis revealed about global finance

Nina Eichacker

INTRODUCTION

In 2008, Iceland's financial crisis appeared to surprise Western media and economists. However, Iceland's financial development in the 1990s and early 2000s ought to have concerned observers and Icelandic policy-makers. Despite Icelandic fundamentals indicating potential for crisis, historic precedence of financial liberalization resulting in crises, and prominent reports by policy-makers, academics and industry about the likelihood of a crisis, Icelandic and international bankers continued to engage in large transactions. The Icelandic krona continued to appreciate, internationally respected economists wrote reports praising Iceland's financial sector, and credit rating agencies increased the country's bond ratings. Why did so many fail to predict Iceland's financial crisis?

This question is important for several reasons. First, if Iceland's financial sector could heat up as profoundly as it did with little apparent public notice, it suggests that there is little to stop something similar from occurring again, in Iceland or elsewhere. Further, the costs of the financial crisis in Iceland have been substantial, despite how favorably Iceland's economic performance may have been in 2008 as compared with other European countries that experienced financial crises. Finally, emphasizing that large-scale financial crises can occur in developed countries that seem to have good public integrity is important for insuring against the costs of such crises in the future.

Existing literature explores the causes of Iceland's financial crisis in 2008. These studies have mainly identified the origins of the crisis in excess consumption, monetary policy, and corrupt or fraudulent activity. These studies tell isolated stories of how Icelandic government policies, banking excess, and household behavior helped doom the Icelandic economy. However, this literature lacks a broader analysis that places the crisis in a historical and institutional context that allows an exploration of factors that allow crises to develop, namely large-scale irrational exuberance, moral hazard, and inadequate global financial supervision before the 2008 financial crisis at the domestic and the international level. This chapter develops a unified narrative that links Iceland's developing country financial crisis narrative with the developed country financial crisis narrative. Additionally, this chapter identifies the institutional short-sightedness of investors as Iceland's investment banking sector grew, and shows the potential for "mistakes" to repeat on a grand scale if academics, policymakers, and private sector actors are unobservant in the future.

The chapter is organized as follows. The second section briefly reviews the existing literature about the Icelandic financial crisis, with attention to recurring arguments about institutional changes in Iceland's monetary and financial architecture, and broad theories of the connection between financial liberalization and the onset of financial crisis. The third section compiles monetary and financial data to illustrate the change in Icelandic economic fundamentals prior to the onset of its crisis as well as the effects of the aftermath of the crisis. The fourth section illustrates how irrational exuberance and moral hazard enabled financial sector growth to unsustainable proportions even as a literature developed predicting an imminent Icelandic financial collapse. The final section of the chapter revisits the paradox of Iceland's crisis being a surprise despite ample evidence and past precedent that ought to have alerted more observers than were aware of Iceland's accumulating problems.

LITERATURE REVIEW

This section is divided into three subsections. The first summarizes literature about the theoretical causes of financial crises, the second examines empirical studies of the linkage between financial liberalization and crisis, and the third focuses on analyses of the particulars of the Icelandic financial crisis and the gaps that remain.

Theoretical Causes of Financial Crisis

Analyses of financial crisis focus on different theoretical causes depending on whether a country is considered to be developing or developed. A well-established theoretical and empirical literature supports the idea that rapid liberalization of financial sectors is likely to be associated with the onset of financial crisis, particularly in developing countries that may lack institutional integrity. Minskyian, Keynesian, and behavioral analyses of finance also argue that developed countries are prone to dynamics that increase financial and economic instability as their financial sectors grow relative to the rest of an economy (Keynes, 1933; Minsky, 1982; Shiller, 2000; Shleifer, 2000). This literature helps one understand how the Icelandic economy changed in the years preceding 2008, and why the economy was vulnerable to a financial crisis.

Monetary policy that targets inflation is associated with increasing interest rates as aggregate demand and GDP increase; as the economy expands and prices rise, central bankers raise interest rates, which should theoretically stem domestic investment and borrowing. These policies may have the unintended effect of encouraging more investment in the domestic economy from foreign interests who pursue higher yields and appreciating currencies. As a result, proponents of inflation-targeting monetary policy may still caution against its application too abruptly in emerging economies in order to prevent potential bubbles from forming (Mishkin and Herbertsson, 2011). While capital account liberalization may increase domestic access to credit and promote more domestic investment, there are simultaneous risks of hot inflows as domestic GDP grows, and capital flight in the event of a downturn. Conventional development and international finance literature cautions against rapid capital account liberalization until a country has a sufficiently robust financial regulatory apparatus to hedge against potential capital surges and sudden stops (Eichengreen and Leblang, 2003; Jeanne, Subramanian and Williamson, 2012). The Icelandic central bank's reorientation of monetary policy in the 1990s and the subsequent change in foreign direct investment (FDI) and overall capital flows into that country highlight the importance of understanding this connection.

Keynes (1933), Minsky (1982), behavioral finance theorists like Shiller (2000) and Shleifer (2000), and systemic risk analysts like Adrian and Shin (2008) and others model the linkage between financial expansion and crisis. Keynes argued that herd behavior could result in adverse economic outcomes, and Minsky argued that economies open to all capital flows were prone to financial booms and subsequent financial fragility as economies would overheat. Shiller and Shleifer have written about irrational exuberance and bias of market participants preventing financial actors from recognizing downturns that are imminent or have begun, increasing the costs of ensuing crashes for all. Adrian and Shin and others argue that the substantial shift toward market-oriented finance, shadow banking and wholesale finance have created vulnerabilities throughout the financial system, increasing systemic risk, potential likelihood of crisis and the costs of financial crisis. These dynamics were all present during the lead up to and onset of the Icelandic financial crisis.

Studies of the Linkage Between Financial Liberalization and Crisis

An extensive literature examines the historical and empirical context of financial liberalization and crisis. Bordo et al. (2001), Grabel (2003), Kindleberger and Aliber (2005), and Reinhart and Rogoff (2009) describe the correlation between financial liberalization and crisis as well as the recurring nature of financial crises throughout history in both developed and emerging markets. Econometric analyses by Bordo et al. (2001), Eichengreen and Arteta (2000), Rodrik (2005), and Barrell et al. (2010), among others, demonstrate the causal link between financial liberalization and the incidence of financial crisis using various econometric techniques, country samples, and time periods. The overwhelming conclusion of these authors is that financial liberalization in developing states that lack sophisticated financial regulatory institutions bear risks of financial crisis if they liberalize too rapidly, and that the costs of these crises are likely to inhibit economic growth.

An extensive literature has investigated the likelihood of financial crisis in developed economies. Jordà, Schularick and Taylor (2011), Forbes and Warnock (2012), and Broner et al. (2013) have written about the correlation between credit bonanzas and the onset of financial crisis in developing and developed economies. Systemic risk is associated with trends such as the increasing prevalence of shadow banking and securitization. This implies increasing uncertainty about asset values and risk levels as banks move assets off their balance sheets and partake in novel securitization techniques, which is more likely in developed financial systems. Adrian and Shin (2008), Acharya and Schnabl (2010), and Adrian and Ashcraft (2012) have performed econometric analyses that support the notion that increased systemic risk is associated with financial crisis in a broad sense. Ang and Longstaff (2013), Schüler (2003), and Engle, Jondeau and Rockinger (2015) have also demonstrated that European states with presumably sophisticated financial institutions have had greater likelihood and incidence of financial crisis as systemic risk, financialization, and securitization have increased. Given these dynamics it is important to consider the nature of the global financial architecture in the twenty-first century, as well as the leverage, capital, and financial dynamics of Iceland's financial sector before the 2008 crisis.

Prominent Analyses of Iceland's Crisis

The Icelandic financial crisis had its origins in monetary and regulatory policy. In the 1990s, the Icelandic government and central bank liberalized the Icelandic banking sector, setting the stage for large capital inflows. As inflows increased Icelandic banks increased their trading activity and acquisition of foreign assets, thereby increasing their profits (Lewis,

2009; Benediktsdottir, Danielsson and Zoega, 2011; Johnsen, 2014). The Icelandic government encouraged Icelanders to buy shares in Icelandic banks, which also pushed up the banks' share prices.

As capital flows increased, Icelandic gross domestic product (GDP) increased as well, contributing to currency appreciation and inflation. The Icelandic krona (ISK) appreciated after large-scale capital inflows, further encouraging foreign investment in Icelandic markets. Icelanders also began to engage in currency carry trades to finance purchases of expensive imports (Lewis, 2009). When foreign investors reduced their lending to Icelandic banks, Iceland's big three banks introduced international retail banks, and households in other parts of Europe opened accounts to take advantage of Iceland's interest rates. These monetary dynamics and financial activities extended the scope of those affected by Iceland's financial boom and bust.

Conservative politicians and business interests worked together to transform Icelandic finance from fundamentally stability oriented to risk-loving by European standards (Wade and Sigurgeirsdottir, 2010, 2012). Conflicts of interest grew as Icelandic banks bought shares of media companies, and media companies bought shares in investment companies, reducing the media's incentive to report unfavorable news about the industry (Andersen, 2010; Wade and Sigurgeirsdottir, 2010, 2012; Arnarson et al., 2011).

Corporate governance of the financial sector failed to recognize or prosecute fraud (Johnsen, 2014). When Icelandic banks were unable to borrow enough in international markets to cover their liabilities, they developed "love letters." These were "new unsecured bonds in the domestic market at a favorable rate," issued in ISK that banks exchanged and resold with other Icelandic banks; subsequently, these bonds were issued in euros, which Icelandic banks exchanged and resold to Eurozone banks (ibid.). Moody's credit rankings of Iceland's banks actually improved as the financial sector grew, on the assumption that the Central Bank of Iceland would act as a lender of last resort in the event of a crisis. Improved ratings on Icelandic bonds motivated more investment in the Icelandic financial sector.

International exuberance about Iceland's financial sector and currency had consequences for Iceland's domestic economy (Lewis, 2009). The influx of capital into a relatively young financial system generated growth that regulators could not have handled, even if they had cared to limit it. Despite their relative inexperience, Iceland's financial actors' willingness to engage in highly leveraged borrowing and investment in tandem with willingness of European partners to lend and invest large sums in the Icelandic banks fomented growth and exacerbated the domestic and international costs of Iceland's inevitable crisis.

This literature taken together tells a compelling story about the causes of Iceland's crisis, but it fails to reveal what Iceland's financial boom and bust says about the broader global economy. Since Iceland's banks and economy could not have grown as it did without international participation, it is important to understand how outside investors failed to heed warnings of the crisis to avoid complicity in financial bubbles or to motivate stability-minded policies. The rest of this chapter addresses the warning data and reports that outside investors and institutions should have recognized as signs of a bubble as well as the reasons why those outsiders were likely to ignore those signals.

EMPIRICAL ANALYSIS

Before the 2008 crisis, Icelandic capital account and inflation data resembled that of a developing rather than a developed economy. Once the Icelandic central bank shifted to a solid inflation-targeting policy regime, inflation rates began to rise as interest rates rose, capital inflows increased, and exchange rates appreciated. These rising capital inflows increased the instability of Icelandic financial and economic systems, particularly since Icelandic banks used those funds to invest heavily in domestic and international securities and shares. These processes reflected the experiences of other developing economies that shifted from stability-minded to inflation-targeting monetary policies, and it set the stage for other changes in Icelandic finance that precipitated the eventual financial crisis. As these dynamics developed, Icelandic banks increased their credit and financial intermediation and increased turnover in security and equity markets. This increased systemic risk in the Icelandic financial sector. This pairing of developing and developed economy trends toward crisis exacerbated the costs of Iceland's subsequent financial crisis.

From 1984 until 1995, the Icelandic central bank shifted from stability-focused monetary policy, which restricted capital flows and maintained very low interest rates, to a regime that targeted inflation, and rapidly increased interest rates. From the early 1990s through 2008, average Icelandic interest rates for general lending and CPI indexed securities approximately doubled (Statistics Iceland, 2016). This contrasted with a period of low interest rates in US and European markets and encouraged increasing capital inflows to Icelandic banks, which increased from roughly 30 percent of GDP in the early 1990s to more than 450 percent of GDP in 2008 (BIS Statistics, 2016). From 2000 until 2008, the Icelandic exchange rate fell by 30 percent against the dollar. Iceland's appreciating currency was accompanied by increasing imports and a rising current account deficit. These changes in foreign liabilities increased Icelandic vulnerability to crisis. Finally, these changes were associated with rising Icelandic inflation from 2.1 percent in 2003, to 12.4 percent in 2008, as the central bank failed to sterilize the price effects of the increasing capital inflows (Statistics Iceland, 2016).

Iceland's inflation-targeting and capital account liberalization policies had precedent in Latin American and Turkish experiences in the 1990s and early 2000s. The Southern Cone states of Chile, Uruguay, and Argentina rapidly liberalized their financial sectors while reorienting monetary policy to inflation targeting in the 1970s and 1980s. The end result was an influx of hot money, appreciation of interest rates, and overvalued exchange rates (Diaz-Alejandro, 1985). As these states' terms of trade improved, current account deficits and national debt grew. Iceland's process of financial liberalization after trade liberalization generated similar capital flow and exchange rate dynamics. As Icelanders purchased more imports, and firms borrowed more from international capital markets, the economy became more vulnerable to sudden stops in foreign capital. In the moment that hot inflows ceased in Chile, Argentina, and Uruguay, the downturns were rapid and substantial.

Turkey is another example of a state that liberalized trade and capital flows in an attempt to court economic growth, following a period of strong economic regulation and financial repression. It also experienced hot money flows, inflation targeting–induced exchange rate appreciation, and financial crises. After an initial rapid liberalization of the capital account that resulted in various scandals in the late 1970s, the Turkish government proceeded with subsequent liberalization more gradually. It liberalized the foreign exchange regime in 1984, and then created an interbank market "for short-term borrowing. . .in 1986," followed by the central bank's initiation of open market operations in 1987, and eventually "[reopened] the Istanbul Stock Exchange" (Boratav and Yeldan, 2006). In 1989, the Turkish state eliminated capital controls, and "full convertibility of the Turkish lira was realized at the beginning of 1990" (ibid.). These changes set the course for increasing waves of foreign capital inflows but ambiguous real sector consequences. Gross inflows to domestic banks rose between 1990 and 1995, before dropping from 1996 to 1998, and then they resumed at high volumes in 1999. Gross bank inflows grew from $50 billion in 1991 to $120 billion in 1995; under the disinflation policy of 2000, gross capital inflows were $209 billion and gross capital outflows were $204 billion (ibid.).

Turkey eventually experienced three major financial crises in the 1990s and early 2000s. These occurred in 1994, between 1998 and 1999, after the downgrade of the Turkish credit rating prompted by contagion effects in the global crisis in Russia and East Asia, and in 2000–01, after several banks' failures triggered a subsequent episode of capital flight. In 1994, capital outflows were 4.8 percent of Turkish gross national product (GNP); in 1998, they were 3.9 percent of GNP, and eight banks were essentially nationalized. In 2000, the Turkish central bank lost "nearly $7 billion" in reserves and 52 percent of its "net external assets" (ibid.). Iceland's financial losses following the sudden stop of lending from large US investment banks were larger, particularly given the size of the Icelandic population; the parallel experience of economic destabilization after financial liberalization holds.

Taken together, these experiences reflect Frederic Mishkin's advice that inflation-targeting monetary policy and capital account liberalization could be associated with financial instability and should be pursued cautiously in developing economies that lacked sophisticated financial regulatory institutions (Mishkin, 2000; Jeanne et al., 2012). Iceland's rapid financial liberalization, together with inflation-targeting policies that would entice large-scale foreign investment, should have been a signal to domestic and international financial actors of the risk of sudden stops and financial crisis. That it did not indicates that Iceland was different despite its rational lack of financial regulatory sophistication.

Between 2002 and 2008, Icelandic demand for financial assets increased across the Icelandic economy, and holdings of securities and shares increased as a share of these holdings, as shown in Figures 3.1 and 3.2.

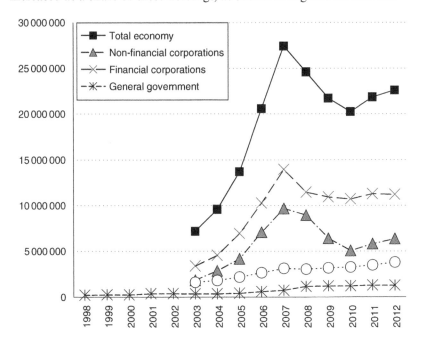

Source: OECD Statistics.

Figure 3.1   Icelandic financial asset holdings, by sector (millions of ISK)

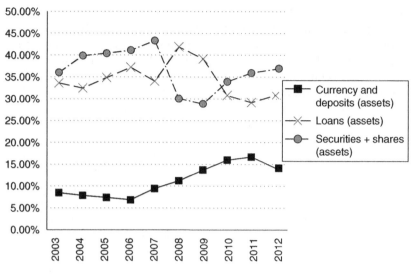

Source: OECD Statistics.

Figure 3.2   Shares of financial assets in Iceland's total economy

Economy-wide issuance of securities and shares also increased over this period. These dynamics increased the Icelandic population's vulnerability to credit and financial crises that might affect those assets and liabilities.

Icelandic financial corporations' behavior also increased the systemic risk of the Icelandic economy. Financial corporations issued more loans, securities, and shares in this period while increasing their borrowing and debt issuance over financial corporations' liabilities. These dynamics increased banks' vulnerability to financial and real sector shocks, as well as international vulnerability to those shocks. Icelandic credit intermediation, the share of loans held as financial corporations' assets relative to borrowing by non-financial firms, the general government, households and non-profits, increased in this period (Figure 3.3).

These ratios and trends indicate the growing importance of the Icelandic financial sector relative to the rest of the Icelandic economy, and the increasing vulnerability of the economy to financial crisis.

Increasing securitization by the Icelandic financial sector also increased the economy's vulnerability to systemic risk and financial crisis. Icelandic issuance of securities and shares increased, as well as increasing bank (and total economy) holdings of securities and shares. Turnover of Icelandic security markets, particularly securities, equities, and housing-related bonds, increased substantially in this period (Figure 3.4).

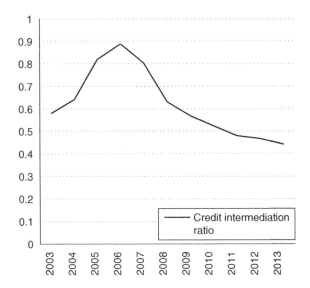

Source: OECD Statistics.

Figure 3.3   Icelandic credit and financial intermediation ratios

The increased scope of activity increased asset prices and short-term growth of holdings, which amplified the magnitude of losses in a crisis. Though Icelandic banking profits rose during this period, those profits depended on banks' willingness to trade with other Icelandic banks and the Icelandic public's willingness to purchase those banks' shares (Lewis, 2009; Sigurjonsson, 2011; Johnsen, 2014)

This section has shown Icelandic economic trends that indicated a growing bubble. These should have signaled financial interests about Iceland's financial instability, and increased oversight within and outside of Icelandic markets. These trends also reflected dynamics that led to crises in developing economies. However, these trends failed to sway international investors, indicating a disconnect between Iceland's assumed financial sophistication and its regulators' ability to prevent a large-scale crisis. The next section of this chapter investigates how the global reaction to Iceland's financial performance also reflected Keynesian and Minskyian assumptions about financialization and crisis as well as behavioral finance theories of irrational exuberance and moral hazard.

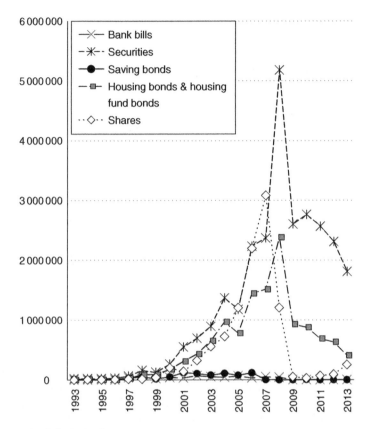

Source: Statistics Iceland.

Figure 3.4 *Trading in Icelandic financial markets – turnover in millions of ISK*

POST-KEYNESIAN STORIES

Narrative accounts of Icelandic institutional change before 2008 also demonstrated its propensity for a financial crisis. Despite analysis from Danske Bank, the IMF, and the OECD demonstrating the fragility of Iceland's financial sector, reports by academics like Robert Wade, and the negative credit assessments by Fitch, Icelandic banks continued to trade as they had in the early 2000s. International banks continued to lend to Icelandic banks. Even after a small-scale funding crisis in 2006, Icelandic banks continued to accrue international retail banking business. This section discusses how positive reports by economists and the credit rating agency

Moody's assuaged investor and consumer confidence, allowing Icelandic banks to continue to grow, as well as how these reports demonstrated conventional assumptions about Iceland's institutional integrity and lack of state corruption. Public critiques of Iceland's rapid financialization and bubble economy failed to alert industry interests, illustrating Keynesian and Minskyian theories of what causes financial crises, namely irrational exuberance, as well as the importance of moral hazard in understanding the build-up to Iceland's crisis.

Iceland's lack of transparent information about its financial sector parallels the common story about developing counties' propensity for financial crises. Reports by Mishkin and other mainstream economists, paid for by Iceland's Chamber of Commerce, specifically cited Iceland's institutional integrity in their arguments that Iceland should not be considered at risk of financial crisis (Mishkin and Herbertsson, 2011). In fact, the Icelandic Special Commission Report (SIC, 2010) and others have identified the Icelandic government's role in threatening to defund public Icelandic institutions and agencies that published reports contradicting the narrative of a robust financial infrastructure and growth (Wade and Sigurgeirsdottir, 2010).

Domestic media coverage of Iceland's financial health reflected the consequences of increased financial and corporate shareholding in Iceland's economy. Before 2008, the Icelandic media consistently underpublished reports critical of the Icelandic financial sector, while publishing more stories praising Iceland's big three banks (Andersen, 2010). Sigurjonsson (2011) identified the cause of this disparity in cross-ownership of company shares between Icelandic financial actors and institutions and Icelandic media institutions. The interconnectedness of these industries created conflicts of interest for Icelandic financial institutions, the Icelandic public, and the international financial community.

Moral hazard also bolstered the international financial community's trust in Iceland. Moody's decision to upgrade Iceland's credit rating after Fitch had downgraded it increased confidence in Icelandic finance. Moody's decision to improve Iceland's credit rating stemmed from the agency's assessment that Iceland demonstrated such financial leverage that its central bank was certain to bail out the big three banks in the event of financial crisis as the lender of last resort. Iceland's financial system was assumed to be "too big to fail," an example of moral hazard with international consequences.

Events in Iceland again paralleled the experience of Southern Cone states in the 1980s. Privatization of banks in the Southern Cone did not make them more efficient; it made them less risk-averse. Chilean banks invested in risky ventures and appeared to invest in firms to which they were connected politically (Diaz-Alejandro, 1985; Corbo and de Melo, 1987). Moral hazard increased in these states as well. Argentina's central bank offered guarantees on bank deposits, encouraging more capital inflows; Chile's central bank ultimately guaranteed deposits to preserve the integrity of its banking system after an initial wave of panics early in the liberalization process. Foreign governments' willingness to use their leverage to ensure that governments or central banks would insure their investments in emerging markets guaranteed moral hazard problems for developing countries considering financial liberalization (Diaz-Alejandro, 1985). Despite the lack of an official claim that the Central Bank of Iceland would act as lender of last resort, Icelandic banks and foreign investors behavior implied a similar trust that no government would allow its banks to enter insolvency (Johnsen, 2014).

The overwhelming trust in Iceland's governing bodies, reporters, and financial institutions in the face of unfavorable reports and data illustrates an unwillingness of eager parties to consider the possibility of Iceland's financial sector's failure. They also demonstrate why financial actors aware of problems in Icelandic finance were hesitant to speak out or eager to profit from internal knowledge of Iceland's inevitable financial collapse. Observers that voiced problems could assume they would be pilloried by Icelandic government and financial institutions and ignored by international investors. If, on the other hand, they could profit from their knowledge, shorting Icelandic banks would be a rational reaction (Lewis, 2009).

ICELAND'S PARADOX

Given prolific empirical and narrative evidence of Icelandic financial instability from academic, public and private sources, why should Iceland's financial crisis have been a surprise for the broader global economy? This chapter points to three factors. First, the prevailing notion that Iceland's economy should succeed in the wake of monumental financial change, given its status as a Western European state with supposedly robust institutions, increased institutional trust in Icelandic banks despite Iceland's rapid growth and short history of financial liberalization. Second, Iceland's crisis also illustrates the power of irrational exuberance and moral hazard to diminish caution about the risks of rapid financial expansion and crisis, and the tendency of investors to assume the best despite evidence to the contrary. Finally, Iceland's crisis reveals the inherent instability created by rapid financialization. When a country adopts a financial approach to economic growth that deregulates banks, encourages international capital inflows through inflation-targeting monetary policy, and promotes wide-scale acquisition of shares and securities in those financial institutions by banks, households, non-financial firms, and the government, financial firms appear to be artificially profitable, and conflicts of interest develop that weaken the stability of the financial sector and broad economy.

Though a substantial literature has emerged since 2008 explaining the particulars of the Icelandic financial crisis, little attention has been paid to what Iceland's crisis reveals about global economic dynamics. This chapter has demonstrated how Iceland's rapid financialization created systemic risks for the Icelandic economy as a whole, illustrating Keynesian and Minskyian arguments that financial systems are inherently prone to crisis without adequate regulatory apparatuses to counteract that tendency. The Icelandic central bank's decision to change the course of policy from stability promotion to inflation targeting set the stage for rising interest rates, a precipitous increase in capital flows and prices, and asset bubbles in the housing market. The Icelandic government's policy to promote non-financial firms' and households' purchase of shares in Icelandic banks created perverse incentives for the banks to raise their share prices and increased the scope of losses in the event of the banks' decline. Together these processes increased Icelandic instability and increased the costs of the inevitable financial crisis.

This chapter also demonstrates the global prevalence of behavioral finance theories of irrational exuberance and moral hazard. Investors and banks had access to data demonstrating trends toward instability, and to analyses illustrating the risks of investing in Iceland's financial system and economy at large. Many continued to follow the advice of economists like Mishkin and Herbertsson (2011) and Portes, Baldursson and Olafsson (2011) who argued that Iceland's financial sector was robust and stable, and that Iceland should not be assumed to have the same financial risks as developing economies despite the newness of its supercharged financial system. Alternately, they followed the rationale set forth by Moody's, that Iceland's financial system was so large that it was guaranteed to be bailed out by the Central Bank of Iceland in the event of some disaster. Whatever the source of confidence in Iceland's economy and financial sector these outside investors' continued willingness to lend to Iceland increased the leveraged state of Icelandic banks and the scope and costs of the eventual financial crisis.

This willful ignorance or irrational exuberance extended to historical experience. Iceland's government orchestrated a remarkably fast liberalization of the state's financial sector alongside a reorientation of national monetary policy from being stability oriented to targeting inflation. Historically, there have been many instances of states pursuing these sorts of policies and then incurring financial crises in short order. The national and international unwillingness to compare Iceland's policy actions and history to that of developing economies like Turkey and Latin America demonstrates a bias in favor of Western European economies. The lack of comparison with developing economies also betrays the assumption that Icelandic institutions were ready for the job of supervising a radically transformed financial sector that embraced the newest financial technologies, the risks of which were underestimated even in sophisticated financial centers like Switzerland, London, and Wall Street. Further, evidence that the Icelandic government actively repressed the publication of data and narratives counter to the story of a commanding and successful Icelandic financial sector, and the Icelandic media's general unwillingness to publish unflattering stories give lie to the notion that Western European states' financial institutions and governments can be trusted to ensure the public welfare and reveal information that may have adverse consequences for the domestic economy or financial interests.

These three lessons from Iceland's crisis indicate the need for the following policies moving forward. First, in an era of unprecedented financial complexity, any state that liberalizes or changes the fundamental premise of monetary policy rapidly should be subject to increased scrutiny. Iceland is not unique as a country that liberalized its financial sector and redirected its monetary policy rapidly and later experienced unsustainable financial growth and crisis. Its fate as a supposedly sophisticated Western state indicates the broader need for scrutiny of financial markets at the domestic and international levels. The consequences for Iceland's population also demonstrate that, while some actors and institutions may recognize the potential for financial crisis and act in ways that maximize their profits, the broader public must be aware of the changes of their new financial landscapes. Greater financial literacy across the economy can help local populations insure against broader economic losses in the event of a crisis that originates in the private sector. Finally, states should reconsider finance-led growth strategies since the costs of financialization, given moral hazard and irrational exuberance, increase rapidly without meaningful oversight. Iceland's experience illustrates the effects of such to the rest of the world.

REFERENCES

Acharya, V. and P. Schnabl (2010), "Do global banks spread global imbalances? Asset-backed commercial paper during the financial crisis of 2007–2009," *IMF Economic Review*, **58**, 37–73.

Adrian, T. and A.B. Ashcraft (2012), "Shadow banking regulation," *FRB of New York Staff Report No. 559.*

Adrian, T. and H.S. Shin (2008), "Financial intermediaries, financial stability, and monetary policy," *Federal Reserve Bank of New York Staff Report No. 346.*

Andersen, A. (2010), "The watchdog that didn't bark," *Reykjavik Grapevine*, 8 October.

Ang, A. and F.A. Longstaff (2013), "Systemic sovereign credit risk: Lessons from the US and Europe," *Journal of Monetary Economics*, **60**(5), 493–510.

Arnarson, M., Þ. Kristjánsson and A. Bjarnason et al. (2011), *The Icelandic Economic Collapse: A Systems Analysis Perspective on Financial, Social and World System Links*, University of Iceland Multi-Disciplinary Report.

Barrell, R., E.P. Davis, D. Karim and I. Liadze (2010), "Bank regulation, property prices, and early warning systems in OECD countries," *Journal of Banking and Finance*, **34**, 2255–64.

Benediktsdottir, S., J. Danielsson and G. Zoega (2011), "Lessons from a collapse of a financial system," *Economic Policy*, **26**, 183–235.

BIS Statistics (2016) [website], accessed October 2016 at https://www.bis.org/statistics/index.htm.

Boratav, K. and E. Yeldan (2006), "Turkey, 1980–2000: Financial liberalization, macroeconomic (in)stability, and patterns of distribution," in L. Taylor (ed.), *External Liberalization in Asia, Post-Socialist Europe, and Brazil*, Oxford: Oxford University Press, pp. 417–45.

Bordo, M., B. Eichengreen and D. Klingebiel et al. (2001), "Is the crisis problem growing more severe?," *Economic Policy*, **16**(32), 51–82.

Broner, F., T. Didier, A. Erce and S.L. Schmukler (2013), "Gross capital flows: Dynamics and crises," *Journal of Monetary Economics*, **60**(1), 113–33.

Corbo, V. and J. de Melo (1987), "Lessons from the Southern Cone policy reforms," *The World Bank Research Observer*, **2**(2), 111–42.

Diaz-Alejandro, C. (1985), "Good-bye financial repression, hello financial crash," *Journal of Development Economics*, **19**(1), 1–24.

Eichengreen, B. and C. Arteta (2000), "Banking crises in emerging markets: Presumptions and evidence," *UC Berkeley: Center for International and Development Economics Research Papers, No. C00-115*.

Eichengreen, B. and D. Leblang (2003), "Capital account liberalization and growth: Was Mr. Mahathir right?," *International Journal of Finance and Economics*, **8**(3), 205–24.

Engle, R., E. Jondeau and M. Rockinger (2015), "Systemic risk in Europe," *Review of Finance*, **19**(1), 145–90.

Forbes, K.J. and F.E. Warnock (2012), "Capital flow waves: Surges, stops, flight, and retrenchment," *Journal of International Economics*, **88**(2), 235–51.

Grabel, I. (2003), "Averting crisis? Assessing measures to manage financial integration in emerging economies," *Cambridge Journal of Economics*, **27**(3), 317–36.

Jeanne, O., A. Subramanian and J. Williamson (2012), *Who Needs to Open the Capital Account?*, Washington, DC: Peterson Institute.

Johnsen, G. (2014), *Bringing Down the Banking System*, New York: Palgrave Macmillan.

Jordà, Ò., M. Schularick and A.M. Taylor (2011), "Financial crises, credit booms, and external imbalances: 140 years of lessons," *IMF Economic Review*, **59**(2), 340–78.

Keynes, J.M. (1933), "National self-sufficiency," *The Yale Review*, **22**, 755–69.

Kindleberger, C. and R. Aliber (2005), *Manias, Panics, and Crashes: A History of Financial Crises*, Hoboken, NJ: Wiley.

Lewis, M. (2009), "Wall Street on the tundra," *Vanity Fair*, March 3, accessed July 25, 2018 at http://www.vanityfair.com/politics/features/2009/04/iceland200904?currentPage=1.

Minsky, H. (1982), *Can "It" Happen Again? Essays on Instability and Finance*, Armonk, NY: M.E. Sharpe, Inc.

Mishkin, F.S. (2000), "Inflation targeting in emerging market countries," *NBER Working Papers No. w7618*.

Mishkin, F.S. and T. Herbertsson (2011), "Financial stability in Iceland," in R. Aliber and G. Zoega (eds), *Preludes to the Icelandic Financial Crisis*, London: Palgrave Macmillan, pp. 107–59.

OECD Statistics (2016) [website], accessed October 2016 at https://stats.oecd.org/.

Portes, R., F. Baldursson and F. Olafsson (2011), "The internationalization of Iceland's financial sector," in R. Aliber and G. Zoega (eds), *Preludes to the Icelandic Financial Crisis*, London: Palgrave Macmillan, pp. 160–240.

Reinhart, C.M. and K.S. Rogoff (2009), *This Time Is Different: Eight Centuries of Financial Folly*, Princeton, NJ: Princeton University Press.

Rodrik, D. (2005), "Growth strategies," in P. Aghion and S.N. Durlauf (eds), *Handbook of Economic Growth, Volume 1*, Amsterdam: Elsevier, pp. 967–1014.

Schüler, M. (2003), "How do banking supervisors deal with Europe-wide systemic risk?," *ZEW Discussion Paper No. 03-03*.

Shiller, R. (2000), *Irrational Exuberance*, Princeton, NJ: Princeton University Press.

Shleifer, A. (2000), *Inefficient Markets: An Introduction to Behavioral Finance*, Oxford: Oxford University Press.

SIC (2010), *Report of the Special Investigation Commission*, accessed July 25, 2018 at https://www.rna.is/eldri-nefndir/addragandi-og-orsakir-falls-islensku-bankanna-2008/skyrsla-nefndarinnar/english/.

Sigurjonsson, T. (2011), "Privatization and deregulation: A chronology of events," in R. Aliber and G. Zoega (eds), *Preludes to the Icelandic Financial Crisis*, London: Palgrave Macmillan, pp. 26–40.

Statistics Iceland (2016) [website], accessed October 2016 at https://www.cb.is/statistics/.

Wade, R. and S. Sigurgeirsdottir (2010), "Lessons from Iceland," *New Left Review*, **65**, 5–29.

Wade, R. and S. Sigurgeirsdottir (2012), "Iceland's rise, fall, stabilization, and beyond," *Cambridge Journal of Economics*, **36**, 127–44.

4. Reanalyzing the gender-specific effects of the Great Recession

Sana Khalil

INTRODUCTION

The subprime mortgage crisis that began in the United States eventually unraveled as the worst global economic crisis – the Great Recession – since the Great Depression of the 1930s. The literature has described several factors to explain the causes of the Great Recession, most prominent being the pace of financial deregulations and excessive financial innovations that catalyzed an unnatural boom that ended in a crisis (Crotty and Epstein, 2009). Countries hit the hardest in terms of an upsurge in unemployment rates over 2008–10 include Denmark, Estonia, Greece, Iceland, Ireland, and Latvia. A comparison of harmonized unemployment rates for these countries shows that Estonia posted the highest increase in the unemployment rate, which rose from 5.5 percent in 2008 to 16.7 percent in 2010, an increase of 203 percentage points. Other countries worst hit by the crisis were Iceland (153 percent), Latvia (151 percent) and Ireland (117 percent) (OECD, 2018a).

To this end, an important but understated issue worthy of discussion concerns the gender impacts of the Great Recession. Crisis theories that have described its distributional dynamics do not converge to a united whole and predict differential impacts of crises for men and women. One theory posits that since women are used as employment buffers – called in when demand increases but pushed back when demand shrinks – women's unemployment rates may rise more than that of men's during recessionary phases. Thus, women might experience a greater loss in employment, earned income, and overall wealth during recessions (Humphries, 1988 [2010]). However, an argument running counter to this theory is that women's concentration in female-dominated occupations – which tend to be cyclically robust – may shield women's employment relative to that of men's.

Since there is no definitive theoretical model of these relations, the issue of the gender impacts of recessions becomes an empirical question.

In this respect, men's and women's labor market experiences from the Great Recession can be treated as a litmus test. Similar to the previous two recessions in the US, men's unemployment rates rose faster than women's during the Great Recession. Due to this phenomenon, these recessions have come to be known as "man-cessions" (Wall, 2009). However, as I argue in this chapter, this observation can be misleading on many accounts. I argue that although men and women showed substantial differences in their vulnerabilities to the recession, within-gender differences were much more pronounced. Additionally, gender impacts of crises derive from differences in men's and women's unique, socially and culturally drawn positions, job structures, family models and welfare systems.

With regard to labeling the Great Recession a "man-cession," although crude comparisons of the data from advanced economies may lead to a simplistic conclusion that men fared worse than women – in terms of job losses – comparison of intra-country and intra-group heterogeneities suggests that the burden of the recession fell on the weaker groups within each gender category. Women on the lower rungs of employment and in low-income categories, and single mothers, fared disproportionately worse than women in high-skilled, high-income categories (Albelda, 2014). Additionally, disparities in men's and women's responses to second-round effects of the recession need to be counted toward overall gender impact of the Great Recession. Although, manufacturing and construction sectors took an immediate hit from the recession, in terms of job losses, second-round effects – particularly, the ensuing austerity measures in many countries in Europe – seem to have shifted the cost of the recession back to women.

In this vein, this chapter brings together a comparative strand of analyses underlying the distributional dynamics of the Great Recession to form a reanalysis of its gender impacts on labor markets in selected OECD countries. It argues that gender regimes shaped by family policies and cultural factors can mediate the effects of crises on the economic situation of men and women. Additionally, both family policies and cultural factors can help explain why men's employment recovered faster than that of women's. Paid parental leave systems may have mediated some of the distributional dynamics across gender lines due to their implications for sexual division of labor.

The structure of this chapter is as follows. The next section lays out a brief description of frameworks helpful in understanding the gender impacts of recessions and draws on selected literature to argue that simplistic comparisons of indicators from paid employment may be misleading. The third section attempts to develop a comparative outlook of the gender impacts of the Great Recession in the context of family policies. In the conclusion, I highlight that both cultural factors and family policies can explain differential experiences of men and women in crises, across countries.

REVIEW OF FRAMEWORKS AND COMPARATIVE LITERATURE

Theoretical Frameworks

This section attempts to bring together various strands of analyses, posited in the selected literature, about the frameworks and the distributional impact of the Great Recession – and crises in general – on the employment situation of men and women.

As noted by Humphries (1988 [2010]), hypotheses that explain women's employment outcomes over crisis periods fall into three main categories:

1. The "flexible reserve"[1] or buffer hypothesis suggests that women are a flexible reserve, drawn into the labor market during economic upturns and pushed back during economic downturns – that women's employment is procyclical. The theoretical perspective for this prediction is based on human capital theory that suggests that relatively lower human capital endowments and lower levels of job-specific skills may reduce the incentive for firms to hoard female workers during economic downturns (Oi, 1962). The buffer hypothesis assumes that the discouraged worker effect will dominate in a recession and predicts a decline in women's unemployment and labor force participation rates – more discouraged women than men leave the labor market. This hypothesis, however, runs into a major problem. Crises may also alter firms' demand for job-specific skills and, in general, influence the labor cost/human capital trade-off. From this perspective, if firms, compelled by the recessionary pressures, aggressively cut back their labor costs, hoarding female workers would make sense – women's employment should therefore rise more than men's. However, firms may also employ female workers in unstable employment forms or areas that require frequent adjustment – for example, temporary and part-time jobs. A recession may, therefore, lead to an increase in the share of unstable employment; hence, even if women's employment increases over a downturn, it is crucial to focus on the qualitative aspects of such gains – the nature of job stability and employment conditions.

2. According to the substitution hypothesis, during times of economic hardship, employers' quest to cut costs and to increase the flexibility of production leads to substitution of female workers for relatively more expensive male workers. During a downturn, firms may be pressured to convert some of the high-paid stable jobs into low-paid, less stable jobs; thus, substitution of female workers for male workers may result in deepening of gender differentials in terms of segregation and wage gap during a recession. The substitution hypothesis predicts a strong added-worker effect for women's participation in the labor force: increased female labor force participation and lower unemployment rates relative to that of male rates.

3. Finally, the segmentation hypothesis emphasizes the role of socially constructed boundaries in shaping job structures in the labor markets – for example, sex-typing of jobs.[2] Theoretically, women's employment trends over business cycles will relate more to the trends in sectoral and occupational structures than business cycles themselves. The segmentation hypothesis predicts that, in a recession, women's unemployment rates will reduce relative to men's as women's employment is relatively stable due to its concentration in less cyclically sensitive sectors.

Bettio and Verashchagina (2014) point to yet another idea, that during economic crises the group with lower employment protection serves as a natural flexible buffer; hence, women, due to their prevalence in temporary employment, may be more vulnerable to the combined effects of economic downturns and labor market segmentation. If employment protection differs among employees, such legislations may reinforce disparities in bargaining power between the "insiders" – tenured, adult, skilled workers who have more favorable employment opportunities – and the "outsiders" – untenured, younger workers who have less favorable employment conditions. Women may be perceived as outsiders due to their more frequent exits and entries into the labor market and the relative unstable nature of their job contracts.

While the buffer hypothesis has popular currency among some analysts (Beechey, 1977), its predictions – concerning the "disposable" nature of women's labor in times of economic hardship – have been called into question by the experiences of men and women in past crises. For example, Humphries's (1988 [2010]) analysis of women's employment experiences in three post–World War II recessions in the United States (1971, 1975 and 1982) shows that the employment situation deteriorated less for women than for men. Testing for cyclical sensitivity of female employment by running the regressions of percentage change in women's employment on the percentage change in total employment, Humphries finds that the buffer hypothesis is only supported at the intermediate stage of integration of women in each sector and industry division. Women tend to occupy more cyclically volatile jobs when their employment penetrates beyond clerical tasks. Women's employment becomes less cyclically volatile when their employment occupies a major share in an industry.

Theoretically, the sex-typing of jobs can be rigid and strong in the short run; therefore, women's employment behavior over the cycle is strongly influenced by sectoral and occupational patterns of job losses in a recession. Given that crises tend to have a relatively more distinct sectoral impact than occupational (Bettio et al., 2012), sectoral segregation may, to some extent, shield women's employment.

Gender impacts of the crises may also be shaped by the unequal position of men and women in relation to productive and reproductive spheres, and the gendered structure of welfare systems. Social norms that construct expected gender roles, underpin the differences in labor market attachments in terms of the nature and types of jobs held by men and women (Elson, 1999; Folbre, 2001; Khalil, 2018). Because women are disproportionately more represented in temporary and part-time jobs, they face higher job insecurity. Although part-time workers may also be covered by permanent contracts in some countries, they may still be excluded from career accession (Tomlinson, 2006). Women may, therefore, have higher turnover rates due to poor job quality (Felstead and Gallie, 2004).

Last but not least, last-in, first-out seniority layoffs, as typical in the United States, may also render women more vulnerable to unemployment as women's average job tenure intervals are lower than men's. If turnover rates are higher for women than for men, women's employment may be expected to undergo greater adjustment than men's employment in response to changes in demand. Houseman and Abraham (1993) estimate elasticities – over one, three, and 12-month periods – for male and female employment with respect to changes in output for Japan and the United States. Their results from the manufacturing sector showed that female workers served as buffers in Japan during the crisis periods of 1970s and 1980s. They argue that women's relatively higher quit rates than men's was one reason women's employment faced greater adjustment to changes in demand.

Suffice it to say that the relationship between female employment and economic recessions is ambiguous at best. If women's paid labor constitutes a flexible and cheap source of labor, akin to Marx's notion of a reserve army (Bruegel, 1979), their participation in paid work is expected to rise during periods of economic recession and decrease in times of economic expansion – consistent with the substitution hypothesis. On the other hand, women's perceived status, arising from prevalent social and cultural norms, as caregivers first and labor force participants second, may play out in terms of employers' perceptions of women as less worthy of employment during times of economic hardship.

Turning to the crude comparisons of men's and women's unemployment rates in the aftermath of the Great Recession, men's unemployment rates did rise faster than women's in several countries hit by the recession. This pattern provides a simplistic conclusion that the Great Recession may be a "man-cession," an observation many analyses have made (Wall, 2009; Şahin, Song and Hobijn, 2010). However, a closer analysis of intra-country and intra-group dynamics is essential to understand how gender impacts of the recession played out. In this respect, it is crucial to examine to what extent the theoretical approaches, presented in this section, are applicable to the gender impacts of crises. This is what follows in the next section.

Empirical Studies

Empirical studies on gender-specific effects of the crisis in terms of its impact on the productive sphere has provided contradictory results. That men were hit harder than women in terms of job losses of the Great Recession is not entirely misplaced insofar as we rely on the first-round effects of the Great Recession on broader axes of gender. Since the hardest-hit sectors – manufacturing and construction as well as high-paid financial sector branches – were male dominated, gender occupational and sectoral segregation does seem to have protected women's employment relative to men's. Sierminska and Takhtamanova (2011) use the term "man-cession" to describe their findings from the experience of the US economy that men fared worse than women in the early years of the Great Recession in terms of higher job-separation probabilities, lower job-finding probabilities and higher unemployment rates relative to women.

If we look at the experiences of middle-income countries, similar observations have been cited (Cho and Newhouse, 2013). Cho and Newhouse examine 17 middle-income countries and suggest that the negative employment effects were stronger for men, particularly for youth. They cite two main factors for this pattern: first, men's concentration in the hardest-hit industrial sector; second, men's higher initial rate of employment.

Notwithstanding the broad conclusions forwarded by much of the analyses, it is rather simplistic to brand the Great Recession as a "man-cession," as the term starkly ignores the heterogeneity in cross-country experiences and in within-gender impacts. Grown and Tas (2011) use US data to delve into demographics within gender categories and show that African-American males and females, Hispanic males and females, young females and single women were hit the hardest by the recession.

It is important to note that women's employment situation in the Great Recession was relatively worse than that in previous recessions – that women's employment may have become relatively more vulnerable in economic downturns. Grown and Tas note that women lost ten times more jobs in the Great Recession than in the previous two recessions, while men lost about 2.3 times more jobs. The authors argue that simple male–female comparisons of unemployment rates yield partial conclusions and misleading policy options as the race/ethnicity and class status of households matters in analyzing the burden of the crisis.

Much of the literature on the effects of the Great Recession overlooks intergroup inequality – an important aspect in understanding how dominant groups can shift the costs of recessions to subordinate groups. Dymski, Hernandez and Mohanty (2013) and Arestis, Charles and Fontana (2013) address this lacuna in two different contexts. Dymski, Hernandez and Mohanty (2013) explore interesting race/gender/power aspects of the Great Recession in the United States by investigating the overinclusion of women and minority groups in subprime mortgage lending. They argue that historically disproportionately excluded groups were granted equal access to mortgage lending. Female-headed households and minority households – especially African-American households – were disproportionately and predatorily targeted for subprime credit. Racial and gender inequalities produce differential social power, which in turn is exploited by lenders – an aspect central to the political economy of subprime lending and consequently the subprime crisis. On the other hand, Arestis, Charles and Fontana (2013) show that, in the case of United States, financialization has been neither race nor gender neutral, which subsequently corresponded to stratification effects of the Great Recession. Testing the gender and race stratification of the US labor markets, as a result of the Great Recession, Arestis, Charles and Fontana show that the wage premium for individuals working in managerial and financial occupations for the period 1983–2009 was unequally distributed – men took an increasing share of the finance wage premium at the expense of women. On average, White and Hispanic men reaped a disproportionate share of the finance wage premium. There is more to investigate with regard to how social norms create identity preferences that link managerial and financial occupations to high earnings, which are in turn linked to the social status of the dominant groups.

To shed some light on the unpaid sector, intra-country studies on the effects of the crisis show that the crisis exacerbated preexisting gender inequalities within households, especially in terms of unequal burden of unpaid labor. Losses in household income in times of economic crisis lead to adjustments both in the paid and unpaid work hours. As a result, women are often the bearers of unequal burden of increased work time – by working longer paid hours to compensate for the loss in household income and by increasing unpaid labor to compensate for the fall in household goods and services that were previously procured from the market. The burden of extra unpaid labor during periods of economic turmoil depends particularly on the gender division of labor within the household.[3] Kaya Bahçe and Memiş (2013) provide an important observation in this regard. In order to examine how individual work time in Turkey changed due to the 2008–09 crisis, Kaya Bahçe and Memiş use the Turkish time-use survey of 2006 and show that a 1 percent increase in their spouse's unemployment risk raises women's paid and unpaid labor time by 22 minutes per day.[4] This raises the question of whether the gender restructuring of paid and unpaid work contributed to women being overworked and men being underworked. For example, during the Asian financial crisis, restructuring in gender composition of paid work in Philippines created overwork for women, as their paid work hours increased along with household production, and forced idleness for men due to unemployment (Lim, 2000).

On the other hand, findings with regard to the redistribution of paid and unpaid work hours from the United States show that the 2008–09 recession narrowed the gap in paid and unpaid labor for married men and women. Consistent with the added-worker effect, mothers substituted paid work for unpaid labor while fathers' paid work hours and total workload reduced and leisure time increased (Berik and Kongar, 2013).

In sum, the overview from this section suggests that although at cross-country level the Great Recession appeared to be a "man-cession," in several advanced countries insofar as comparisons are drawn from paid work, studies on the intra-country, intra-group, and unpaid work reveal that inter-sectionality played an important role in shaping the burden of the crisis.

GENDER-SPECIFIC EFFECTS OF THE GREAT RECESSION IN THE CONTEXT OF FAMILY POLICIES: EUROPE VERSUS THE UNITED STATES

Gender impacts of the Great Recession can be organized along three foci: first-round effects were prominent in the financial sector, primarily influencing the productive sectors; the second-round effects translated via their impacts on household adjustment to the economic contraction, thereby encompassing the reproductive sector; and the third-round effects transpired through consequent austerity measures (crisis-induced budget deficits and cuts, and longer-run adjustments) were particularly conspicuous in the reproductive sector (Fukuda-Parr, Heintz and Seguino, 2013).

In this context, it is inadequate to try to identify the gender impacts of the Great Recession in the abstract: the structures underpinning the organization of the family – in essence, family policies that shape gender regimes – need to be analyzed in relation to the gender impacts of the Great Recession. Social reproduction (the family) and production (the economy) are not autonomous structures. While the structure of the economy influences demand-side constraints for women's paid work, organization of the family creates supply-side pressures and constraints concerning women's integration in paid labor (Folbre, 1994, 2008).

This section aims to draw comparisons between the experiences of men and women in the Great Recession in the United States and selected European countries based on varieties of gender regimes as reflected by family policies.[5] The approach adopted in this section links the analysis of gender-specific effects of the crisis to differences in institutions of family models that underwrite the social construction of gender relations, which in turn interact with wider social, political, and economic factors. Gender-specific economic outcomes are embedded in the institutional settings that shape differences in vulnerability to the crises and adjustment paths. To keep the analysis to a manageable size, this chapter will limit the focus to family policies due to its implications for gender relations concerning paid and unpaid work.

Thévenon (2011) provides a comparative analysis of family-friendly policies across OECD countries in terms of three main types of family support: leave entitlements, cash transfers, and provision of childcare services. Thévenon divides European countries into five main categories in terms of generosity of family policies. In group 1 are countries that provide limited assistance to families on all three types of family support; this includes Poland, Portugal, Spain, Italy, and Greece. Group 2 comprises countries that provide short parental leave and target the support to low-income, single-parent families with preschool children; it includes Austria, Netherlands, UK, and USA. In group 3, high financial support is offered but limited support is given to dual-earner families with children under age 3; countries in this group are Germany, France, Norway, and Denmark. Group 4 consists of countries that provide long leave but low cash benefits and childcare for children under age 3; Hungary falls under this category. Finally, group 5 consists of countries that provide continuous, strong support for working parents of children under age 3; Finland and Sweden are included in this category. The gender regimes as depicted, in part, by the nature of family policies, reflect the specificities of the welfare state and the rubrics of family model that are closely linked with the extent of women's integration in paid work.

Two factors concerning the role of family policies in shaping women's labor supply during and after the crisis may be relevant for our discussion. On one hand, as family-friendly policies may be conducive to an environment of relatively higher fertility rates (Thévenon, 2011), the pre-crisis structure of family-friendly policies in many European countries may have created a resurgence of traditional family values in terms of concentration of women in temporary and part-time work – since such policies allow combining paid work with unpaid domestic labor (Algan and Cahuc, 2003; Karamessini, 2008; Khalil, 2018).[6] In this regard, discouraged worker effect for women can be expected to be stronger in countries with generous family policies as women may retire to the reproductive sphere during periods of economic slack. On the other hand, in the aftermath of the crisis, ensuing austerity measures including cutbacks in social provisions concerning childcare support programs[7] may compel women to enter paid work to make up for the lost family income. In this context, the effect of culture, family policies and crises on women's employment is complex to predict. Nevertheless, observations from the post-recession experiences of OECD countries seems to support the latter argument. The share of male breadwinner households declined sharply in favor of female breadwinner households (Bettio et al., 2012). The role of added-worker effect is particularly important in this regard; family-friendly policies can soften the impact of the crisis by shielding the households' overall well-being and relate to a weaker added-worker effect.

Table 4.1 provides a comparison of men's and women's pre- and post-crisis labor force participation (LFP) rates for 15–64-year-olds (percentage in same age group) for the groups of countries according to Thévenon's (2011) family-policy categorization. The first point to note is that in many countries women's LFP rates rose from 2007 to 2009 relative to men's rates. From 2007 to 2009, the ratio of male LFP rate and female LFP rate declined for a majority of countries; comparing these figures for the period 2009 to 2016, this decline appears to have persisted throughout the period. The decline in this ratio mainly appears to be due to a higher increase in women's LFP rate relative to men's rate.

Overall, the figures in Table 4.1 appear to refute the buffer hypothesis – the claim that women's paid work increases during bad times and recedes during good times does not seem to hold water for the majority of countries during the periods covered in the analysis. However, a counterargument could be that many countries in Europe are still undergoing second-round effects and hence it is too early to make a call concerning women's employment behavior. Notwithstanding, if we look at the case of the USA, where effects from the Great Recession have arguably subsided to a significant extent, the buffer hypothesis also does not find support from the figures shown in Table 4.1. In the case of the USA, contrary to the predictions of

Table 4.1   *Men and women's labor force participation rates (15–64-year-olds), percentage in same age group*

Country	2007			2009			2016		
	Men	Women	Ratio[a]	Men	Women	Ratio	Men	Women	Ratio
Group 1									
Poland	70	56.5	1.24	71.8	57.8	1.24	75.7	62	1.22
Portugal	79.2	68.7	1.15	78.2	68.9	1.13	77.2	70.5	1.10
Spain	82.6	62.8	1.57	82	66	1.24	80.5	70.2	1.15
Italy	74.3	50.6	1.51	73.5	51.1	1.44	74.8	55.2	1.36
Greece	78.4	54.8	1.43	78.5	56.5	1.39	76.2	60.4	1.26
Group 2									
Austria	80	67.1	1.19	80	68.7	1.16	80.7	71.7	1.13
Netherlands	83.8	70.4	1.19	84.6	72.3	1.19	84.4	75	1.13
UK	83.3	69.8	1.21	83.2	70.2	1.17	83.4	73	1.13
USA	81.7	69.1	1.18	80.4	69	1.19	78.8	67.3	1.14
Group 3									
Germany	81.8	69.4	1.18	82.2	70.4	1.17	82.2	73.6	1.12
France	74.7	64.9	1.15	75	65.7	1.08	75.6	67.9	1.11
Iceland	91.6	83.6	1.10	88.4	82	1.06	91.8	86.2	1.06
Norway	81.8	75.9	1.08	81.4	76.5	1.09	80.3	75.9	1.06
Denmark	83.7	76.4	1.10	83.6	76.8	1.23	82.6	77.2	1.07
Group 4									
Hungary	68.6	54.9	1.25	67.7	55	1.23	76.9	63.5	1.21
Group 5									
Finland	77.4	73.9	1.05	75.8	73.5	1.03	77.9	74.1	1.05
Sweden	81.4	76.8	1.06	81.3	76.4	1.06	83.9	80.2	1.05

Note: a. The ratio is calculated as male LFP rate divided by female LFP rate.

Source: OECD (2018b).

the buffer hypothesis, women's LFP rate remained almost unchanged (69 percent) from 2007 to 2009; men's LFP rate, on the other hand, declined from 81.7 percent to 80.4 percent.

To look at the question of whether men experienced a stronger hit, Table 4.2 presents a comparison of unemployment rates for men and women before and after the crisis to examine whether men experienced a stronger hit relative to women in terms of a spike in unemployment rates.

Several features in Table 4.2 are worthy of attention. First, in terms of the immediate effects of the crisis, unemployment figures for men and

Table 4.2   *Unemployment rates for men and women (15–64-year-olds)*
              before and after the Great Recession

Country	2007		2009		2016	
	Men	Women	Men	Women	Men	Women
Group 1						
Poland	9.1	10.4	7.9	8.8	6.2	6.3
Portugal	7	10.1	9.4	10.7	11.5	11.5
Spain	6.5	10.7	17.7	18.2	18.2	21.5
Italy	5	7.9	6.8	9.3	11.1	12.9
Greece	5.3	13	7.1	13.4	19.9	28.3
Group 2						
Austria	4.1	4.8	5.8	5.5	5.8	5.9
Netherlands	3.2	4.1	3.7	3.8	5.6	6.5
UK	5.6	5	8.9	6.6	5.1	4.8
US	4.8	4.6	10.5	8.2	5	4.8
Group 3						
Germany	8.6	8.9	8.2	7.4	4.5	3.8
France	7.3	8.1	8.7	8.8	10.1	9.6
Iceland	2.3	2.4	8.9	5.8	3.2	3.2
Norway	2.6	2.5	3.7	2.7	5.6	4.1
Denmark	3.5	4.2	6.8	5.4	6	6.8
Group 4						
Hungary	7.2	7.8	10.4	9.8	5.2	5.1
Group 5						
Finland	6.5	7.3	9.1	7.6	9.2	8.7
Sweden	6	6.5	8.8	8.1	7.5	6.7

Source: OECD (2018a).

women (15–64-years-old) for the year 2009 show that women in group 1 experienced higher unemployment rates than men compared to other groups.

In this group, women's unemployment rates were much higher than men's unemployment during the pre-crisis period. The crisis of 2008 appears to have narrowed the gender gap in unemployment rate whereby men's unemployment rose disproportionately more than that of women's, from 2007 to 2009. On the other hand, all the countries except the Netherlands in group 2 exhibited higher male unemployment rates relative to the female rate. A similar pattern is depicted for groups 3, 4, and 5 where all the countries except France – where male unemployment rate rose slightly more than female unemployment – had higher male unemployment rates relative to the female rate.

Second, the gender gap in unemployment rate was much larger during the pre-crisis period for the countries in group 1 (see Italy and Greece's gender gap in unemployment rates for 2007). This situation persisted over the crisis and although the immediate effects of the crisis narrowed the gender gap in 2009, the gap widened again over the recovery period. For most countries in the rest of the four groups, female unemployment rates were higher than male unemployment rates over the pre-crisis period. The Great Recession narrowed this gap during the crisis and over the period of recovery.

Third, for several countries – UK, USA, Germany, Iceland, Hungary – recovery in the unemployment rates for 2016 appear to be larger for men relative to that of women although men's unemployment seems to have recovered more quickly than women's. Reductions in male unemployment rates appear to be phenomenal in the UK (from 8.9 percent in 2009 to 5.1 percent in 2016) and the USA (from 10.5 percent in 2009 to 5 percent in 2016). For all the countries except Poland in group 1, male and female unemployment rates are stubbornly high, which may correspond to ensuing sovereign debt crisis in these countries (see Lane, 2012).

The second-round effects for group 1 countries, especially Greece, Italy, and Spain, suggest that women's unemployment rates have persistently remained higher than men's. In the case of Greece, the gender gap in unemployment rate widened from 7.7 in 2007 to 8.4 in 2016. Similarly, Netherlands, Denmark and Austria posted relatively higher unemployment rates for women than men in 2016, suggesting that women fared worse than men from the second-round effects of the crisis. This is consistent with the observation that the second-round effects of the Great Recession have started echoing in the services sector where women's employment is predominant. In Spain, women's unemployment rates have consistently surpassed men's. Due to Spain's rigid two-tiered labor market, employers find it cheaper to cut back on temporary employment, retaining full-time employees; this practice has been associated with the perennial problem for Spanish women's high unemployment rates (Lahey and de Villota, 2013). In 2011, an ambitious plan was introduced to restructure the two-tiered labor market that compelled employers to either retain permanent, full-time employees amid falling demand or face large penalties for dismissing them in place of temporary workers. However, the figures for 2016 suggest that despite the introduction of the new plan, Spanish women's high unemployment rate has persisted. In the case of Portugal, job losses due to the crisis for men and women were not uniformly distributed throughout the years following the crisis, 2009 being the worst year for men – brought about mainly by contraction of the manufacturing and construction sector – and 2011 the worst year for women – the losses were mainly concentrated in agriculture and manufacturing (Ferreira, 2014). In 2011, men and women lost almost the same number of jobs; as of 2016, men and women's unemployment rates were similar at 11.5 percent.

In sum, the label of "man-cession" for the Great Recession does not hold water if we include the second-round effects; two key developments, as shown in Table 4.3, point to a counter-trend. First, the second-round effects in many European countries that are undergoing sovereign debt crisis – especially, Spain, Italy, and Greece – seem to have impacted women more than men insofar as relative unemployment rates are compared. Second, men's unemployment rates recede faster than women's; however, there is significant cross-country heterogeneity in these trends.

The extent to which men's and women's labor market outcomes varied in response to the crisis may also depend on the types of gender regimes that shape the dynamics in both the productive and the reproductive spheres. One way of looking at these gender regimes would be to examine the gendered nature of their family policies, especially parental leave systems. Due to their implications for gender division of labor (in both paid and unpaid work), parental leave policies carry substantial gendered impacts on labor markets (Folbre, 2001; Hartmann and Rose, 2004).

Parental leave has direct and substantial effects on the supply of women's paid labor, although its overall impact on women's employment is ambiguous. On one hand, paid leave entitlement gives the right to mothers to return to their old jobs after giving birth to a child. Additionally, since having a job in the first place is the primary qualification for a parental leave, paid leave may act as an incentive for women to join paid labor as it protects potential mothers against the fear of unemployment and hence loss of income during their childbearing and childcare period. On the other hand, paid parental leave entitlements may encourage women to stay out of the labor force longer than they otherwise would. It may also raise the expected cost to employers of employing women of childbearing age and discourage them from hiring women[8] (Blau and Kahn, 2013), and/or encourage employers to restrict women to temporary forms of employment – this is particularly relevant in the case of countries where employers share the burden of paid leave entitlements along with public social security.

Table 4.3 shows paid leave entitlements for mothers and fathers in selected OECD countries as of 2016. Countries where employers share the burden of paid leave entitlements include Greece, Netherlands, the UK, Germany and Denmark. An important point worth mentioning

Table 4.3 Comparison of paid leave entitlements, Europe versus USA, 2016

Country	(a) Total unpaid parental leave for mothers	(b) Total paid leave available to mothers[a]		(c) Total paid leave available to fathers		(d) Source of paid leave payments	(e) Women's labor force participation (15–64-year-olds)	(f) Gender share of part-time employment
	Length (weeks)	Length (weeks)	Average payment rate (%)[b]	Length (weeks)	Average payment rate (%)[c]			
Group 1								
Poland[d]	See note d	52	80	2	100	SS[e]	62	68.2
Portugal	13	30.1	67.7	22.3	56.3	SS	70.5	62.5
Spain	140	16	100	2.1	100	SS	70.2	72.8
Italy	23	47.7	52.7	0.4	100	SS	55.2	73.6
Greece	13	43	54.2	0.4	100	Mixed[f]	60.4	61.9
Group 2								
Austria	96	60	85.3	8.7	80	SS	71.7	78.3
Netherlands	13	16	100	0.4	100	Mixed	75	73.3
UK	53	39	30.9	2	20.2	Mixed	73	74.1
USA	12	0	0	0	0		67.3	
Group 3								
Germany	120	58	73.4	8.7	65	Mixed	73.6	78.1
France	142	42	44.9	28	20.1	SS	67.9	74.7
Iceland	13	26	59.7	13	59.7	SS	86.2	65.1
Norway	52	91	49.4	10	97.9	SS	75.9	67.1
Denmark	31	50	53.6	2	53.6	Mixed	77.2	57.7

Table 4.3 (continued)

Country	(a) Total unpaid parental leave for mothers	(b) Total paid leave available to mothers[a]		(c) Total paid leave available to fathers		(d) Source of paid leave payments	(e) Women's labor force participation (15–64-year-olds)	(f) Gender share of part-time employment
	Length (weeks)	Length (weeks)	Average payment rate (%)[b]	Length (weeks)	Average payment rate (%)[c]			
Group 4								
Hungary[g]	See note g	160	44.9	1	100	SS	63.5	64.8
Group 5								
Finland	14	161	25.2	9	62.9	SS	74.1	60.8
Sweden	45	55.7	62.3	14.3	76	SS	80.2	61.8

Notes:

a. Total paid leave available to mothers includes total paid maternity leave and paid parental and homecare leave.
b. Average payment rate refers to the proportion of past earnings replaced by the benefits over the duration of the paid leave.
c. Average payment rate refers to the proportion of past earnings replaced by the benefits over the duration of the paid leave.
d. In the case of Poland, mothers are allowed to take 52 weeks of paid leave; maternity leave comprises 20 weeks paid at 100% of total salary with additional six weeks of maternity leave available upon request. The rest of the leave counts toward parental leave, paid at 60% of average earnings.
e. Social security.
f. Mixed = Social security and employers.
g. In Hungary, mothers can take up to three years of paid leave during which 24 weeks are paid with 70% of average earnings.

Sources:

Kovács, Polese and Morris (2017) (source of note g); Ray, Gornick and Schmitt (2010); information for Poland and Hungary was also from the author's research.

Columns (b)–(c): OECD family database.
Columns (e)–(f): OECD (2018b).

here is that where paid leave entitlements are disproportionately tilted in favor of mothers, traditional gender norms and norms concerning gender division of labor may deepen. This may be the case for Greece, Italy, and Netherlands where total paid leave available for fathers is less than a week. Greece (60.4) and Italy (55.2) have lowest female labor force participation rates among other countries, as depicted in Table 4.3. In the case of the Netherlands, women have relatively higher employment rates but lower working hours, as around 75 percent of Dutch women work part-time and only a quarter of women express a preference for a full-time job.[9]

Family policies that aim to address the conflicts between family care and labor market participation interact with cultural factors in shaping women's paid and unpaid employment. Such policies have gendered implications – that they may reflect and promote traditional ideals of care; for instance, parental leave (paid or unpaid) may reinforce the notion that it is mothers' primary responsibility to act as caregivers first and labor force participants second (Budig, Misra and Boeckmann, 2012). Prolonged leave policies may lead to longer absence of mothers from paid employment after childbirth and may, thereby, foster an adoption of the male breadwinner model upon reentry (Berghammer, 2014). That is, paid parental leave policies have the effect of reinforcing women's specialization in care. To the extent that women's perceived responsibilities toward family care are read by employers as a negative influence on their paid work effort, employers may engage in statistical discrimination against women. In this context, both family policies and cultural factors mediate the effect of crises on men and women's employment. For instance, in the cases of Spain, Italy, and Greece where cultural support for the male breadwinner model is high (Algan and Cahuc, 2003; Budig et al., 2012), gender gaps in unemployment rates appear substantially higher than other countries over the years covered (see Table 4.3). This relates to the findings that the employment rate of women is almost double in Anglo-Saxon (USA, UK, Australia, Canada, Ireland, New Zealand) and Scandinavian countries (Denmark, Finland, Norway, Sweden) compared to Mediterranean countries (Greece, Italy, Portugal, Spain, Turkey) (Algan and Cahuc, 2003).

To summarize, the discussion from this section attempts to develop an understanding of the effects of the Great Recession on labor market outcomes of men and women along two axes. First, going back to the frameworks for the relation between crises and women's employment, the interaction of culture and family policies would mediate the effect of both the substitution and segmentation hypotheses and women's employment can be expected to fare better or worse than men's accordingly. Second, both family policies and cultural factors can help explain why men's employment recovers faster than women's.

CONCLUSION

Comparative analysis of the gender-specific effects of the Great Recession provided in this chapter suggests that the label of "man-cession" for the Great Recession does not hold water if the overall effects of the crisis are taken into account. Although men's employment took the immediate hit in terms of relatively higher job losses than women, this effect may have reversed in the second-round effects where women's employment seems to have suffered more.

The extent to which men's and women's labor market outcomes varied in response to the crisis may also depend on the types of gender regimes that shape the dynamics in both the productive and the reproductive spheres. Gender regimes, partly explained by the gendered nature of family policies, especially parental leave systems, have implications for gender division of labor – in both paid and unpaid work. Parental leave policies, along with cultural factors, exert gendered impacts on labor markets and, therefore, can mediate the effect of crises on men and women's labor market outcomes.

NOTES

1. This is further supported by the observation that female turnover rates tend to be comparatively higher than male.
2. Whitehead (1979) and Elson (1999) emphasize the idea that labor market institutions are "bearers of gender" in the sense that employer–employee relation is embedded under the rubric of social stereotypes that assign gender roles in terms of "being the boss," "men's work" and "women's work."
3. Earlier literature on intra-household time allocation assumed that division of paid and unpaid labor is exogenously determined (Becker and Murphy, 1992); in contrast, feminist scholars argue that along with other intra-household interactions, time allocation is also endogenously determined by factors such as patriarchal relations, social biases, ethical principle and so on (Bittman et al., 2003).
4. The change in women's unpaid labor was found to be substantially higher in urban settings.
5. The selection of countries is partly based on availability of literature on their experiences in the Great Recession and partly to allow direct comparison with the United States in terms of economic development.
6. This may correspond with the perceived characteristic of women's position as caregivers first and labor force participants second.
7. For example, childcare benefits were retrenched in the United Kingdom as well as other family-related measures. Germany reduced parental allowance and compensation for paid parental leave. Netherlands also experienced cutbacks in childcare benefits (Kersbergen, Vis and Hemerijck, 2014).
8. Employers may fear erosion of firm-level skills due to the intermittent nature of women's employment during their childbearing and childcaring years.
9. Dutch News (2017), "Dutch women work part-time even in their 20s with no kids," 31 January, accessed 17 July 2018 at http://www.dutchnews.nl/news/archives/2017/01/dutch-women-work-part-time-even-in-their-20s-with-no-kids/.

REFERENCES

Albelda, R. (2014), "Gender impacts of the 'Great Recession' in the United States," in K. Karamessini and J. Rubery (eds), *Women and Austerity: The Economic Crisis and the Future for Gender Equality*, New York: Routledge, pp. 82–101.

Algan, Y. and P. Cahuc (2003), "Job protection and family policies: The macho hypothesis," unpublished paper, University of Paris I.

Arestis, P., A. Charles and G. Fontana (2013), "Financialization, the Great Recession, and the stratification of the US labor market," *Feminist Economics*, **19**(3), 152–80.

Beechey, V. (1977), "Some notes on female wage labor in capitalist production," *Capital and Class*, **1**(3), 45–66.

Becker, G.S. and K.M. Murphy (1992), "The division of labor, coordination costs, and knowledge," *The Quarterly Journal of Economics*, **107**(4), 1137–60.

Berghammer, C. (2014), "The return of the male breadwinner model? Educational effects on parents' work arrangements in Austria, 1980–2009," *Work, Employment and Society*, **28**(4), 611–32.

Berik, G. and E. Kongar (2013), "Time allocation of married mothers and fathers in hard times: The 2007–09 US recession," *Feminist Economics*, **19**(3), 208–37.

Bettio, F. and A. Verashchagina (2014), "Women and men in the 'Great European Recession'," in K. Karamessini and J. Rubery (eds), *Women and Austerity: The Economic Crisis and the Future for Gender Equality*, New York: Routledge, pp. 57–81.

Bettio, F., M. Corsi and C. D'Ippoliti et al. (2012), *The Impact of the Economic Crisis on the Situation of Women and Men and on Gender Equality Policies*, Brussels: European Commission.

Bittman, M., P. England and N. Folbre et al. (2003), "When does gender trump money? Bargaining and time in household work," *American Journal of Sociology*, **109**(1), 186–214.

Blau, F.D. and L.M. Kahn (2013), "Female labor supply: Why is the United States falling behind?," *American Economic Review*, **103**(3), 251–6.

Bruegel, I. (1979), "Women as a reserve army of labour: A note on recent British experience," *Feminist Review*, **3**(1), 12–23.

Budig, M.J., J. Misra and I. Boeckmann (2012), "The motherhood penalty in cross-national perspective: The importance of work–family policies and cultural attitudes," *Social Politics*, **19**(2), 163–93.

Cho, Y. and D. Newhouse (2013), "How did the Great Recession affect different types of workers? Evidence from 17 middle-income countries," *World Development*, **41**, 31–50.

Crotty, J. and G. Epstein (2009), "Avoiding another meltdown," *Challenge*, **52**(1), 5–26.

Dymski, G., J. Hernandez and L. Mohanty (2013), "Race, gender, power, and the US subprime mortgage and foreclosure crisis: A meso analysis," *Feminist Economic*, **19**(3), 124–51.

Elson, D. (1999), "Labor markets as gendered institutions: Equality, efficiency and empowerment issues," *World Development*, **27**(3), 611–27.

Felstead, A. and D. Gallie (2004), "For better or worse? Non-standard jobs and high involvement work systems," *The International Journal of Human Resource Management*, **15**(7), 1293–316.

Ferreira, V. (2014), "Employment and austerity: Changing welfare and gender regimes in Portugal," in K. Karamessini and J. Rubery (eds), *Women and*

Austerity: The Economic Crisis and the Future for Gender Equality, New York: Routledge, pp. 207–27.

Folbre, N. (1994), "Children as public goods," *The American Economic Review*, **84**(2), 86–90.

Folbre, N. (2001), *The Invisible Heart: Economics and Family Values*, New York: The New Press.

Folbre, N. (2008), *Valuing Children: Rethinking the Economics of the Family*, Cambridge, MA: Harvard University Press.

Fukuda-Parr, S., J. Heintz and S. Seguino (2013), "Critical perspectives on financial and economic crises: Heterodox macroeconomics meets feminist economics," *Feminist Economics*, **19**(3), 4–31.

Grown, C. and E. Tas (2011), "Gender equality in US labor markets in the 'Great Recession' of 2007–10," in M. Starr (ed.), *Consequences of Economic Downturn*, New York: Palgrave Macmillan, pp. 167–86.

Hartmann, H. and S. Rose (2004), *Still a Man's Labor Market: The Long-Term Earnings Gap*, Washington, DC: Institute for Women's Policy.

Houseman, S.N. and K.G. Abraham (1993), "Female workers as a buffer in the Japanese economy," *American Economic Review*, **83**(2), 45–51.

Humphries, J. (1988 [2010]), "Women's employment in restructuring America: The changing experience of women in three recessions," in J. Rubery (ed.), *Women and Recession*, London: Routledge.

Karamessini, M. (2008), "Continuity and change in the Southern European social model," *International Labour Review*, **147**(1), 43–70.

Kaya Bahçe, S.A. and E. Memiş (2013), "Estimating the impact of the 2008–09 economic crisis on work time in Turkey," *Feminist Economics*, **19**(3), 181–207.

Kersbergen, K., B. Vis and A. Hemerijck (2014), "The Great Recession and welfare state reform: Is retrenchment really the only game left in town?," *Social Policy and Administration*, **48**(7), 883–904.

Khalil, S. (2018), "Gender gaps in part-time and involuntary part-time employment: Why do women work part-time involuntarily?," unpublished conference paper, 44th Annual Conference – Eastern Economic Association, March 2018, Boston, USA.

Kovács, B., A. Polese and J. Morris (2017), "Adjusting social welfare and social policy in Central and Eastern Europe: Growth, crisis and recession," in P. Kennett and N. Lendvai (eds), *Handbook of European Social Policy*, Cheltenham, UK and Northampton, MA, USA: Edward Elgar Publishing, pp. 194–217.

Lahey, K.A. and P. de Villota (2013), "Economic crisis, gender equality, and policy responses in Spain and Canada," *Feminist Economics*, **19**(3), 82–107.

Lane, P.R. (2012), "The European sovereign debt crisis," *Journal of Economic Perspectives*, **26**(3), 49–68.

Lim, J.Y. (2000), "The effects of the East Asian crisis on the employment of women and men: The Philippine case," *World Development*, **28**(7), 1285–306.

Oi, W.Y. (1962), "Labor as a quasi-fixed factor," *Journal of Political Economy*, **70**(6), 538–55.

Organisation for Economic Co-operation and Development (OECD) (2018a), "LFS by sex and age: Unemployment rate," accessed 17 July 2018 at https://stats. oecd.org/Index.aspx?DataSetCode=LFS_SEXAGE_I_R.

Organisation for Economic Co-operation and Development (OECD) (2018b), "LFS by sex and age: Labor force participation rate," accessed 17 July 2018 at https://stats.oecd.org/Index.aspx?DataSetCode=LFS_SEXAGE_I_R.

Ray, R., J.C. Gornick and J. Schmitt (2010), "Who cares? Assessing generosity and gender equality in parental leave policy designs in 21 countries," *Journal of European Social Policy*, **20**(3), 196–216.

Şahin, A., J. Song and B. Hobijn (2010), "The unemployment gender gap during the 2007 recession," *Current Issues in Economics and Finance*, **16**(2), 1–7.

Sierminska, E. and Y. Takhtamanova (2011), "Job flows, demographics, and the Great Recession," in K. Tatsiramos and S.W. Polachek (eds), *Who Loses in the Downturn? Economic Crisis, Employment and Income Distribution*, Bingley: Emerald Group Publishing Limited, pp. 115–54.

Thévenon, O. (2011), "Family policies in OECD countries: A comparative analysis," *Population and Development Review*, **37**(1), 57–87.

Tomlinson, J. (2006), "Part-time occupational mobility in the service industries: Regulation, work commitment and occupational closure," *The Sociological Review*, **54**(1), 66–86.

Wall, H. (2009), "The 'man-cession' of 2008–09: It's big, but it's not great," *The Regional Economist*, **18**(4), 4–9.

Whitehead, A. (1979), "Some preliminary notes on the subordination of women 1," *The IDS Bulletin*, **10**(3), 10–13.

PART II

Managing international capital flows: Costs
and dilemmas

5.   Capital controls in a time of crisis*

Ilene Grabel

INTRODUCTION

The implosion of the United States' highly liberalized, liquid, and internationally integrated financial system severely damaged the case that neoclassical economists had made for several decades that the country's financial system was the ideal to which all other countries should aspire. The global crisis has posed a particularly strong challenge to true believers in the universal desirability of unrestrained international private capital flows, a central component of the financial liberalization prescription.

During the long neoliberal era, capital controls were largely discredited as a vestigial organ of wrong-headed, dirigiste economic meddling. And so it was that until the global crisis, one had to look to the work of the Keynesian minority within the academic wing of the economics profession and to the world's heretical governments, central banks, and finance ministries for forceful, consistent support of the management of international capital flows. Enter the global financial crisis. Many extraordinary things happened during the crisis, one of which is that Keynesian-inflected ideas about the legitimacy and necessity of managing international capital flows began to infuse the work of a broader set of economists in academia and in the policy community. Notably, views on capital controls at the International Monetary Fund (IMF) evolved significantly during the crisis, though in some respects (and as I will argue below) this was a grudging evolution revealing of continuing discomfort (see Chwieroth, 2014; Gallagher, 2014; Grabel, 2011, 2015b; Moschella, 2014). The new view recognizes that capital controls are a "legitimate part of the policy toolkit" (to borrow a now oft-cited phrase from IMF research on the subject during the crisis) (e.g., Ostry et al., 2010). Greater tolerance for controls is also reflected in the pronouncements of officials associated with other multilateral institutions, important figures in the world of central banking, analysts at credit rating agencies, in reports in the financial press, and in the recent research of economists that one would not have associated with Keynesian thought.

A large group of developing and emerging economies and several countries on the European periphery implemented far-reaching, heterogeneous controls on capital inflows and outflows in response to diverse economic challenges. From a pre-crisis vantage point, the boldness, range, and creativity of the policy interventions across a significant swath of economies was unexpected. But a longer-run perspective on what appears to be the "new normal" (Grabel, 2011) situates the new openness and policy practice in the context of a longer-run process of legitimation that began slowly and unevenly after the East Asian financial crisis of the late 1990s (Abdelal, 2007; Chwieroth, 2010, Moschella, 2009). Hence, the global crisis has intensified a process of legitimation that predated it. The complex processes of change can most accurately be understood as "messy," uneven, contested, and evolving. That said, the degree of ideational and practical change around capital controls is far greater and more consistent than in the years following the East Asian crisis. In the language of marketing, capital controls have been "rebranded" during the global crisis.

The rebranding of capital controls has occurred against a broader backdrop of uncertainty and economic, political, and ideational change. This state of affairs – which I have elsewhere termed "productive incoherence" – constitutes the broader environment in which thinking and practice on capital controls are evolving (Grabel, 2011). By productive incoherence I refer to the proliferation of responses to the crisis by national governments, multilateral institutions, rating agencies and the economics profession that have not yet congealed into a consistent vision or model. Instead, and in response to diverse economic challenges, we find a proliferation of strategies that defy encapsulation in a unified narrative. I argue that incoherence is productive because it has widened the policy space to a greater and more consistent degree than in the years following the East Asian crisis (cf. Chwieroth, 2015; Gallagher, 2014; Moschella, 2014).

How are we to account for this extraordinary evolution regarding capital controls?[1] In what follows I examine five factors that, in my view, must appear in any comprehensive account. These include: (1) the rise of increasingly autonomous developing states, largely as a consequence of their successful response to the Asian crisis; (2) the increasing confidence and assertiveness of their policymakers in part as a consequence of their relative success in responding to the global crisis at a time when many advanced economies have and are still stumbling; (3) a pragmatic adjustment by the IMF to an altered global economy in which the geography of its influence has been severely restricted, and in which it has become financially dependent on its former clients; (4) the intensification of the need for capital controls by countries facing a range of circumstances – not just those that confront financial fragility or implosion and those that have been buffeted by the spillover effects of policy choices in wealthy econo-mies, but also those that fared "too well" during the first many years of the crisis; and (5) the evolution in the ideas of academic economists and IMF staff. I will also explore in passing, important tensions that have emerged in conjunction with rebranding. Paramount in this regard are attempts to develop a hierarchy in which controls are more acceptable if they focus on inflows and are implemented only as a last resort, are temporary, targeted, and non-discriminatory. Less acceptable are those that target outflows and are blunt, comprehensive, lasting, and discriminatory. In addition, tensions have emerged over the question of whether controls should be used by capital-source rather than just capital-recipient countries.

Others have earlier sought to rebrand controls, though these efforts did not prove sticky outside the Keynesian minority. For instance, Epstein, Grabel and Jomo (2004) use the term "capital management techniques" to refer to two complementary (and often overlapping) types of financial policies: capital controls and those that enforce prudential management of domestic financial institutions. Ocampo (2003, 2010) has long used the term "capital account regulations" to refer to a family of policies that includes capital controls. The IMF now refers to capital controls matter of factly as "capital flow management" techniques (IMF, 2011b). IMF rebranding is particularly significant. The new, entirely innocuous term is suggestive of a neutral, technocratic approach to a policy instrument that had long been discredited as a vestigial organ of wrong-headed, dirigiste economic meddling in otherwise efficient markets.

THE ORIGINS OF CHANGE: CAPITAL CONTROLS AND THE EAST ASIAN CRISIS

The Asian crisis stimulated new thinking about capital flow liberalization. Key mainstream economists, such as Bhagwati (1998) and Feldstein (1998), began to be openly critical of the way in which powerful interest groups and the IMF used the Asian (and other) crises to press for capital account liberalization, and caused others to reassess the case for capital liberalization (Krugman, 1998; Obstfeld, 1998). IMF research staff started to change their views on capital controls, albeit subtly, unevenly, and inconsistently. In the post-Asian crisis context, the center of gravity at the Fund and in the academic wing of the economics profession shifted away from an unequivocal, fundamentalist opposition to any interference with the free flow of capital to a tentative, conditional acceptance of tempo-rary, "market-friendly" inflows controls (Prasad et al., 2003). Academic literature on capital controls after the Asian crisis reflected this gradually evolving view (Chwieroth, 2010, ch. 8; Epstein et al., 2004; Kaplan and Rodrik, 2001; Magud and Reinhart, 2006).

Despite the modest intellectual progress on capital controls that began after the Asian crisis, controls remained an exceptional and contested measure. But things begin to change during the global crisis, when circumstances coalesce so as to legitimate controls to a far greater and more consistent degree.

The evolution in thinking and practice on capital controls during the global crisis represents an important turn in the direction of post-World War II support for the measure. Capital controls were the norm in developing and wealthy countries in the decades that followed World War II (Helleiner, 1994). In the first several decades of its existence, the IMF supported capital controls, a position that was consistent with and reflected the views of the economics profession (and notably, the views of John Maynard Keynes) and public figures (such as the US Treasury's Harry Dexter White). Both Keynes and White not only saw capital controls as a central feature of postwar economic policy, but also understood that controls on both sending and receiving ends could be warranted, and that cooperation by capital source and recipient countries was essential (see Horsefield, 1969, pp. 31, 65; Steil, 2013, pp. 134, 150).

REBRANDING CAPITAL CONTROLS DURING THE GLOBAL CRISIS

Several factors have facilitated the resurrection and legitimation of capital controls during the global crisis. In the interests of clarity, I discuss these factors separately in what follows, even though I see them as fully interdependent and cumulative.

Increasing State Autonomy in the Global South and East

Dismal experiences with the IMF, especially during the Asian crisis, led policymakers in the developing world to pursue strategies that would minimize the chance of future encroachments on their policy autonomy. The chief way in which this goal was operationalized was through the self-insurance provided by the overaccumulation of currency reserves. Self-insurance strategies collectively promote resilience and even what Nassim Taleb (2012) refers to as "antifragility," or the ability to thrive in periods of instability. This strategy of building antifragility was validated during the first many years of the global crisis.

Between 2000 and the second quarter of 2013, developing and emerging economies added about US$6.5 trillion to their reserve holdings, with China accounting for about half this increase (Prasad, 2014a). Emerging and developing economies (with reserves of US$7.7 trillion in 2014) accounted for 72 percent of the increase in global reserves between 2000 and 2014 (IMF COFER, author calculation).

The resources held by a group of developing countries help to create an environment wherein policymakers have the material means to enjoy increasing policy autonomy relative to the IMF. Not least, this has meant that policymakers have been able to deploy capital controls without worrying about negative reactions by the IMF or investors. The resilience and even the antifragility and the policy space created by these resources may prove essential if current turbulence intensifies.

Increasing Assertiveness in the Developing World

During the global crisis, developing country policymakers took advantage of their increased autonomy in a variety of ways. The use of capital controls was one and perhaps the most dramatic "indicator" of increased autonomy, and we consider this matter below. But we turn now to a brief consideration of three other indicators of increasing assertiveness: the use of countercyclical macroeconomic policies; innovation in financial architecture; and new activism at the IMF.

Countercyclical policies

The developing countries that have enjoyed the ability to protect and even expand their autonomy during the global crisis used the resulting policy space to pursue a range of countercyclical macroeconomic policies. Ocampo et al. (2012) conclude that when we look across the developing world we find diverse, uneven countercyclical policy responses. This is a radical departure from the past insofar as developing country policymakers generally had no alternative but to implement strongly procyclical policies, most often as per the conditions of IMF assistance. Policymakers could implement countercyclical and other protective policies that were previously unavailable to them precisely because of the enabling effects of prior reserve accumulation strategies.

The sheer scale of the crisis, the bold rhetoric around the need for new strategies to combat it, and the range of unorthodox policy responses pursued across the globe may have provided broader validation for the protective national policy responses pursued in the developing world. The G-20's brief "Keynesian moment" in 2008–09 opened space for capital controls and countercyclical responses in the developing world. Similarly, the IMF's rhetorical attention to pro-poor spending during the crisis began to legitimate countercyclical responses (Grabel, 2013b). Expansionary monetary policies in the USA and other wealthy countries likewise helped to normalize protective responses to the crisis in the developing world. What the IMF's Lagarde termed the rise of "unconventional monetary policies" (i.e., negative interest rates) in a number of wealthy countries provided cover for other unorthodox policies, such as capital controls. Finally, the rising chorus of criticism around the cross-border spillover effects of monetary policy decisions (especially by the USA) have made capital controls appear as a reasonable protective response.

Architectural innovations
As with the Asian crisis, the global crisis promoted interest in the expansion of existing and the creation of new institutions that deliver liquidity support and long-term project finance in ways that complement the IMF and the World Bank, respectively. The initiatives have been given life by the economic and political environment in which many developing country policymakers found themselves during the global crisis.

These initiatives range from reserve pooling arrangements such as the Chiang Mai Initiative Multilateralisation among members of the Association of Southeast Asian Nations (ASEAN)+ Japan, China, and South Korea, the Latin American Reserve Fund, the Arab Monetary Fund, and the Contingent Reserve Arrangement (CRA), which involves Brazil, Russia, India, China, and South Africa (the BRICS); to development or project/infrastructure finance banks, such as the Development Bank of Latin America, the New Development Bank (NDB) of the BRICS, and the China-led Asian Infrastructure Investment Bank and the One Belt, One Road initiative; to hybrid arrangements that have both liquidity support and project finance facilities, such as the Eurasian Fund for Stabilization and Development among members of the Eurasian Economic Community.[2]

Collectively, these innovations indicate the extent to which developing country governments have been stimulated by the crisis to pursue architectural initiatives that express an increasing self-confidence and a desire for autonomy from the Bretton Woods institutions (BWIs). Moreover, it is conceivable that recent changes in IMF views and practice on capital controls stem partly from attempts to protect the institution's franchise from actual or potential competition from these institutional innovations.

New lenders, renewed pressures
The increasing assertiveness of developing countries is also given expression in the new and historically unprecedented role that they have taken on

at the IMF. Developing countries were twice called upon to and did in fact commit funds to the institution (in April 2009 and June 2012). The new commitments reflect evolving power dynamics in the global economy and the IMF's evolving relationships with former clients. It is not inconsequential that most of the IMF's new lenders have been utilizing capital controls during the crisis, and more broadly have pursued various forms of dirigiste economic policy.

At the same time that developing countries took on a new role at the IMF they became more assertive in pressing the long-standing case for reform of the institution's formal governance. The 2012 contributions to the IMF by the BRICS were pointedly conditioned on governance reform, particularly implementation of the very modest governance reforms agreed to in 2010 (Giles, 2012). The US Congress blocked implementation of these reforms until December 2015, and this long period of gridlock was explicitly referenced when the BRICS announced in July 2014 that they would launch the NDB and CRA.

The IMF's Constrained Geography of Influence

An important consequence of the Asian crisis and subsequent changes in the global economy was the loss of purpose, standing and relevance of the IMF. Prior to the global crisis, demand for the institution's resources was at an historic low. During the crisis itself, developing countries did their best to stay clear of IMF oversight.

The global crisis nonetheless reestablished the IMF's central place as first responder to financial distress. The Fund was able to leverage its prior experience in responding to financial distress. Notably, the restoration of the IMF was largely due to events in and on the periphery of Europe rather than across the developing world (Lütz and Kranke, 2014). The April 2009 G-20 meeting not only gave the IMF pride of place in crisis response efforts, but also yielded massive funding commitments to the institution.

The IMF's staff face the challenges of protecting its restored franchise and image in an environment in which many of its former clients have pursued strategies that insulate them from the institution, are among its lenders, and have exercised increasing assertiveness in several domains. The IMF has been forced to negotiate to retain the influence that, until the East Asian crisis, it was able to take for granted. This negotiation is especially apparent in the domain of capital controls, where the IMF has often responded after the fact to unilateral decisions made by national authorities. Even where it retains substantial authority, its economists are responding to capital controls in ways that diverge from past practice (Grabel, 2015b).

Winners, Losers, Spillovers, and Capital Controls

During 2009–14, developing and emerging countries received net capital inflows of US$2.2 trillion (Stiglitz and Rashid, 2016). The vast inflows meant that many developing countries were confronted with surges of liquidity, asset bubbles, inflationary pressures, and currency appreciations. That the market capitalization of stock exchanges in Mumbai, Johannesburg, São Paulo, and Shanghai nearly tripled in the years that followed the global crisis is just one indicator of the fragility induced by these inflows (ibid.). Expansionary monetary policies in wealthy countries fed this flood of capital to developing country markets. In a departure from the old script, capital controls were necessitated by the side-effects of the relative success with which many developing countries navigated the global crisis and their own good fortune when it came to commodity prices and economic growth. This success, coupled with economic weakness and low returns on assets in wealthy countries, drove investors and speculators to developing country markets. The use of capital controls by what we might think of as "winning economies" has, in my view, contributed importantly to the legitimation of this policy instrument in the eyes of policymakers, the IMF, the international investment community, and the neoclassical core of the economics profession.

Now the tide is turning. In 2015, net capital outflows from the developing world exceeded US$600 billion, which was more than 25 percent of the capital inflows that they received during the previous six years (ibid.). Taking previously unrecorded flows into account, the Institute for International Finance (IIF) estimates that total net capital outflows from developing and emerging economies amounted to US$735 billion in 2015. By comparison, total net outflows from developing and emerging economies as a whole were valued at US$111 billion in 2014 (IIF, 2016), and East Asian economies experienced net capital outflows of only US$12 billion in 1997 (ibid.).

In this context, some developing countries have abandoned or loosened the inflow controls that they put in place during good times, and some have begun to implement new controls, particularly on outflows. These new controls have been implemented in response to the accelerating pace of outflows and the combined effects of slowing growth, falling commodity and asset prices, weakening currencies, and reserve disaccumulation. The excess liquidity and asset bubbles generated during good times have inevitably given way to public and private debt overhangs, which are aggravated by the locational mismatch that is made worse by the weakening of developing country currencies. In addition, these pressures have been both induced and magnified by the unsettled state of international financial markets and the spillover effects of the monetary policy environment in wealthy countries (i.e., negative interest rates, Federal Reserve tapering and tightening). In this new environment we have reason to expect familiar, vicious macroeconomic cycles in the developing world. The experience with and the widening of policy space around capital controls may well pay dividends in the coming period.

"Too much of a good thing"

Policymakers in a large set of developing countries deployed capital controls to mitigate the financial fragility and vulnerabilities induced by the large capital inflows that they received during much of the global crisis. In several country settings, controls were "dynamic" (as per Epstein et al., 2004) such that policymakers tightened, broadened, or layered new controls over existing measures as new sources of financial fragility and channels of evasion were identified and/or when existing measures proved too tepid to discourage undesirable financial activities. Controls were also removed as circumstances changed.

Brazil is a notable exemplar of dynamic capital controls. The country is an interesting case because the government (particularly former Finance Minister, Guido Mantega) staked out a strong position on policy space for controls throughout the crisis, and because the IMF's response to the country's controls exemplifies the evolution and equivocation in the views of Fund staff.

In late October 2009, Brazil began to utilize capital controls by imposing a tax on inflows of portfolio investment. They were intended to slow the appreciation of the currency in the face of significant capital inflows. Brazil imposed a 2 percent tax on money entering the country to invest in equities and fixed-income investments and later a 1.5 percent tax on certain trades involving American Depository Receipts, while leaving foreign direct investment untaxed. The IMF's initial reaction to Brazil's inflow controls was mildly disapproving. A senior official said: "These kinds of taxes provide some room for maneuver, but it is not very much, so governments should not be tempted to postpone other more fundamental adjustments. Second it is very complex to implement those kinds of taxes, because they have to be applied to every possible financial instrument," adding that such taxes have proven to be "porous" over time in a number of countries (cited in Subramanian and Williamson, 2009). In response, Subramanian and Williamson (2009) indicted the IMF for its doctrinaire and wrong-headed position on the Brazilian controls, taking the institution to task for squandering the opportunity to think reasonably about capital controls. A week later the IMF's then Managing Director, Dominique Strauss-Kahn, reframed the message on Brazil's controls. The new message was, in a word, stunning: "I have no ideology on this"; capital controls are "not something that come from hell" (cited in Guha, 2009).

The Brazilian government continued to strengthen and layer new controls over existing measures during October 2010 and July 2011. These included controls that specifically targeted derivative transactions and others that closed identified loopholes as they became apparent.[3] For example, in October 2010, the tax charged on foreign purchases of fixed-income bonds was tripled (from 2 to 6 percent), the tax on margin requirements for foreign exchange derivatives was increased, and some loopholes on the tax on margin requirements for foreign investors were closed. Despite an array of ever-increasing controls, IMF economists called its use of controls "appropriate" in an August 2011 review of Brazil (Ragir, 2011). Brazilian policymakers began to narrow some capital controls in December 2011, though at the same time continued to extend others.

Many other developing countries implemented and adjusted controls on outflows and especially on inflows during propitious economic times. Some strengthened existing controls, while others introduced new measures. For some countries (such as Argentina, Ecuador, Venezuela, China, and Taiwan) these measures are part of broader dirigiste approaches to policy. For most other countries (e.g., Brazil, South Korea, Indonesia, Costa Rica, Uruguay, the Philippines, Peru, and Thailand), controls were part of a dynamic, multi-pronged effort to respond to the challenges of attracting too much foreign investment and carry trade.

In December 2008, Ecuador doubled the tax on currency outflows, established a monthly tax on the funds and investments that firms kept overseas, discouraged firms from transferring US dollar holdings abroad by granting tax reductions to firms that reinvest their profits domestically, and established a reserve requirement tax (Tussie, 2010). In October 2010, Argentina and Venezuela implemented outflow controls. Argentina's controls were strengthened in October 2011. The country's capital and exchange controls were lifted in December 2015 following the presidential election of Mauricio Macri. Venezuelan capital and currency controls remain in force.

Peru began to impose inflow controls in early 2008. The country's central bank raised the reserve requirement tax four times between June 2010 and May 2012. The May 2012 measures included a 60 percent reserve ratio on overseas financing of all loans with a maturity of up to three years (compared to two years previously) and curbs on the use of a particular derivative (Yuk, 2012). What is particularly interesting about Peru's measures is the way in which they were branded by the central bank. In numerous public statements, the Central Bank President maintained that the country did not need capital controls even while it implemented and sustained its reserve requirement tax (Quigley, 2013).

In August 2012, Uruguay imposed a reserve requirement tax of 40 percent on foreign investment in one type of short-term debt (Reuters, 2012). Like Peru, its bilateral agreement with the USA could have made this control actionable. Currency pressures also induced Costa Rica to use capital controls for the first time in 20 years. The country began to use controls in September 2011 when it imposed a 15 percent reserve requirement tax on short-term foreign loans received by banks and other financial institutions (LatinDADD-BWP, 2011). In January 2013, the Costa Rican President began to seek Congressional approval to raise the reserve requirement tax to 25 percent, while also seeking authorization to increase from 8 percent to 38 percent a levy on foreign investors transferring profits from capital inflows out of the country.

In another sign of changing sentiments during the crisis, the rating agency Moody's recommended that South East Asian countries use controls to temper currency appreciation (Magtulis, 2013). Indeed, numerous Asian countries deployed new or strengthened existing controls during good times.

For instance, in November 2009, Taiwan imposed new inflow restrictions and at the end of 2010, controls on currency holdings were strengthened twice (Gallagher, 2011). In 2010, China added to its existing and largely quantitative inflow and outflow controls (ibid.). In 2013, China's State Administration of Foreign Exchange (SAFE, which is the unit within the central bank that manages the renminbi) took new steps to control "hot money" flows (Monan, 2013).

In June 2010, Indonesia announced what its officials termed a "quasi capital control" via a one-month holding period for central bank money market securities (raised to six months in 2011) and new limits on the sales of central bank paper by investors and on the interest rate on funds deposited at the central bank. During 2011, it reintroduced a 30 percent cap on short-term foreign exchange borrowing by domestic banks, and raised a reserve requirement on foreign currency deposits (Batunanggar, 2013). The awkward labeling of controls in Indonesia suggested its government was still afraid of the stigma that long attached to capital controls.

Thailand introduced a 15 percent withholding tax on capital gains and interest payments on foreign holdings of government and state-owned company bonds in October 2010. In December 2012, the Philippines announced limits on foreign currency forward positions by banks and restrictions on foreign deposits (Aquino and Batino, 2012).

As in Brazil, Korean authorities took a dynamic, layered approach to capital controls, while also targeting the particular risks of derivatives. But unlike Brazil, authorities reframed these measures as macroprudential and not as capital controls (see Chwieroth, 2015). In 2010, Korean regulators began to audit lenders working with foreign currency derivatives, placed a ceiling on the use of this instrument, and imposed a levy on what it termed "non-core" foreign currency liabilities held by banks. In 2011, Korea also levied a tax on holdings of short-term foreign debt by domestic banks, banned "naked" short selling, and reintroduced a 14 percent withholding tax on foreign investment in government bonds sold abroad and a 20 percent capital gains tax on foreign purchases of government bonds (ADB, 2011; Lee, 2011).

"Stopping the bleeding"

Some countries have and are using capital controls during the global crisis for the more customary reason of stemming a financial or economic collapse. In these cases, the IMF has tolerated controls on capital outflows. This is notable insofar as the Fund and the neoclassical heart of the economics profession have long seen outflow controls as far worse than inflow controls.

Iceland's policymakers put outflow controls in place to slow the implosion of the economy before signing an agreement with the IMF in October 2008. The agreement made a very strong case for the extension of these controls as a means to restore stability and to protect the krona (IMF, 2012a; Sigurgeirsdóttir and Wade, 2015). In public statements on the matter, the IMF's staff repeatedly said that the country's outflow controls were crucial to prevent a collapse of the currency, that they were temporary, and that it was a priority to end all restrictions as soon as possible. The IMF's mission chief in the country commented that "capital controls as part of an overall strategy worked very, very well" (Forelle, 2012), and the institution's Deputy Managing Director stated that "unconventional measures (as in Iceland) must not be shied away from when needed" (IMF, 2011a). The rating agency, Fitch, praised the country's "unorthodox crisis policies" when announcing that it had raised its credit rating to investment grade in February 2012 (Valdimarsson, 2012). It should be said that neoliberals in the country did not share this enthusiasm for the unorthodox response or the IMF's advice (Danielsson and Arnason, 2011).[4]

The IMF's characterization of and role in strengthening Iceland's outflow controls marked a dramatic precedent and revealed a fundamental change in thinking about capital controls. The December 2008 agreement with Latvia allowed for the maintenance of pre-existing restrictions arising from a partial deposit freeze at the largest domestic bank (IMF, 2009b). Soon thereafter, a Fund report acknowledged that Iceland, Indonesia, the Russian Federation, Argentina, and Ukraine all put outflow controls in place to "stop the bleeding" related to the crisis (IMF, 2009a). The report neither offers details on the nature of these controls nor commentary on their ultimate efficacy, something that suggests that controls – even and most notably on outflows – are being destigmatized by the context in which they are being used, and by the Fund's and, in the cases of Cyprus and Greece, the EU's and the European Central Bank's measured reaction to them.[5] Indeed, a report by the IMF's Independent Evaluation Office (IEO, 2015) takes note of the institution's greater tolerance for outflow controls during the global financial crisis as exemplified by its support for outflow controls in Iceland, Cyprus, and Latvia.[6]

Cyprus was the first country in the Eurozone to implement capital controls during the global crisis. The IMF and the EU did not flinch when stringent outflow controls were implemented as the country's economy imploded in March 2013. Cyprus's capital controls evolved in the months that followed the March collapse and after it began to receive support in May 2013 under an IMF Extended Fund Facility. Capital controls began to be removed in March 2014, and the remaining controls were lifted in April 2015. Standard and Poor's upgraded Cyprus's sovereign debt rating in September 2015, and in doing so cited the removal of capital controls (Zikakou, 2015). Greece became the second Eurozone country to implement capital controls. Stringent outflow controls were put in place at the end of June 2015 once Eurozone leaders announced that they would not extend Greece's then current assistance package, and that the European Central Bank (ECB) would cap emergency liquidity assistance to the country's banks.

"Taper tantrums" and the new outflow rout

Beginning in 2013, developing countries again began to adjust, experiment, and/or create space for diverse types of capital controls against the backdrop of growing financial fragility, weakening economies, depreciating currencies, and turmoil induced by international policy spillovers. New or tightened capital controls were implemented by policymakers in the context of the growing fragility in 2015 and early 2016. Some controls that were put in place in good times were loosened or abandoned.

For example, in June 2013, Brazil eliminated some remaining capital controls that were left over from the country's heady days. It reduced the tax on overseas investments in domestic bonds from 6 percent to zero, and removed a 1 percent tax on bets against the dollar in the futures market (Biller and Rabello, 2013; Leahy and Pearson, 2013). In March 2014, Costa Rica put in place a framework for new capital controls aimed at giving the central bank the ability to curb speculative money flows from abroad (Reuters, 2014). And, in an indication of changing sentiments in challenging times, the Governor of the Bank of Mexico, Agustín Carstens, said in January 2016 that it might soon be time for central bankers in the developing world "to become unconventional" to stem the vast tide of capital outflows (Wheatley and Donnan, 2016). (This is particularly notable since as recently as 2015 he had spoken strongly against capital controls; see below.)

China's strategy of "managed convertibility" has become increasingly difficult for officials to navigate in the wake of growing national and global economic turbulence and missteps by national policymakers, particularly involving decisions to devalue the currency. This strategy involves a complex mix of liberalizing capital controls to increase the convertibility of the renminbi (RMB) and increase its flow and use across borders, while also tightening existing and implementing new controls to protect the economy and the currency from volatile capital flows (Subacchi, 2015). Liberalizing capital controls was also necessitated by policymakers' long-held goal of having the IMF agree to include the RMB in the Special Drawing Rights basket alongside other currencies that it had long designated as having "global reserve currency" status. In November 2015, China achieved this (largely symbolic) goal. Against this backdrop and in a series of announcements in 2014, the country's policymakers eased some capital controls, such as those that restricted domestic investors from investing in foreign stocks and properties, firms from selling RMB-denominated shares abroad, and doubling the daily range in which the RMB could trade (Barboza, 2014; Bloomberg, 2014). After the surprise decision to allow the RMB to devalue in August 2015, SAFE expended up to US$200 billion in reserves defending the currency during the next month, increased monitoring and controls on foreign exchange transactions, and imposed a 20 percent reserve on currency forward positions (Anderlini, 2015). And following another round of large capital outflows in January 2016, SAFE implemented several new, ad hoc, and stringent capital controls.

In August 2013, India implemented capital controls on some types of outward flows. These restricted the amount that Indian-domiciled companies and residents could invest abroad (*Financial Times*, 2013). Interestingly, then Governor of the Reserve Bank of India, Duvvuri Subbarao, took pains to explain that these measures should not be labeled as capital controls (despite the obvious point). In his last speech as Central Bank Governor, he said of these measures: "I must reiterate here that it is not the policy of the Reserve Bank to resort to capital controls or reverse the direction of capital account liberalization," and he emphasized that the measures did not restrict inflows or outflows by non-residents (Reuters, 2013b). Market observers nevertheless dubbed them as "partial capital controls" (Ray, 2013). When the new Governor of the Reserve Bank of

India, Raghuram Rajan, took his place in September 2013, he promptly rolled back the new outflow controls (ibid).

Tajikistan deployed several types of outflow controls during 2015 and 2016 in the context of the turmoil induced by falling oil prices. These involve administrative measures that attempt to stabilize the currency, closure of private currency exchange offices, the requirement that ruble-denominated remittances be converted to the national currency, restrictions on foreign currency transactions, and termination of the direct sale of foreign currency to the population (IntelliNews, 2016; National Bank of Tajikistan, 2015; UNCTAD, 2015). Here, too, authorities attempted to brand these measures as something other than capital controls. Indeed, First Deputy Chairman of the country's central bank, Nuraliev Kamolovich, denied that these moves amounted to capital controls in an interview with the *Financial Times* (Farchy, 2016).

In December 2014, the Russian government put outflow controls in place, though these are being referred to in the country's press as "informal" capital controls. The government set limits on net foreign exchange assets for state-owned exporters; required that large state exporting companies report to the central bank weekly and reduce net foreign exchange assets to the lower level that prevailed earlier in the year; and the central bank installed supervisors at currency trading desks of top state banks (Kelly, Korsunskaya and Fabrichnaya, 2014).

Ukraine deployed several outflow controls in February 2014. These measures include a ceiling on foreign currency purchases by individuals; a ban on buying foreign exchange to invest overseas or repay foreign debt early; a five-day waiting period before companies can receive the foreign exchange that they have purchased; and a limit on foreign currency withdrawals from bank deposits (to around US$1500 per day; Strauss 2014).

The case of Azerbaijan is illustrative of the continued tensions over capital controls within some countries and also of the rating agencies' new measured responses to them. In January 2016, the country's parliament passed a bill that would impose a 20 percent tax on foreign currency outflows and allow repayment of dollar loans up to US$5000 at the exchange rate that prevailed prior to the currency's devaluation. The country's President, Ilham Aliyev, rejected the bill the next month. In doing so he said that "[it] was a mistake to tax foreign-currency outflows as it would scare away foreign investors" (Agayev, 2016). In the period between the parliament's passage and Aliyev's rejection, the rating agencies had a measured reaction to the prospect of outflow controls. Standard and Poor's lowered the countries rating, but cited low oil prices in doing so, and Fitch did not change their rating, saying that "the introduction of the capital controls does not 'automatically' have consequences for the country's sovereign rating" (Eglitis, 2016; *Financial Times*, 2016).

Beginning in late 2014, Nigeria began to implement outflow controls as falling oil prices and a concomitant drop in foreign reserves destabilized its economy. In December 2014, limits on currency trading were imposed. And starting in April 2015 and continuing through the year, new outflow controls were put in place. These included restrictions on access to hard currency and cross-border payments, daily limits on foreign ATM withdrawals, and restrictions on access to dollars (Ferro, 2014; Johnson, 2015; Reuters, 2015).[7] In February 2016, the IMF's Lagarde began to call publicly on the government to remove capital and exchange controls, abandon the currency peg, and borrowing from an old script, to pursue fiscal discipline and structural reform to bolster growth (Reuters, 2016).

Similar pressures, dissimilar responses, and legal constraints
Not all policymakers have responded to the pressures induced by large inflows, outflows, and policy spillovers with capital controls. Policymakers in some countries that enjoyed high inflows during much of the global crisis, such as Turkey, Chile, Mexico, and Colombia, publicly rejected inflow controls. Instead they increased their purchases of dollars and used expansionary monetary policy. These divergent responses to similar pressures reflect many factors, not least of which are differing internal political economies and the resilience of the view that central banks must signal their commitment to neoliberalism.

There is far more to the matter of resisting capital controls than the long half-life of neoliberalism, however. Some countries simply cannot introduce capital controls – either on inflows or outflows – because of bi- or multilateral trade and investment treaties with the USA (such as the North American Free Trade Agreement, NAFTA, and the Dominican Republic–Central American Free Trade Agreement), the EU, and the OECD (Gallagher, 2012, 2014, ch. 8; Shadlen, 2005; Wade, 2003). The scope of these constraints would have been expanded if the Trans-Pacific Partnership (TTP) had not been aborted.[8]

Governments face other restrictions on controls from the obligations to liberalize financial services under the WTO (Gallagher, 2012). Article 63 of the Lisbon Treaty of the EU enforces open capital accounts across the union and requires that members do not restrict capital transactions with other countries. However, Cyprus and Greece are members of the EU, and they did deploy stringent outflow controls in 2013 and 2015 (respectively). Indeed, the EC and the ECB gave their blessing to capital controls on the grounds that they were temporary and essential to preventing large-scale investor exit and the collapse of the banking system. Other restrictions appear in the OECD's Code of Liberalisation of Capital Movements, though since it is not a treaty the obligations are not actionable (Abdelal, 2007; Gallagher, 2012).

At the time when many of these agreements were negotiated, their restrictions on capital controls no doubt seemed redundant since controls were effectively blocked by the effective constraints imposed by the IMF, rating agencies and investors. Today, however, in the face of reversals by the previous enforcers of neoliberalism, the provisions are consequential. Chile's refusal to use controls during the global crisis may have had as much to do with its 2004 trade agreement with the USA as with neoliberal ideology. The US–Chile Free Trade Agreement exposes the country to lawsuits by investors who are able to demonstrate that they are harmed by controls. Mexico's situation is similar. Here neoliberal views are backed up by the strictures in NAFTA that threaten to punish any change in its policy stance.[9] By contrast, Brazil was free to utilize controls during the global crisis because it has not signed bilateral treaties with the USA.

Reframing controls as something other than controls seems to be one viable avenue in cases where policymakers do not have the appetite to push the limits of trade/investment agreements (as with Peru and Uruguay), or where they otherwise fear the anti-free market stigma), hence, Korea's macroprudential measures;[10] Indonesia's quasi-controls; Tajikistan's denial that it is using controls; India's use of partial controls, and the Central Bank Governor's message to foreign investors; and Azerbaijan's President blocking capital controls because of the perceived reaction by foreign investors.[11]

Revising the rule book
Since 2008, many developing countries have implemented controls without seeking permission from the IMF. For many (but not all) countries, controls were a response to the costs of their relative economic success during much of the global crisis. It is hard to imagine that capital controls could have been rebranded as legitimate policy tools as quickly and deeply as has been the case had it not been for the divergent effects of the crisis across the globe, and the initiatives of many of the winners from the crisis to assert control over financial flows. Just as history is written by the victors, so may it be the case that the rebranding and relegitimizing of a forbidden policy tool depends primarily on the practices and strategies of those countries whose success grants them the latitude and confidence, and the influence over other countries, not just to "cheat" in a policy domain but to revise the rule book completely. Thus, whether the IMF and the economics profession have changed fundamentally on capital controls matters less than the context in which they are being utilized.

Outflow controls have also been legitimized by widespread acknowledgement of their success in Iceland and elsewhere. Outflow controls are nevertheless still seen in a different light than inflow controls, but the crisis has catalyzed a degree of rethinking on this controversial instrument as well. It may be that outflow controls become necessary in more national contexts if present turbulence accelerates, as seems likely. This may test the limits of the policy space around this tool.

The rebranding of controls has also been facilitated by the fact that carry trade pressures caused central bankers in wealthy countries to reconsider their long-held opposition to capital controls. For example, the head of the Swiss National Bank announced that it was considering controls on foreign deposits when the currency was under pressure, though these have not been used (Ross and Simonian, 2012). A top Bundesbank official signaled a softening in its traditional position in stating that "limited use of controls could sometimes be appropriate" to counter currency pressures (Reuters, 2013a). Moreover, the emergence of unconventional monetary policies and the growing discussion of their spillover effects may have triggered recognition that desperate times require desperate measures. This may reflect what Benlialper and Cömert (2016) term a broadening of central bank practice and policy targets during the crisis.

The Economics Profession, the IMF, and the New Pragmatism on Capital Controls

Today, IMF staff economists and leading academic economists have taken steps toward elaborating a theoretical and empirical case for capital controls.

Neoclassical economics and capital controls

Two views on capital controls have predominated among academic economists who advocate neoliberalism. The first, and minority view, is associated with libertarian thought. From the libertarian perspective, controls are a violation of investor rights. The case against them is therefore impervious to new empirical evidence or a change in economic conditions. In contrast, neoclassical welfarist critics have long held that capital controls are counterproductive.

The neoliberal case against capital controls seems to have lost some of its luster during the global crisis, though some ardent defenders have been left standing. For instance, in a discussion of inflow controls, Mexico's Central Bank Governor, Agustín Carstens, said: "[C]apital controls. . .don't work, I wouldn't use them, I wouldn't recommend them" (Carstens, 2015). In the same speech he indicted outflow controls: "when investors come in [to a new country] they first look to see where the exit is and if it doesn't exist, they won't come in."[12] Some neoliberals (as we have seen earlier) have rebuked the IMF for its support of capital controls in Brazil and Iceland, and others, such as Cline (2010), have rebuked the IMF for its new acceptance of controls. The conservative US think tank, the Heritage Foundation, has been sharply critical of the IMF's recent acceptance of capital controls, and in an Issue Brief highlights with horror a 2012 speech made by the IMF's Lagarde in praise of Malaysia's 1998 controls (Olson and Kim, 2013).

Despite this notable camp of holdouts, we find evidence within neoclassical thought of a new pragmatism concerning capital controls. Prior to the global crisis, neoclassical economists almost universally held that controls were costly interventions in the market because they raise the cost of capital, especially for small and medium-sized firms, and generate costly evasion strategies (Edwards, 1999; Forbes, 2005). Capital controls were therefore imprudent since developing countries could hardly afford new sources of inefficiency and distributional disparities.

Recent research in neoclassical economics challenges the critique by emphasizing the negative externalities associated with highly liberalized international financial flows, particularly in the absence of international coordination of monetary policies. The research has helped to legitimize capital controls, particularly targeted, temporary controls, and some of this research also offers support for international policy coordination and/ or regulations on capital flows in both source and recipient countries.

There are three dimensions to the new academic research. The first strand is associated with the work of Korinek (2011), and is termed the "new welfare economics of capital controls." It assumes that in an environment of uncertainty, imperfect information and volatility, unstable capital flows have negative externalities on recipient economies (Aizenman, 2009; Korinek, 2011). In this approach, liberalized short-term capital flows are recognized to induce ambient risk that can destabilize economies. Inflow controls induce borrowers to internalize the externalities of risky capital flows, and thereby promote macroeconomic stability and enhance welfare (Korinek, 2011).

A second strand of research, associated with Korinek (2011, 2014) and Rey (2014, 2015), emphasizes the way in which capital controls protect developing countries from the international spillover effects of monetary policy in wealthy countries, and it explicitly takes up the absence of multilateral mechanisms to coordinate monetary, capital control, and other prudential policies. Research by Korinek and Rey provides rigorous academic support for the claims of Brazil's Mantega and India's Rajan (among others) regarding currency wars and spillover effects. An article in *The Economist* put the connection between these spillover effects and capital controls quite clearly: "QE [quantitative easing] has helped to make capital controls intellectually respectable again" (*The Economist*, 2013).

Korinek (2013) argues that the negative international spillover effects of expansionary monetary policy during the global crisis highlights the need for multilateral coordination. An IMF Staff Discussion Note (in which Korinek is one of the authors) extends these themes (Ostry, Ghosh and Korinek, 2012). The report argues that coordination of capital controls between source and recipient is welfare improving since the costs of controls increase at an increasing rate with the intensity of controls. Thus, a more efficient outcome is to spread the costs of controls across countries so that no one country shoulders all the costs. In a similar vein, using data from 1995 to 2012, Ghosh, Qureshi and Sugawara (2014) find that imposing capital controls on both source and recipient countries can achieve a larger decrease in the volume of flows, or the same decrease with less intrusive measures on either end. Thus, international coordination achieves globally more efficient outcomes, and what they term costly "capital control wars" can be avoided.

Rey's (2015) work is also motivated by the unwelcome international spillover effects of wealthy country monetary policy. These spillover effects necessitate use of targeted capital controls on inflows and outflows, particularly since she sees international coordination on monetary policy spillovers as being "out of reach." Capital controls are necessary to protect developing countries from what she terms the "global financial cycle," that is, the instability triggered by large, sudden inflows associated with carry trade activity and their equally sudden exit (ibid.). In a lecture at the IMF, former Federal Reserve Chair Bernanke criticized Rey and Mantega by name for being too willing to portray policymakers in developing countries as "passive objects of the effects of Fed policy decisions" (Bernanke, 2015, especially pp. 24, 30, 33, 36, 44), and argued that international cooperation on monetary policy was neither necessary nor appropriate. Bernanke (ibid.) endorsed the use of targeted capital controls to tackle the unwelcome international spillover effects of monetary policy, though he also noted the importance of regulatory and other macroprudential measures.

Other neoclassical economists have wrestled with the international spillover effects of monetary policy and capital controls during the crisis. Nobel Laureate, Michael Spence, wrote of the troubling "financial protectionism" that was occasioned by expansionary monetary policy in rich countries. He (and his co-author) worried that such financial protectionism would accelerate as the era of cheap capital came to a close (Dobbs and Spence, 2011). But despite characterizing controls as financial protectionism, Spence spoke favorably about their utility in developing countries during a 2010 speech at the Reserve Bank of India. There he called capital controls on such flows "essential as part of the process of maintaining control" in developing countries, and also noted that most of the high-growth developing countries have had capital controls (Spence, 2010).

A third strand of new neoclassical research is empirical and substantiates the theoretical claims of the welfarist approach. Ghosh and Qureshi (2016) review a large body of empirical evidence that shows that inflow controls change the composition of capital inflows and do not discourage investors. Even Forbes, a longstanding critic of controls, finds that Brazilian taxes on foreign purchases of fixed-income assets between 2006 and 2011 achieved one of its key goals of reducing the purchase of Brazilian bonds (Forbes et al., 2011). Another type of empirical work involves "meta-analysis" of a large volume of existing studies. Magud and Reinhart (2006) find that inflow controls enhanced monetary policy independence, altered the composition of inflows, reduced real exchange rate pressures, and did not reduce the aggregate volume of net inflows. (See also the survey in Magud, Reinhart and Rogoff, 2011, which includes studies conducted in the early years of the global crisis.)[13]

Empirical research by economists outside the profession's mainstream reaches beyond the tepid, conditional endorsement of capital controls that we find in the recent work of neoclassical economists (e.g., Epstein, 2012; Erten and Ocampo, 2013; Gallagher, 2014; Grabel, 2015b). Erten and Ocampo (2013) provide what is perhaps the most expansive support for the achievements of a range of capital controls, including those on outflows. Using data from 51 emerging and developing economies from 1995 to 2011, they find that capital controls that target inflows, outflows, and foreign exchange-related measures were associated with lower foreign exchange pressures, and reduced exchange rate appreciation. They also find that these three types of measures enhanced monetary policy autonomy; that increasing their restrictiveness in the run-up to the global crisis reduced the growth decline during the crisis (and thereby enhanced crisis resilience); and that countries that used these measures experienced less overheating during post-crisis recovery when a new surge in capital inflows occurred.

The IMF and capital controls
The evolution in thinking on capital controls by academic economists is reflected in and reinforced by developments at three overlapping levels of practice at the IMF: research, official statements by key officials, and policy recommendations by its staff. We find continued evidence of discomfort or tension around capital controls that is reflected in efforts to

develop a hierarchy among types of capital controls and the circumstances under which they are most acceptable.

In February 2010, a team of IMF economists published a thorough survey of econometric evidence that commended inflow controls for preventing crises and ultimately reducing the risk and severity of crisis-induced recessions, and for reducing fragility by lengthening the maturity structure of countries' external liabilities and improving the composition of inflows (Ostry et al., 2010). These findings pertain to controls prior to and after the Asian crisis, as well as during the global crisis. After Ostry et al. (2010) was released, prominent IMF watchers praised the Fund for finally embracing a sensible view of controls. For example, Ronald McKinnon stated, "I am delighted that the IMF has recanted" (cited in Rappeport, 2010); former IMF official Eswar Prasad states that the paper represented a "marked change" in the IMF's advice (cited in Wroughton, 2010), while Dani Rodrik stated that the "the stigma on capital controls (is) gone," and that the report "is a stunning reversal – as close as an institution can come to recanting without saying, 'Sorry, we messed up'" (Rodrik, 2010). Rodrik also noted that "[j]ust as John Maynard Keynes said in 1945 – capital controls are now orthodox" (cited in Thomas, 2010). No less telling is the sharp rebuke to Ostry et al. (2010) by Cline (2010), which is illustrative of the discomfort that "true believers" in capital liberalization have with what they see as the Fund's troubling, wrong-headed new embrace of controls.

Research on controls spilled out from various quarters of the IMF through 2011–15. The IMF's crisis-induced research on controls culminated in a December 2012 report of the Executive Board, which the IMF terms the "institutional view" (IMF, 2012b, 2012c). The institutional view report (IMF, 2012c) makes clear that inflow and outflow surges induce instability; that countries should not consider capital liberalization prematurely; that temporary, targeted, and transparent inflow and even outflow controls may be warranted during turbulence, though they should not discriminate against foreign investors; that countries retain the right under Article VI to put controls in place; and that the IMF's new, more permissive stance on controls may conflict with and be subsumed by trade and other agreements. Particularly notable is the fact that the report refrains from denigrating capital controls as a last resort measure – a theme that had recurred throughout IMF research in 2010 and 2011 – and that it sanctions the deployment of outflow controls during crises.

There is clear evidence in the institutional view of the IMF's continued effort to "domesticate" the use of controls in the language around targeted, transparent, temporary, and non-discriminatory measures. Moreover, arguments in the report continue to be guided by the view that capital liberalization is ultimately desirable, though claims to this effect are more nuanced than in the past.[14] Not least, the report rejects the presumption that this is the right policy for all countries at all times. Tensions over these and other matters among members of the IMF's Executive Board were given an oblique airing in a Public Information Notice released by the Fund, and more directly in press accounts, many of which focused on criticisms of the report by Paulo Nogueira Batista, then IMF Executive Director for Brazil and ten other countries (IMF, 2012b). Criticism by Nogueira Batista also focused on the failure of the institutional view to consider the role of push factors from wealthy countries and the IMF's lack of even-handedness (Prasad, 2014b, p. 195). That said, the fact that the IMF has shifted the discussion of capital controls away from straight economics and toward the legal and institutional conditions required for their success is further evidence that the most stubborn form of resistance to controls on economic grounds has been overcome.[15]

The IMF continues to wrestle with the interpretation and practical implications of its own institutional view. An April 2013 Staff Guidance Note aimed at providing guidance as to how IMF staff should interpret the institutional view (IMF, 2013). The Guidance Note reiterates that "staff advice should not presume that full liberalization is an appropriate goal for all countries at all times," made allowance for "a temporary re-imposition" of [capital flow measures] under certain circumstances, but reiterates that they should be "transparent, targeted, temporary, and preferably non-discriminatory" (pp. 9–10, 16). Despite the growing acknowledgement of spillover effects, the Guidance Note rejects the view that capital source countries should be expected to take spillover effects into account (p. 17). A December 2015 report prepared for IMF staff (IMF, 2015) probes what the institutional view and the 2013 Guidance Note mean specifically for outflow controls. In doing so, the 2015 report says that outflow controls (like inflow controls) should be transparent, temporary, lifted once the crisis conditions abate, and should seek to be non-discriminatory, though it does acknowledge that sometimes residency-based measures may be hard to avoid (IMF, 2015, fn. 1). The report also observes that unlike capital controls on inflows, temporary controls on outflows generally need to be comprehensive and adjusted to avoid circumvention (p. 3), and that "re-imposition of [capital controls] on outflows can be appropriate and consistent with an overall strategy of capital flow liberalization. . .even in non-crisis-type circumstances if premature or improperly sequenced liberalization. . .outpaced the capacity. . .to safely handle the resulting flows" (p. 4).

The Talmudic process of interpreting the institutional view that has followed its release reflect not just hedging and discomfort, but also deep internal conflicts within and outside the IMF around its development (see the IMF's IEO, 2015, p. 9, fn. 15; and Gallagher, 2014, ch. 6). The IEO (2015) notes that it is uncertain whether implementation of this view will result in consistent IMF advice on capital controls, owing to the fragile nature of the consensus that sustains it, the resilience of internal conflict around the matter, and the constraints on controls in trade and investment agreements. Preliminary evidence suggests a basis for cautious optimism: the 2015 IEO report reviews the IMF's Article IV reports from January 2006 to August 2014, and finds that staff advice on capital controls was more discouraging in the early part of this period, and more supportive and even encouraging of such measures from 2010 on (p. 12).

Beyond the research, public statements by current and former officials at the BWIs beginning in 2009 further illustrate the normalization, lingering ambivalence, and attempt to domesticate the use of controls. For instance, former IMF First Deputy Managing Director, John Lipsky, acknowledged in a December 2009 speech that temporary "(c)apital controls also represent an option for dealing with sudden surges in capital flows" and that "[a]bove all, we should be open-minded" (Lipsky, 2009). Public statements by the IMF's Strauss-Kahn illustrate well the grudging evolution in the IMF's views. In public statements in 2009, Strauss-Kahn emphasized the costs of capital controls, and that they tend to lose effectiveness over time (IEO, 2015, box 3). But in a July 2010 speech he reframed his message: "[I]t is. . .fair that these countries would try to manage the inflows" as a last resort against inflow-induced asset bubbles (Oliver, 2010); and later in the year he reiterated what was by then the new mantra that capital controls are a legitimate part of the toolkit (IEO, 2015, p. 16; Strauss-Kahn, 2010). In 2010, the Director of the Fund's Western Hemispheric department made a case (unsuccessfully) for the utility of controls in Colombia owing to the appreciation of its currency (Crowe, 2010). The IMF's Lagarde spoke in 2012 and 2014 of the utility of temporary, targeted capital controls (IEO, 2015, box 3); and in March 2015 she observed that there is scope for greater cooperation in connection with monetary policy spillovers (Lagarde, 2015).

Given the unevenness of the IMF's position on capital controls after the Asian crisis, the research, policy advice and statements coming from key officials during the global crisis mark by its standards a minor revolution. Change at the Fund has been uneven, to be sure, with one step back for every two steps forward. None of this should be surprising. We should expect that deeply established ideas hang on despite their apparent disutililty (Grabel, 2003a). We should expect to find continuing evidence of tension and equivocation in research by academic economists and in future IMF reports and practice. But for now, at least, welfarist arguments for controls have been embraced at the top of the profession, and this is apt to continue to cast a long shadow over the IMF and beyond. More importantly, and as I have argued throughout, change at the IMF and in the economics profession is only one of a larger set of factors that have legitimated capital controls.

SUMMARY AND CONCLUSIONS

In the end, whether the IMF's new openness on capital controls fades with the crisis may not matter insofar as the institution has been rendered less relevant as it faces increasingly autonomous and assertive developing country members (some of which emerged as its lenders earlier in the crisis). The fact that economies that performed relatively well during the crisis successfully utilized controls has eliminated the long-standing stigma around the instrument. That the Fund has also acknowledged the utility of outflow controls in countries in crisis also makes it harder to envision a return to pre-2008 views, something that may turn out to be quite important if the current instability continues to deepen.[16]

As with most rebranding exercises there is uncertainty about whether the new framing will prove sufficiently sticky, especially in the context of tensions and countervailing impulses at the IMF and elsewhere, a resilient bias within economics against state management of economic flows, and new attempts to assert outflow controls in times of distress that would run counter to the interests of powerful financial actors. For now, though, there seems to be substantial momentum propelling increasing use of and experimentation with the flexible deployment of capital controls, in some cases with IMF support and most other cases without IMF resistance. The widening of policy space and the practical experience with capital controls gained during the global crisis may prove consequential in the coming period. Even if the problems of "doing too well" fade across the developing world (as seems likely), the experiments with controls on capital inflows during better times may pay important dividends in the challenging times ahead. A critical test of recent and ongoing experiences with capital controls will occur in future crises, as states rely on and adjust fledgling practices and policies in hopes of dampening instability and otherwise managing turbulence better than they had over the course of previous crises. The coming period may test – sooner rather than later – the resilience of the new openness to controls.

In my view, it is critical that efforts be made to maintain and expand the opportunity that has emerged in the crisis environment for national policy-makers to experiment with capital controls and to adjust them as circumstances warrant. Hence, the pressing policy challenge today is to construct regimes that expand national policy autonomy to use capital controls while managing cross-border spillover effects. This certainly suggests abandoning (or, at the very least, renegotiating) the strictures on capital controls in existing and pending bilateral, and multilateral trade and investment agreements. It also suggests the need (ideally) to develop frameworks for burden sharing and international cooperation in the case of spillover effects. Moreover, historical and recent experience show that capital controls on inflows and outflows should be thought of not as a last resort, but rather as a permanent and dynamic part of a broader prudential, countercyclical toolkit to be deployed as internal and external conditions warrant; and that there are circumstances wherein controls may need to be blunt, comprehensive, significant, lasting, and discriminatory rather than modest, narrowly targeted, and temporary (Epstein et al., 2004; Erten and Ocampo, 2013; Fritz and Prates, 2014; Grabel, 2003b, 2004; Rodrik, 2015).[17]

Any regime that seeks to develop a framework for capital controls should err on the side of generality, flexibility, and permissiveness; should involve and promote cooperation by both capital source and recipient countries; and should embody an even-handed acknowledgement that monetary policies, like capital controls, have positive and negative global spillover effects that necessitate some type of burden sharing. It is therefore heartening that the crisis appears to have occasioned the rediscovery of the views of Keynes and White,[18] and that these views have been given new life by the widespread use and rebranding of capital controls in many national contexts and by the related attention to currency wars and policy spillovers. Reconsideration of these matters by leading policymakers, neoclassical economists, and IMF researchers has also shifted neoclassical economists and the IMF quite far from their blanket embrace of capital liberalization prior to the Asian crisis.

The spread of capital controls and the conflict over spillovers also highlight the problems associated with the absence of global policy coordination. Brazil's former finance minister raised this matter on many occasions. More recently, India's Central Bank Governor, Raghuram Rajan, in October 2015 began to be openly critical of IMF support of the easy money policies in wealthy countries, the tide of competitive and nationalist monetary easing, and the IMF's failure to flag the negative spillover effects of such measures (*Times of India*, 2015). In this context, Rajan has proposed that the IMF (and possibly the G-20 and Bank for International Settlements, BIS) study this matter seriously, and develop a system for passing judgment on unconventional monetary policies and the severity of their spillovers in relation to their possible effects on growth. This might involve a panel of "eminent academics" appointed by the IMF, G-20 and/or BIS who would rate polices using a color-coded (red/green/

orange light system) (Krishnan, 2016), or might involve the IMF passing such judgments itself (Rajan, 2016).

In this environment of disruption, economic and institutional change, intellectual aperture, and uncertainty we find a productive expansion of policy space for capital controls and a movement away from the reification of capital flows and other aspects of financial liberalization within neoclassical economics, something that may ultimately be seen as an important legacy of the global crisis. This change, messiness, and uncertainty exemplify what I see as the productive incoherence of the present environment.

NOTES

* Reprinted/adapted by permission from Springer Nature: Palgrave Macmillan, *Financial Liberalisation: Past, Present and Future*, by P. Arestis and M. Sawyer (eds) © 2017. I thank George DeMartino, Philip Arestis, and Malcolm Sawyer for invaluable comments on this chapter. I also thank Jeff Chase, Denise Marton Menendez, Meredith Moon, and Alison Lowe for excellent research assistance.

1. Discussion in this chapter draws heavily on, though extends and updates, discussion in Grabel (2011, 2015b) and parts of Grabel (2003b, 2013b, 2013c) and Grabel and Gallagher (2015). See Grabel (2017, ch. 7) for further discussion of capital controls and the global financial crisis.

2. See Grabel (2013a, 2015a, 2017, ch. 6) for an examination of these and other initiatives.

3. Fritz and Prates (2014) see controls on derivatives as distinct from (though complementary to) capital controls and prudential financial regulations.

4. Temporary outflow controls turned out to be rather long-lived – indeed, the central bank and the finance ministry began phasing them out in 2016.

5. See Chwieroth (2015) on the process of destigmatizing capital controls.

6. The IEO (2015, p. 13) noted that staff did not approve of outflow and exchange controls in 2008 in Ukraine (see also Saborowski et al., 2014).

7. Thanks to Michael Akume for research on Nigeria.

8. A separate annex to the TPP allows Chile alone to maintain or enact capital controls that are consistent with its own domestic laws to ensure financial stability.

9. NAFTA includes a balance of payments exception that allows controls when the host states "experience serious balance of payments difficulties, or the threat thereof," but controls must be temporary and non-discriminatory (Gallagher, 2014, p. 181).

10. Korea's 2007 free trade agreement with the USA allows temporary controls under certain circumstances.

11. In some cases, this reframing may be less instrumental than I suggest. Chwieroth (2015) argues that Korean authorities see the measures they put in place during the global crisis as prudential and consistent with their acceptance of the norm of liberalization. I should add here that the renormalization of capital controls may involve rebranding, the focus of this chapter, and/or reframing of capital controls as something other than capital controls. The former represents a more direct assault on the preexisting neoliberal ideology, and is expected where states have achieved substantial policy autonomy. The latter amounts to "cheating" – attempting to use a strategy that is not permitted under the neoliberal rules of the game without admitting it. We should expect this strategy in cases where states have not achieved substantial policy autonomy.

12. Recall that (as earlier noted) Carstens (2015) spoke more catholically about controls in January 2016.

13. Adair Turner, former chair of the UK's Financial Services Authority, takes note of

the enduring resilience of the liberalization ideal despite empirical evidence (Turner, 2014). Ghosh and Qureshi (2016) root the demonization of inflow controls in a "guilt by association" with outflow controls. They endorse the former, whereas they distance themselves from the latter, which they see as broad based and difficult to reverse.

14. See Fritz and Prates (2014) for a critique of the institutional view on these and other grounds.
15. Chwieroth (2014) argues that the greater equivocation on controls in the institutional view reflects the fact that official documents require member state approval, whereas reports such as Staff Position Notes do not.
16. Another possibility is that conflict over controls has decisively shifted from the economic to the legal arena of investment and trade agreements as I suggested earlier.
17. Stiglitz and Rashid (2016) take what I see as a more modest view, such that current and coming turbulence in developing economies may necessitate quick action that includes targeted and time-bound capital controls, especially on outflows.
18. On these views, see Horsefield (1969, pp. 31, 65) and Steil (2013, pp. 134, 150).

REFERENCES

Abdelal, R. (2007), *Capital Rules: The Construction of Global Finance*, Cambridge, MA: Harvard University Press.

Agayev, Z. (2016), "Azeri leader rejects bill to tax outflows of foreign currency," *Bloomberg*, February 10, accessed March 22, 2016 at http://www.bloomberg. com/news/articles/2016-02-10/azeri-leader-rejects-bill-to-tax-outflows-of-foreign-currency.

Aizenman, J. (2009), "Hoarding international reserves versus a Pigovian tax-cum-subsidy scheme: Reflections on the deleveraging crisis of 2008–09, and a cost benefit analysis," *NBER Paper No. 15484*, accessed July 18, 2018 at http://www. nber.org/papers/w15484.

Anderlini, J. (2015), "Beijing clamps down on forex deals to stem capital flight," *Financial Times*, September 9, accessed March 22, 2016 at http://www.ft.com/ intl/cms/s/0/0f825e12-56cf-11e5-a28b-50226830d644.html.

Aquino, N. and C. Batino (2012), "Philippines joins Korea in restraining currency gains: Economy," *Bloomberg*, December 26, accessed March 22, 2016 at http:// www.bloomberg.com/news/articles/2012-12-26/philippines-imposes-currency-forward-caps-to-restrain-peso-surge.

Asian Development Bank (ADB) (2011), *Asian Capital Markets Monitor*, accessed December 6, 2015 at http://www.adb.org/publications/asia-capital-markets-monitor-august-2011.

Barboza, D. (2014), "China's central bank allows its currency more volatility," *New York Times*, March 15, accessed March 22, 2016 at http://www.nytimes. com/2014/03/16/business/international/chinas-central-bank-raises-the-volatility-of-its-currency.html.

Batunanggar, S. (2013), "Macroprudential framework and measures: The Indonesian experience," in R. Maino and S. Barnett (eds), *Macroprudential Frameworks in Asia*, Washington, DC: International Monetary Fund, pp. 121–9.

Benlialper, A. and H. Cömert (2016), "Central banking in developing countries after the crisis: What has changed?," *IDEAS Working Paper Series, No. 1*, accessed February 26, 2016 at http://www.networkideas.org/working/jan2016/01_2016.pdf.

Bernanke, B. (2015), "Federal reserve policy in an international context," Mundell-Fleming Lecture at the International Monetary Fund, Washington, DC, November 5, accessed March 22, 2016 at http://www.imf.org/external/np/res/seminars/2015/arc/pdf/Bernanke.pdf.

Bhagwati, J. (1998), "The difference between trade in widgets and dollars," *Foreign Affairs*, **77**(3), 7–12.

Biller, D. and M.L. Rabello (2013), "Brazil dismantles capital control as real drops to four year low," *Bloomberg*, June 12, accessed March 22, 2016 at http://www.bloomberg.com/news/articles/2013-06-13/brazil-dismantles-capital-control-as-real-drops-to-four-year-low.

Bloomberg (2014), "China outlines plan to ease capital curbs, push yuan," October 10, accessed March 22, 2016 at http://www.bloomberg.com/news/articles/2014-10-09/china-outlines-plans-to-ease-capital-controls-boost-use-of-yuan.

Carstens, A. (2015), "Speech at the session on capital inflows, exchange rate management and capital controls at the Conference on Rethinking Macro Policy III: Session 5. Capital inflows, exchange rate management and capital controls," April 15, 2015, accessed March 22, 2016 at http://www.imf.org/external/mmedia/view.aspx?vid=4176918093001.

Chwieroth, J. (2010), *Capital Ideas: The IMF and the Rise of Financial Liberalization*, Princeton, NJ: Princeton University Press.

Chwieroth, J. (2014), "Controlling capital: The International Monetary Fund and transformative incremental change from within international organizations," *New Political Economy*, **19**(3), 445–69.

Chwieroth, J. (2015), "Managing and transforming policy stigmas in international finance: Emerging markets and controlling capital inflows after the crisis," *Review of International Political Economy*, **22**(1), 44–76.

Cline, W. (2010), "The IMF staff's misleading new evidence on capital controls," *PIIE, Realtime Economic Issues Watch*, February 24, accessed March 22, 2016 at http://blogs.piie.com/realtime/?p=1351.

Crowe, D. (2010), "Colombia central bank rules out capital controls," *Colombia Reports*, October 19, accessed April 11, 2016 at http://colombiareports.com/colombia-central-bank-rules-out-capital-controls/.

Danielsson, J. and R. Arnason (2011), "Capital controls are exactly wrong for Iceland," *Voxeu.org*, November 14, accessed March 22, 2016 at http://www.voxeu.org/article/iceland-and-imf-why-capital-controls-are-entirely-wrong.

Dobbs, R. and M. Spence (2011), "The era of cheap capital draws to a close," *Financial Times*, accessed February 26, 2016 at http://www.ft.com/cms/s/0/1478bc50-2d70-11e0-8f53-00144feab49a.html-axzz41OPv4o3d.

Edwards, S. (1999), "How effective are capital controls?," *Journal of Economic Perspectives*, **13**(4), 65–84.

Eglitis, A. (2016), "Azerbaijan credit rating cut to junk by S&P after oil plunge," *Bloomberg*, January 29, accessed March 22, 2016 at http://www.bloomberg.com/news/articles/2016-01-29/azerbaijan-credit-rating-cut-to-junk-by-s-p-after-oil-s-collapse.

Epstein, G.A. (2012), "Capital outflow regulation: Economic management, development and transformation," in K.P. Gallagher, S. Griffith-Jones and J.A. Ocampo (eds), *Regulating Global Capital Flows for Long-Run Development*, Pardee Center Task Force Report, Boston, MA: Boston University, Pardee Center for the Study of the Longer-Range Future, pp. 47–58.

Epstein, G.A., I. Grabel and K.S. Jomo (2004), "Capital management techniques

in developing countries: An assessment of experiences from the 1990s and lessons for the future," *G24 Discussion Paper No. 27*, March 2004, New York and
Geneva: United Nations, accessed July 18, 2018 at http://policydialogue.org/files/
publications/Capital_Mgmt_Epstein.pdf.

Erten, B. and J.A. Ocampo (2013), "Capital account regulations, foreign exchange
pressures, and crisis resilience," *Initiative for Policy Dialogue Working Paper
Series*, October, accessed July 18, 2018 at http://policydialogue.org/files/publica
tions/CAR_Erten_Ocampo_withCS.pdf.

Farchy, J. (2016), "Tajikistan and IMF in talks over bailout," *Financial Times*,
February 23, accessed March 22, 2016 at http://www.ft.com/intl/cms/
s/0/3dd384b0-da48-11e5-98fd-06d75973fe09.html-axzz43lSYfpkX.

Feldstein, M. (1998), "Refocusing the IMF," *Foreign Affairs*, **77**(2), 20–33.

Ferro, S. (2014), "Nigeria brings on capital controls," *Business Insider*,
December 19, accessed March 22, 2016 at http://www.businessinsider.com/
nigeria-imposes-capital-controls-2014-12.

Financial Times (2013), "India's capital crisis," August 15, accessed March 22,
2016 at http://www.ft.com/intl/cms/s/0/d469362e-05af-11e3-8ed5-00144feab7de.
html-axzz40jfKd1Ev.

Financial Times (2016), "Fitch keeps wary eye on Azerbaijan after controls,"
January 22, accessed March 22, 2016 at http://www.ft.com/fastft/2016/01/22/
fitch-keeps-wary-eye-on-azerbaijan-after-capital-controls/.

Forbes, K. (2005), "Capital controls: Mud in the wheels of market efficiency," *Cato
Journal*, **25**(1), 153–66.

Forbes, K., M. Fratzscher, T. Kostka and R. Straub (2011), "Bubble thy neighbor:
Direct and spillover effects of capital controls," paper presented at the 12th
Jacques Polak Annual Research Conference, IMF, November 10–11, accessed
March 22, 2016 at https://www.imf.org/external/np/res/seminars/2011/arc/pdf/
forbes.pdf.

Forelle, C. (2012), "In European crisis Iceland emerges as an island of recovery,"
Wall Street Journal, May 21, accessed March 22, 2016 at http://www.wsj.com/
articles/SB10001424052702304203604577396171007652042.

Fritz, B. and D.M. Prates (2014), "The new IMF approach to capital account
management and its blind spots: Lessons from Brazil and South Korea,"
International Review of Applied Economics, **28**(2), 210–39.

Gallagher, K.P. (2011), "Regaining control? Capital controls and the global
financial crisis," *Political Economy Research Institute Working Paper No. 250*,
University of Massachusetts-Amherst, accessed March 26, 2016 at http://www.
ase.tufts.edu/gdae/policy_research/KGCapControlsPERIFeb11.html.

Gallagher, K.P. (2012), "The global governance of capital flows: New opportunities,
enduring challenges," *Political Economy Research Institute Working Paper, No.
283*, University of Massachusetts-Amherst, accessed July 18, 2018 at http://www.
peri.umass.edu/236/hash/5177c19e45bd73aaf9ae065db58a72cb/publication/512/.

Gallagher, K.P. (2014), *Ruling Capital: Emerging Markets and the Reregulation of
Cross-Border Finance*, Ithaca, NY: Cornell University Press.

Ghosh, A.R. and M.S. Qureshi (2016), "What's in a name? That which we call
capital controls," *IMF Working Paper No. 25*, accessed March 1, 2016 at https://
www.imf.org/external/pubs/ft/wp/2016/wp1625.pdf.

Ghosh, A.R., M.S. Qureshi and N. Sugawara (2014), "Regulating capital flows
at both ends: Does it work?," *IMF Working Paper No. 188*, October, accessed
March 1, 2016 at https://www.imf.org/external/pubs/ft/wp/2014/wp14188.pdf.

Giles, C. (2012), "Brics to create financial safety net," *Financial Times*, May 16, 2014, accessed March 1, 2016 at http://www.ft.com/intl/cms/s/0/bfd6adfe-b9bb-11e1-a470-00144feabdc0.html.

Grabel, I. (2003a), "Ideology, power and the rise of independent monetary institutions in emerging economies," in J. Kirshner (ed.), *Monetary Orders: Ambiguous Economics, Ubiquitous Politics*, Ithaca, NY: Cornell University Press, pp. 25–52.

Grabel, I. (2003b), "International private capital flows and developing countries," in H.-J. Chang (ed.), *Rethinking Development Economics*, London: Anthem, pp. 324–45.

Grabel, I. (2004), "Trip wires and speed bumps: Managing financial risks and reducing the potential for financial crises in developing economies," *G-24 Discussion Paper No. 33*, November 2004, Geneva: UNCTAD.

Grabel, I. (2011), "Not your grandfather's IMF: Global crisis, 'productive incoherence' and developmental policy space," *Cambridge Journal of Economics*, **35**(5), 805–30.

Grabel, I. (2013a), "Financial architectures and development: Resilience, policy space, and human development in the Global South," *Human Development Report Office, Occasional Paper No. 7*, accessed July 18, 2018 at http://hdr.undp.org/sites/default/files/hdro_1307_grabel.pdf.

Grabel, I. (2013b), "Global financial governance and development finance in the wake of the 2008 financial crisis," *Feminist Economics*, **19**(3), 32–54.

Grabel, I. (2013c), "Productive incoherence in a time of crisis: The IMF and the resurrection of capital controls," in M.H. Wolfson and G.A. Epstein (eds), *The Handbook of the Political Economy of Financial Crisis*, Oxford and New York: Oxford University Press, pp. 563–7.

Grabel, I. (2015a), "Post-crisis experiments in development finance architectures: A Hirschmanian perspective on 'productive incoherence'," *Review of Social Economy*, **73**(4), 388–414.

Grabel, I. (2015b), "The rebranding of capital controls in an era of productive incoherence," *Review of International Political Economy*, **22**(1), 7–43.

Grabel, I. (2017), *When Things Don't Fall Apart: Global Financial Governance and Developmental Finance in an Age of Productive Incoherence*, Cambridge, MA: MIT Press.

Grabel, I. and K.P. Gallagher (2015), "Capital controls and the global financial crisis: An introduction," *Review of International Political Economy*, **22**(1), 1–6.

Guha, K. (2009), "IMF refuses to rule out use of capital controls," *Financial Times*, November 2, accessed March 22, 2016 at http://www.ft.com/intl/cms/s/0/80201cce-c7ef-11de-8ba8-00144feab49a.html-axzz43lSYfpkX.

Helleiner, E. (1994), *States and the Reemergence of Global Finance*, Ithaca, NY: Cornell University Press.

Horsefield, J.K. (1969), *The International Monetary Fund, 1945–65, Vol. 3*, Washington, DC: International Monetary Fund.

Independent Evaluation Office of the IMF (IEO) (2015), *IMF's Approach to Capital Account Liberalization, Revisiting the 2005 IEO Evaluation*, accessed July 18, 2018 at http://www.ieo-imf.org/ieo/files/whatsnew/The IMFs Approach to Capital Account Liberalization Revisiting the 2005 IEO Evaluation3.pdf.

Institute for International Finance (IIF) (2016), "Capital flows to emerging markets," January 19, accessed March 1, 2016 at https://images.magnetmail.net/images/clients/IIF_2/attach/CF_0116_Press(3).pdf.

IntelliNews (2016), "Tajik central bank denies termination of ruble transfers,"

February 8, accessed March 22, 2016 at http://www.intellinews.com/tajik-central-bank-denies-termination-of-ruble-transfers-90219/.

International Monetary Fund (IMF) (2009a), *Annual Report on Exchange Rate Arrangements and Exchange Restrictions*, Washington, DC: IMF.

International Monetary Fund (IMF) (2009b), *Review of Recent Crisis Programs*, report prepared by the Strategy, Policy, and Review Department, International Monetary Fund, accessed July 18, 2018 at http://www.imf.org/external/np/pp/eng/2009/091409.pdf.

International Monetary Fund (IMF) (2011a), "How Iceland recovered from its near death experience," *IMF Blog*, accessed May 15, 2013 at http://blog-imfdirect.imf.org/2011/10/26/how-iceland-recovered-from-its-near-death-experience/.

International Monetary Fund (IMF) (2011b), *Recent Experiences in Managing Capital Inflows – Cross-cutting Themes and Possible Policy Framework*, February 14, report prepared by the Strategy, Policy, and Review Department, Washington, DC: IMF, accessed July 18, 2018 at http://www.imf.org/external/np/pp/eng/2011/021411a.pdf.

International Monetary Fund (IMF) (2012a), "Iceland: Ex post evaluation of exceptional access under the 2008 stand-by arrangement," *IMF Country Report No. 12/91*, Washington, DC: IMF, April, accessed July 18, 2018 at https://www.imf.org/external/pubs/ft/scr/2012/cr1291.pdf.

International Monetary Fund (IMF) (2012b), "IMF Executive Board discusses the liberalization and management of capital flows – an institutional view," *Public Information Notice, No. 12/137*, Washington, DC: IMF, December 3, accessed March 1, 2016 at https://www.imf.org/external/np/sec/pn/2012/pn12137.htm.

International Monetary Fund (IMF) (2012c), *The Liberalization and Management of Capital Flows: An Institutional View*, Washington, DC: IMF, November 14, accessed March 1, 2016 at http://www.imf.org/external/np/pp/eng/2012/111412.pdf.

International Monetary Fund (IMF) (2013), "Guidance note for the liberalization and management of capital flows," Washington, DC: IMF, April 25, accessed March 1, 2016 at https://www.imf.org/external/np/pp/eng/2013/042513.pdf.

International Monetary Fund (IMF) (2015), *Managing Capital Outflows – Further Operational Considerations*, staff report issued to the Executive Board, December, accessed March 1, 2016 at https://www.imf.org/external/np/pp/eng/2015/120315.pdf.

International Monetary Fund (IMF) COFER (various years), "Currency Composition of Official Foreign Exchange Reserves (COFER)," Washington, DC: International Monetary Fund.

Johnson, S. (2015), "Emerging market slump raises fears of capital controls," *Financial Times*, September 9, accessed March 22, 2016 at http://www.ft.com/intl/cms/s/3/72c18c2c-554a-11e5-b029-b9d50a74fd14.html#axzz43mCKnnUk.

Kaplan, E. and D. Rodrik (2001), "Did the Malaysian capital controls work?," *NBER Working Paper No. 8142*, Cambridge, MA: National Bureau of Economic Research, accessed March 22, 2016 at http://www.nber.org/papers/w8142.

Kelly, L., D. Korsunskaya and E. Fabrichnaya (2014), "Informal capital controls arrest Russian rouble's slide," *Reuters*, December 24, accessed March 22, 2016 at http://uk.reuters.com/article/uk-russia-crisis-rouble-idUKKBN0K10EE20141224.

Korinek, A. (2011), "The new economics of prudential capital controls: A research agenda," *IMF Economic Review*, **59**(3), 523–61.

Korinek, A. (2013), "Capital controls and currency wars," University of Maryland, unpublished paper, February, accessed March 26, 2016 at http://www.cepr.org/sites/default/files/Korinek_Capital Controls and Currency Wars.pdf.

Korinek, A. (2014), "International spillovers and guidelines for policy cooperation: A welfare theorem for national economic policymaking," paper presented at the 15th Jacques Polak Annual Research Conference, November 13–14, 2014, Washington, DC: IMF, accessed December 16, 2015 at https://www.imf.org/external/np/res/seminars/2014/arc/pdf/korinek.pdf.

Krishnan, U. (2016), "Rajan seeks global color-coded rules to rate monetary policy," *Bloomberg*, March 12, accessed March 20, 2016 at http://www.bloomberg.com/news/articles/2016-03-12/rajan-proposes-global-color-coded-system-to-rate-monetary-policy.

Krugman, P. (1998), "Saving Asia: It's time to get radical," *Fortune*, September 7, 35–6, accessed March, 2016 at http://archive.fortune.com/magazines/fortune/fortune_archive/1998/09/07/247884/index.htm.

Lagarde, C. (2015), "Spillovers from unconventional monetary policy – lessons for emerging markets," speech at the Reserve Bank of India, March 17, accessed March 15, 2016 at https://www.imf.org/external/np/speeches/2015/031715.htm.

LatinDADD-BWP (2011), *Breaking the Mould: How Latin America is Coping with Volatile Capital Flows*, December, LatinDADD-Bretton Woods Project (BWP), accessed March 22, 2016 at http://www.brettonwoodsproject.org/wp-content/uploads/2013/10/breakingthemould.pdf.

Leahy, J. and S. Pearson (2013), "Brazil slashes financial transactions tax," *Financial Times*, June 5, accessed March 22, 2016 at http://www.ft.com/intl/cms/s/0/6c113a7c-cd74-11e2-90e8-00144feab7de.html-axzz40jfKd1Ev.

Lee, C.-H. (2011), "S. Korea to undertake stress test on banks' FX funding-source," *Reuters*, July 25, accessed March 22, 2016 at http://www.reuters.com/article/korea-banks-idUSL3E7IP0KO20110725.

Lipsky, J. (2009), "Building a post-crisis global economy – an address to the Japan Society," New York, December 10, accessed May 14, 2013 at http://www.imf.org/external/np/speeches/2009/121009.htm.

Lütz, S. and M. Kranke (2014), "The European rescue of the Washington Consensus? EU and IMF lending to Central and Eastern European countries," *Review of International Political Economy*, **21**(2), 310–38.

Magtulis, P. (2013), "Moody's backs limited use of capital controls in SEA," *Philippine Star*, February 22, accessed March 22, 2016 at http://www.philstar.com/business/2013/02/22/911570/moodys-backs-limited-use-capital-controls-sea.

Magud, N. and C. Reinhart (2006), "Capital controls: An evaluation," *NBER Working Paper No. 11973*, accessed July 18, 2018 at http://www.nber.org/papers/w11973.

Magud, N., C. Reinhart and K. Rogoff (2011), "Capital controls: Myth and reality – a portfolio balance approach," *NBER Working Paper No. 16805*, accessed July 18, 2018 at http://www.nber.org/papers/w16805.

Monan, Z. (2013), "China's cold eye on hot money," *Project Syndicate*, June 10, accessed March 22, 2016 at http://www.project-syndicate.org/commentary/china-s-new-rules-for-managing-cross-border-capital-flows-by-zhang-monan?barrier=true.

Moschella, M. (2009), "When ideas fail to influence policy outcomes: Orderly liberalization and the International Monetary Fund," *Review of International Political Economy*, **16**(5), 854–82.

Moschella, M. (2014), "Institutional roots of incremental ideational change: The

IMF and capital controls after the global financial crisis," *British Journal of Politics and International Relations*, **17**(3), 442–60.

National Bank of Tajikistan (2015), "The activities of currency exchange offices of physical entities are suspended," accessed July 18, 2018 at http://nbt.tj/en/news/399843/?view_result=Y.

Obstfeld, M. (1998), "Global capital markets: Benefactor or menace?," *Journal of Economic Perspectives*, **12**(4), 9–30.

Ocampo, J.A. (2003), "Capital account and countercyclical prudential regulation in developing countries," in R. Ffrench-Davis and S. Griffith-Jones (eds), *From Capital Surges to Drought: Seeking Stability for Emerging Markets*, Basingstoke: Palgrave Macmillan, pp. 217–44.

Ocampo, J.A. (2010), "Time for global capital account regulations," *Economic and Political Weekly*, **XLV**(46), 32–3.

Ocampo, J.A., S. Griffith-Jones and A. Noman et al. (2012), "The Great Recession and the developing world," in J.A. Alonso and J.A. Ocampo (eds), *Development Cooperation in Times of Crisis*, New York: Columbia University Press, pp. 17–81.

Oliver, C. (2010), "IMF warns on emerging market currency controls," *Financial Times*, July 11, accessed January 12, 2011 at http://www.ft.com/intl/cms/s/0/5ba241aa-8ce9-11df-bad7-00144feab49a.html.

Olson, R. and A.B. Kim (2013), "Congress should query IMF support for capital controls," *Heritage Foundation Issue Brief No. 3949*, accessed March 22, 2016 at http://www.heritage.org/research/reports/2013/05/congress-should-query-imf-support-for-capital-controls.

Ostry, J.D., R.A.R. Ghosh and K. Habermeier et al. (2010), "Capital inflows: The role of controls," *IMF Staff Position Note No. 4*, February 19, accessed July 18, 2018 at https://www.imf.org/external/pubs/ft/spn/2010/spn1004.pdf.

Ostry, J.D., A.R. Ghosh and A. Korinek (2012), "Multilateral aspects of managing the capital account," *IMF Staff Discussion Note No. 10*, September 7, accessed July 18. 2018 at https://www.imf.org/external/pubs/ft/sdn/2012/sdn1210.pdf.

Prasad, E. (2014a), "The dollar reigns supreme, by default," *Finance and Development*, **51**(1), accessed July 18, 2018 at http://www.imf.org/external/pubs/ft/fandd/2014/03/prasad.htm.

Prasad, E. (2014b), *The Dollar Trap: How the US Dollar Tightened Its Grip on Global Finance*, Princeton, NJ: Princeton University Press.

Prasad, E., K. Rogoff, S.-J. Wei and M.A. Kose (2003), "Effects of financial globalization on developing countries: Some empirical evidence," *IMF Occasional Paper No. 220*, September 9, accessed July 18, 2018 at https://www.imf.org/external/pubs/nft/op/220/.

Quigley, J. (2013), "Velarde says he doesn't see need for Peru capital controls," *Bloomberg*, January 25, accessed March 22, 2016 at http://www.bloomberg.com/news/articles/2013-01-25/velarde-says-he-doesn-t-see-need-for-peru-capital-controls-1-.

Ragir, A. (2011), "Brazil's capital controls are 'appropriate' tool, IMF says," *Bloomberg*, August 3, accessed March 22, 2016 at http://www.bloomberg.com/news/articles/2011-08-03/brazilian-capital-controls-are-appropriate-tool-imf-says.

Rajan, R. (2016), "The global monetary non-system," *Project Syndicate*, January 6, accessed March 1, 2016 at https://www.project-syndicate.org/onpoint/unconventional-monetary-policy-weak-growth-by-raghuram-rajan-2016-01?barrier=accesspaylog.

Rappeport, A. (2010), "IMF reconsiders capital controls opposition," *Financial*

Times, February 22, accessed July 18, 2018 at http://www.ft.com/intl/cms/s/0/ ec484786-1fcf-11df-8deb-00144feab49a.html.

Ray, A. (2013), "Capital controls needed to insulate economies from US," *Economic Times*, September 18, accessed March 20, 2016 at https://economictimes.india times.com/news/economy/finance/capital-controls-needed-to-insulate-economies-from-us/articleshow/22679115.cm.

Reuters (2012), "Uruguay cenbank moves to stem peso's appreciation," August 16, accessed March 22, 2016 at http://in.reuters.com/article/uruguay-peso-idINL2E 8JFA4720120815.

Reuters (2013a), "Bundesbank warms to capital controls in currency war debate," January 24, accessed March 22, 2016 at http://in.reuters.com/article/ emerging-currencies-germany-idINL6N0AT3XC20130124.

Reuters (2013b), "India cbank chief says policy not to resort to capital controls," August 29, accessed March 22, 2016 at http://in.reuters.com/article/ india-cbank-governor-idINI8N0EW02N20130829.

Reuters (2014), "Costa Rica president says to use capital controls very selectively," April 2, accessed March 22, 2016 at http://www.reuters.com/article/ costarica-capitalcontrols-idUSL1N0MU20U20140402.

Reuters (2015), "Nigeria's central bank curbs access to foreign currency," June 24, accessed March 22, 2016 at http://www.reuters.com/article/nigeria-currency-idUSL8N0ZA21C20150624.

Reuters (2016), "IMF calls on Nigeria to lift foreign exchange curbs," February 24, accessed March 22, 2016 at http://www.reuters.com/article/nigeria-economy-idUSL8N1631D5.

Rey, H. (2014), "The international credit channel and monetary autonomy," Mundell-Fleming Lecture at the International Monetary Fund, Washington, DC, November 13, accessed December 16, 2015 at https://www.imf.org/external/ np/res/seminars/2014/arc/pdf/Mundell.pdf.

Rey, H. (2015), "Dilemma, not trilemma: The global financial cycle and monetary policy independence," *NBER Working Paper No. 21162*, May, accessed July 18, 2018 at http://www.nber.org/papers/w21162.

Rodrik, D. (2010), "The end of an era in finance," *Project Syndicate*, March 11, accessed August 16, 2015 at http://www.project-syndicate.org/commentary/ the-end-of-an-era-in-finance.

Rodrik, D. (2015), "Global capital heads for the frontier," *Project Syndicate*, March 10, accessed March 22, 2016 at https://www.project-syndicate.org/commentary/ frontier-market-economy-fad-by-dani-rodrik-2015-03?barrier=true.

Ross, A. and H. Simonian (2012), "Swiss eye capital controls if Greece goes," *Financial Times*, May 27, accessed March 22, 2016 at http://www.ft.com/cms/s/0/ d7678676-a810-11e1-8fbb-00144feabdc0.html-axzz43pjftUkY.

Saborowski, C., S. Sanya, H. Weisfeld and J. Yepez (2014), "Effectiveness of capital outflow restrictions," *IMF Working Paper No. 8*, January, accessed March 1, 2016 at https://www.imf.org/external/pubs/ft/wp/2014/wp1408.pdf.

Shadlen, K. (2005), "Exchanging development for market access? Deep integration and industrial policy under multilateral and regional-bilateral trade agreements," *Review of International Political Economy*, **12**(5), 750–75.

Sigurgeirsdóttir, S. and R.H. Wade (2015), "From control by capital to control of capital: Iceland's boom and bust, and the IMF's unorthodox rescue package," *Review of International Political Economy*, **22**(1), 103–33.

Spence, M. (2010), "Keynote address by Professor Andrew Michael Spence," First

International Research Conference of the Reserve Bank of India, Mumbai, February 12, 2010, accessed March 21, 2016 at https://rbidocs.rbi.org.in/rdocs/Content/PDFs/FST130210.pdf.

Steil, B. (2013), *The Battle of Bretton Woods: John Maynard Keynes, Harry Dexter White, and the Making of a New World Order*, Princeton, NJ: Princeton University Press.

Stiglitz, J. and H. Rashid (2016), "Closing developing countries' capital drain," *Project Syndicate*, February 18, accessed March 1, 2016 at https://www.project-syndicate.org/commentary/developing-countries-capital-outflows-by-joseph-e-stiglitz-and-hamid-rashid-2016-02?barrier=true.

Strauss, D. (2014), "Ukraine capital controls stem fall in its currency," *Financial Times*, February 10, accessed March 22, 2016 at http://www.ft.com/intl/cms/s/0/fc4e3cf2-926d-11e3-9e43-00144feab7de.html-axzz41PqgwvuE.

Strauss-Kahn, D. (2010), "Macro-prudential policies – an Asian perspective," speech, Shanghai, China, October 18, accessed July 4, 2011 at http://www.imf.org/external/np/speeches/2010/101810.htm.

Subacchi, P. (2015), "The renminbi goes forth," *Project Syndicate*, December 11, accessed March 10, 2016 at https://www.project-syndicate.org/commentary/renminbi-international-currency-in-the-making-by-paola-subacchi-2015-12.

Subramanian, A. and J. Williamson (2009), "The fund should help Brazil to tackle inflows," *Financial Times*, October 25, accessed March 1, 2016 at http://www.ft.com/cms/s/0/a0c04b34-c196-11de-b86b-00144feab49a.html-axzz43lSYfpkX.

Taleb, N. (2012), *Antifragile: Things That Gain From Disorder*, New York: Random House.

The Economist (2013), "Just in case," October 12, 10–12, accessed March 20, 2016 at http://www.economist.com/news/special-report/21587383-capital-controls-are-back-part-many-countries-financial-armoury-just-case.

Thomas, L., Jr. (2010), "Countries see hazards in free flow of capital," *New York Times*, November 10, B1, accessed March 16, 2016 at http://www.nytimes.com/2010/11/11/business/global/11capital.html?_r=0.

Times of India (2015), "RBI chief Rajan blasts IMF for being soft on easy money policies of west," *Times of India*, October 1, accessed March 1, 2016 at http://timesofindia.indiatimes.com/business/india-business/RBI-chief-Rajan-blasts-IMF-for-being-soft-on-easy-money-policies-of-west/articleshow/49456531.cms.

Turner, A. (2014), "In praise of fragmentation," *Project Syndicate*, February 18, accessed March 22, 2016 at https://www.project-syndicate.org/commentary/adair-turner-criticizes-economists--adherence-to-the-belief-that-the-benefits-of-capital-account-liberalization-outweigh-the-costs?barrier=true.

Tussie, D. (2010), "Decentralizing global finance," *TripleCrisis.com*, April 9, accessed March 10, 2015 at http://triplecrisis.com/decentralizing-global-finance/.

UNCTAD (2015), "Introduction of foreign-exchange controls," *Investment Policy Hub*, March 13, accessed March 22, 2016 at http://investmentpolicyhub.unctad.org/IPM/MeasureDetails?id=2673&rgn=.

Valdimarsson, O. (2012), "Iceland to apply new rules before capital controls are removed," *Bloomberg*, August 27, accessed March 22, 2016 at http://www.bloomberg.com/news/articles/2012-08-27/iceland-to-apply-new-rules-before-capital-controls-are-removed.

Wade, R.H. (2003), "What strategies are viable for developing countries today? The World Trade Organization and the shrinking of 'development space'," *Review of International Political Economy*, **10**(4), 621–44.

Wheatley, J. and S. Donnan (2016), "Capital controls no longer taboo as emerging markets battle flight," *Financial Times*, January 27, accessed March 22, 2016 at http://www.ft.com/intl/cms/s/0/36cfcc66-c41b-11e5-808f-8231cd71622e. html-axzz41OPv4o3d.

Wroughton, L. (2010), "IMF endorses capital controls as temporary measure," *Reuters*, February 19, accessed March 1, 2014 at http://prasad.dyson.cornell. edu/doc/media/Reuters_19Feb2010.pdf.

Yuk, K.P. (2012), "Peru: LatAm's latest currency warrior," *Financial Times*, May 1, accessed March 22, 2016 at http://blogs.ft.com/beyond-brics/2012/05/01/ peru-latams-latest-currency-warrior/.

Zikakou, I. (2015), "S&P upgrades Cyprus after capital control removal," *Greek Reporter*, September 26, accessed March 22, 2016 at http://greece.greekreporter. com/2015/09/26/sp-upgrades-cyprus-after-capital-control-removal/.

6. Easing the trilemma through reserve accumulation? The Latin American case

Luis D. Rosero

INTRODUCTION

The repercussions of the Global Financial Crisis were felt throughout the world, including in Latin America. However, this last set of countries, along with other emerging economies, appears to have been uniquely positioned to weather the recession more effectively and experienced a milder and shortened version of it. After experiencing a short-lived real gross domestic product (GDP) contraction of -1.5 percent (-0.1 percent if we consider only South America) in 2009, the region's GDP swiftly recovered to pre-crisis growth rates in 2010. This impressive performance from one of the traditionally most unstable regions in the world stands in sharp contrast to the much direr experiences of developed economies, particularly the United States and those of Europe, which experienced average GDP contractions of -2.4 percent and -4.1 percent, respectively, during this same year.[1]

One prevailing explanation for this reversal of fortunes is the unprecedented accumulation of international reserves by most emerging market economies, including those in Latin America. This stands in direct contrast to the modest stocks of reserves held by developed nations. By 2009, Latin American countries held foreign reserves of nearly US$594 billion, or 256 percent higher than those held a decade earlier. Arguments in favor of precautionary accumulation of reserves hold that access to liquid reserves allows countries to deter and deal with shocks to their currencies, thus avoiding the painful readjustment processes associated with currency and banking crises. Based on this observation, some in the literature (e.g., Aizenman, 2009) have concluded that enhanced reserve stocks have in fact fulfilled their mission, and more importantly that fears of excessive accumulations proved to be overblown. More recently, Alberola, Erce and Serena (2016) find that, in the context of global financial instability, higher levels of reserves are associated with higher gross inflows and lower gross outflows of capital.

While foreign reserves can serve an important role as buffers in the event of a shock, and perhaps more importantly as deterring signals to potential speculators, they carry a significant opportunity cost (see Rodrik, 2006, among others). Therefore, policy aimed at shielding the domestic economy should not simply follow Mrs. Machlup's hoarding approach to her wardrobe (Machlup, 1966). Reserve accumulation should instead be informed by evidence of its effectiveness at improving the expected outcomes. Given the unprecedented accumulation of costly reserves by developing countries and the ambiguous evidence for their effectiveness, it is critical to evaluate whether reserve accumulation as a strategy does in fact "work."

In this context, and within an empirical framework, this chapter directly tests the effectiveness of foreign reserves in enhancing the policy options at the disposal of policymakers. More specifically, this chapter uses yearly data for the seven largest Latin American countries in the last four decades to directly assess the degree to which reserves contribute to any of the three traditional goals associated with the impossible trilemma of international finance: exchange rate stability, free flows of capital, and effective control over monetary policy. Using vector autoregression analysis (VAR), this chapter finds limited evidence for the presumed benefits of reserve accumulation in advancing the trilemma goals. This analysis shows that, with one key exception, the effect of changes in the relative levels of reserves on any of the three trilemma goals is by and large not statistically different from zero, undermining some of the traditional expectations. However, the few exceptions identified here hint at two key conclusions. First, in line with the traditional optimal reserve demand literature, we find that increases in relative reserves are associated with higher levels of exchange rate stability in instances of hard pegs. Second, our findings suggest that only countries with high levels of reserves obtain benefits in terms of their exchange rate stability and monetary policy independence as a result of increases in holdings of foreign reserves.

LITERATURE REVIEW

Reserves Accumulation Motives

In line with the majority of emerging market countries around the world, Latin American countries have accumulated unprecedented levels of international reserves. This growth in reserves was most pronounced in the period following the turmoil associated with the East Asian financial crisis, and has turned negative only once during a brief reprieve associated with the latest Global Financial Crisis. Research into the motivations for this impressive accumulation of reserves is vast, and can be subdivided into two main views. First, the precautionary approach is based on a perceived necessity to self-insure against external shocks associated with greater exposure to international financial and trade markets (e.g., Heller, 1966; Feldstein, 1999; Aizenman and Lee, 2007). The second approach, known as the mercantilist approach, views reserve accumulation as a by-product of the activities of monetary authorities engaged in currency manipulation to boost the comparative advantage of their countries' exports (Dooley, Folkerts-Landau and Garber, 2005). Despite the differences in motivations, both the precautionary and mercantilist roles of reserves presuppose high liquidity for the assets held, and an implicit intertemporal investment trade-off. Therefore, this extensive accumulation of international reserves comes at a hefty social opportunity cost (Rodrik, 2006).

Views on the Precautionary Efficacy of Reserves

Given the context of high, growing, and costly international reserves, it is sensible to assess the degree to which reserves are actually serving their intended precautionary purpose. Evidence from previous studies suggests a mixed conclusion. Among the works that are in line with the precautionary expectations of reserves, Obstfeld, Shambaugh and Taylor (2009) find that while the level of reserves relative to GDP is not significantly associated (in statistical terms) with depreciations of the exchange rate, the level of "underinsurance" – defined as the ratio of actual reserves to those predicted by their model[2] – is significantly and negatively associated with such depreciations. This suggests that countries that accumulated sufficient reserves were more likely to have better weathered the recent crisis, while those that did not accumulate enough paid the consequences in the form of large currency depreciations. Similarly, in a review of the applicability of traditional leading (i.e., warning) indicators in explaining the latest Global Financial Crisis, Frankel and Saravelos (2012) conclude that international reserves (through different specifications) is one of two consistently significant indicators of crisis vulnerability.[3] Moreover, their findings can be interpreted as suggestive of reserves serving a stabilizing role. For instance, they find that the level of reserves relative to GDP is positively and significantly associated with exchange rate appreciation and changes in industrial production, and negatively and significantly associated with the likelihood of a country resorting to the International Monetary Fund (IMF) for help. Baqir et al. (2010), using cross-sectional data for 57 emerging market countries for the 2008–09 crisis, finds that higher pre-crisis levels of reserves (relative to external financing requirements) were positively and significantly associated with higher percentage changes in real output. Moreover, they conclude that while there are gains to reserve accumulation in terms of output growth, countries face diminishing returns to scale in accruing these gains. That is, countries with little relative reserves benefit more from the protection of reserves than do countries with reserve stocks exceeding 100 percent of short-term debt.[4] Dominguez, Hashimoto and Takatoshi (2012) also find evidence that suggests that countries with higher reserve levels before the Global Financial Crisis benefited from higher post-crisis GDP growth rates.

In contrast, other studies point to less encouraging results with regard to the effectiveness of international reserve holdings in fulfilling their presumed precautionary role. Chief among this part of the literature is a strand that emphasizes the apparent shift by emerging market economies from the "fear of floating"[5] to the "fear of reserve loss" during Global Financial Crisis years. Aizenman and Hutchison (2012) note that despite their unprecedented accumulation of foreign reserves, emerging market countries (including those in Latin America, with the exception of Venezuela) relied more heavily on exchange rate depreciation, rather than reserve drawdowns to counter pressures associated with the latest Global Financial Crisis. Table 6.1 reproduces this evidence for the seven emerging economies in Latin America for the 2008–09 period. Aizenman (2009) suggests that Latin American countries might have been particularly prone to suffering from the "fear of reserve loss" due to their relatively higher exposure to changes in the commodity markets and their lower levels of public and private savings.

Similarly, Artus (2009) finds that emerging market economies opted for conserving their accumulated reserves at the expense of high depreciation

Table 6.1   Exchange market pressure absorption (2008–09)

Country	Exchange Rate Depreciation (%)	Reserve Loss (%)	Exchange Market Pressure (%)
Argentina	17.5	0.86	18.41
Brazil	51.59	8.25	59.84
Chile	18.49	–4.80	13.69
Colombia	42.56	1.55	44.11
Mexico	48.41	5.93	54.34%
Peru	15.66	16.29	31.95
Venezuela	0.00	22.89	22.89

Source: Adapted from Aizenman and Hutchison (2012).

of their currency. Moreover, since in some of these countries reserves stocks were built up as a result of speculative capital inflows, these accumulated reserves are not seen as effective safeguards against capital flight during a reversal of fortunes. Blanchard, Faruqee and Klyuev (2009) reach a similar conclusion, and suggest that the automatic response by emerging markets to further accumulate reserves might harm the prospects for economic recovery, and are likely to accentuate the problems associated with global imbalances.

Other arguments in the literature that question the precautionary benefits of reserve accumulation are based on the distortions caused by these stocks on the monetary base on the holding countries, as well as the implications for the rest of the world in the form of global imbalances. Kletzer (2000) concludes that the accumulation of international reserves may prove counterproductive. The expansion of the monetary base that is usually associated with rising reserves can lead to a change in the fundamentals and consequently lead to the currency depreciations that they are supposed to protect against in the first place. Glick and Hutchison (2009) find that countries with high levels of reserves (e.g., China) face growing challenges in reining in inflationary pressures resulting from monetary base expansions associated with rising international reserve holdings. Attempts to sterilize these expansions in the monetary base not only grow costlier, but also more futile as reserve accumulation grows to some of the unprecedented levels seen in some emerging countries in recent years.[6] In this sense, the accumulation of reserves, rather than providing the expected countercyclical protection may actually lead to distortions in the exchange rate, and more importantly can undermine the country's monetary policy independence.

Reassessing the Benefits of Reserve Accumulation

The unprecedented accumulation of costly international reserves by emerging market countries, along with the apparent ambiguity in terms of the ability of these reserves to serve their intended purposes makes it critical to reassess the extent that reserve accumulation has actually "worked." The remainder of this chapter will consider this question in the context of the past four decades in the seven largest economies in Latin America: Argentina, Brazil, Chile, Colombia, Mexico, Peru, and Venezuela. Most of these countries have experienced directly the havoc associated with global financial instability and have in recent years (except for Venezuela) embraced a strategy of managed flexible exchange rates supported by large stocks of reserves. Moreover, the period considered captures the major periods of instability in the region (e.g., the Lost Decade, contagion effects from the East Asian financial crisis, the Argentinean crisis, as well as the effects of the most recent Global Financial Crisis), and consequently provides a comprehensive view into the effects of varying levels of reserves on these countries' policy instruments and economic outcomes.

To assess the benefits that reserve stocks provide in terms of expanding policy options, this chapter relies on the traditional trilemma framework derived from the Mundell–Fleming model (Fleming, 1962; Mundell, 1963) as a baseline approach. Under the trilemma framework, countries in an open economy are constrained in their ability to simultaneously accomplish the three traditional goals of macroeconomic policymakers: exchange rate stability, monetary policy autonomy, and the free movement of capital flows. Open economies are faced with a choice of two of these goals, at the expense of the third. During the classical Gold Standard era, countries opted for exchange rate stability – in the form of fixed exchange rates – and free movements of capital, while sacrificing monetary autonomy, and thus their ability to implement countercyclical monetary policy (Triffin, 1963). As argued in Obstfeld, Shambaugh and Taylor (2005), that strategy stands in contrast with the international infrastructure that prevailed during the Bretton Woods era when the choice of policy mix was characterized by a return of monetary policy autonomy and stable exchange rates – albeit at the expense of capital account liberalization.

Latin America's recent history in negotiating the policy mix shows that in the 1980s most of the region opted for overvalued exchange rates (mostly in the form of unofficial pegs) and control over its monetary policy. Capital controls – not always binding – were put in place to rein in some of the rising pressures of capital flight. However, adverse conditions in the international financial markets, along with excessively expansionary monetary policy made capital flight and the eventual devaluation of the currency unavoidable. The liberalization process of the 1990s in the region brought with it a re-evaluation of the trilemma policy mix, leading to a new era of capital account liberalization, (mostly) flexible exchange rates, and consequently the rendering of countercyclical monetary policy ineffective. This choice proved particularly costly as integration into the international financial structure entailed further risk exposure to the vagaries of international markets.

In this context, this chapter considers whether international reserves allow countries to "ease the trilemma" by fostering any of its three policy goals. Literature dealing with the direct effects of international reserves accumulation on the three components of the trilemma is limited. Aizenman (2009) claims that the large accumulation of international reserves by emerging market countries has made it possible for them to adopt a "middle-ground" configuration of the trilemma, under which they can afford to have managed exchange rate flexibility, and increasing integration into the world financial markets, while retaining a degree of monetary policy independence. This new prevalent arrangement is argued to have resulted in better outcomes in terms of adjusting to the shocks associated with the last Global Financial Crisis. Similarly, Aizenman, Chinn and Ito (2010) conclude that only in countries with reserves that exceed 21 percent of their GDP, do these reserves allow them to escape the trilemma. On the other hand, Glick and Hutchison (2009), through an analysis of the Chinese case, argue that reserve accumulation can compromise monetary control. This is of particular concern for instances in which sterilization becomes less feasible. Given some of the existing voids and contradicting evidence, this chapter contributes to the literature by explicitly looking at the relationship of reserve accumulation and the policy goals under the trilemma.

METHODOLOGY

Measuring the Trilemma

This analysis makes use of the indices developed in Aizenman, Chinn and Ito (2013) for the three policy choices that countries face under the traditional trilemma approach.[7] Whether in the form of an explicit fixed exchange rate regime (e.g., Argentina's currency board period), or through a managed float, stability of the exchange rate is highly valued by open economies.[8] The index used to capture a country's exchange rate stability (ERS) is calculated for each year as follows:

$$ERS = \frac{0.01}{0.01 + stdev(\Delta log(exchrate))},$$

where the exchange rate is expressed as the price of a unit of US currency in terms of the domestic currency, and the standard deviation measure is based on a yearly calculation of monthly data.[9] An ERS index of one is characteristic of a country with a perfectly fixed exchange rate, while a value of zero corresponds to a country with a pure float of its currency.

While more nuanced, the argument in favor of capital account openness as a policy goal derives from the assumption that free flow of capital allows for interest rate parity, and thus access to more and cheaper financial capital to fund domestic projects in capital-deprived regions.[10] To capture the second policy goal of the trilemma – capital account openness – this chapter relies on the Chinn-Ito index (KAO). This index accounts for *de jure* capital account liberalization, based on reported restrictions on current and capital account transactions, the presence of multiple exchange rates, and the requirement of the surrender of export proceeds. Possible values of this index range from zero to one, with higher values representing instances of countries with a more open capital account.

The third policy goal under the trilemma is that of monetary policy independence. The monetary policy independence index (MPI) is captured by comparing the behavior of domestic short-term interest rates to those of a base country, such that:

$$MPI = \frac{1 - corr(i_i, i_j)}{2},$$

where i_i accounts for the monthly money market interest rate in the Latin American country under consideration, and i_j corresponds to the US monthly money market rate. As with the previous two indices, the MPI index ranges from zero to one, with higher values associated with countries with more control over their monetary policy – as expressed by the divergence of and variation of their interest rate relative to that of the base country.

Historical representations of the three indices under consideration mostly confirm the suspected trade-offs faced under the trilemma approach. Moreover, Figure 6.1 shows the changes in the policy choices adopted in the region. In recent years, most of the largest Latin American countries appear poised to favor monetary policy autonomy and capital account liberalization, at the expense of exchange rate stability. Argentina and Venezuela, by contrast, have opted for maintaining relatively more control over their currency by restraining capital flows into their economies. Starting in 2002 and following the dismantling of its currency board, Argentina's ERS index values increased significantly until 2010. Similarly, Venezuela's ERS index jumped to 1 in 2013 as the country instituted a hard peg to the US dollar. Concurrently, the MPI index values for both countries were decreasing. For other Latin American countries like Brazil, Chile, Colombia, and Peru, the KAO index increased significantly in the early 2000s as they disbanded some of their capital controls, or embraced full capital account liberalization in the case of Peru since 1997. Exchange rate stability, however, was sacrificed during this time in most of these countries with the exception of Peru.

As will be discussed later, these differences in the trilemma mix selection provide an insight into the differing effectiveness of reserve accumulation in easing a country's trilemma constraints. On the whole, there appears to be preliminary evidence for an attempt in the region to adopt moderated

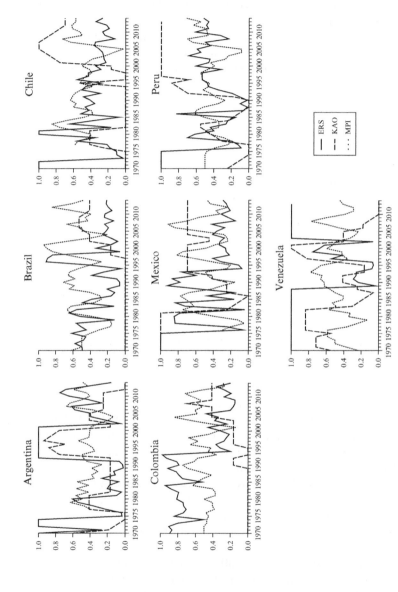

Figure 6.1 Developments in the policy trilemma

114

policy choices, while shying away from policy extremes in either direction. For instance, most countries in the region rely on managed flexible exchange rates, some – albeit more lenient – capital controls, and monetary independence within a context of inflation targeting.

The Role of Reserve Accumulation: Easing the Trilemma?

To assess the effectiveness of international reserve accumulation, this chapter seeks to explore the relationship between each of the indices described above and the relative (to GDP) level of reserves. Before delving into a more formal analysis, this section formalizes the hypothetical expectations and explores underlying trends in the overall data.

In theory, high levels of international reserves allow countries facing devaluation pressures to sustain a given target exchange rate by drawing down these reserves, or more importantly by signaling the ability of the central monetary authority to respond to these pressures. For instance, Obstfeld et al. (2009) find that in the context of the 2008 financial crisis, a country's relative level of international reserves was a good predictor of exchange rate movements. Countries with insufficient levels of reserves were more likely to experience currency depreciation following the crisis. An alternative view of international reserves accumulation suggests that high levels of reserves are a by-product of stable – purposely undervalued – exchange rates. Countries are seen to rely on these undervalued exchange rates aimed at gaining mercantilist advantage for their exports (Dooley et al., 2005). A preliminary look at the relationship between international reserves and the ERS index during the period considered in this chapter suggests that, contrary to our expectations, non-gold international reserves as a share of GDP (RESGDP) have been associated with slightly lower levels of this index (Figure 6.2) in Latin America.

Traditional arguments in favor of capital account openness suggest that in the context of emerging nations like those of Latin America, the elimination of barriers to capital should *ceteris paribus* lead to capital flowing into these countries in search of better returns. Positive net inflows of capital would thus be associated with capital account surpluses, which could finance deficits in the current account or add to existing surpluses in the latter. Consequently, based on the simple accounting of the balance of payments accounts, capital account liberalization should result in additions to a country's stock of international reserves, with other things being held constant. Capital account surpluses are assumed to arise primarily from a combination of pull factors (e.g., inherently higher rates of return on capital) and structural conditions (e.g., lack of capital controls and

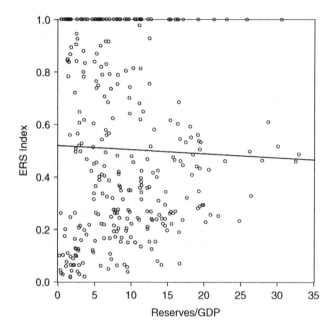

Figure 6.2   Exchange rate stability and reserves (1972–2014)

predictable monetary policy). Conversely, higher levels of international reserves can arguably foster capital account openness by providing a buffer against adverse shocks related to the exposure of more mobile capital flows. In either case, the relationship between reserves and the extent of capital account liberalization would be expected to be positive. A scatter plot of the KAO index and the level of reserves adjusted by the level of GDP (Figure 6.3) provides *prima facie* evidence in support of this positive relationship. Thus, higher relative levels of reserves seem to be associated with instances of more liberalized capital accounts in the countries and period under study.

Higher liquidity in the form of international reserves also provides flexibility in adjusting to shocks, and thus reduces the need to modify monetary policy outcomes. International reserves, when sufficiently available, make the sterilization process associated with defending against exchange rate depreciation credible. In an open economy, a balance of payments deficit introduces depreciation tendencies to the domestic currency, which can be offset by the monetary authority through the sale of foreign assets in exchange for domestic currency. Given the procyclical nature of international capital flows, the resulting decrease in the domestic money supply can be devastating to an already ailing economy. A process

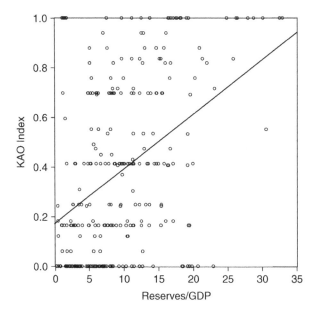

Figure 6.3   Capital account openness and reserves (1972–2014)

of sterilization (through the purchase of domestic financial assets by the central bank), along with the original intervention using foreign reserves, makes it possible to respond to deflationary pressures on the exchange rate, while retaining monetary autonomy by leaving the interest rate target unaffected.

Conversely, when faced with an undesirably appreciated domestic currency, an active central bank has the option of counteracting the resulting upward pressure on the money supply through the sale of domestic financial assets to match increasing foreign reserves acquired in the currency stabilization process. An alternative view of the relationship between international reserves and monetary policy independence emphasizes causality running from the latter to the former. That is, countries that enjoy monetary policy independence can engage in countercyclical monetary policy to address shocks to the internal economy, and thus ensure more stability in the current and financial accounts. Figure 6.4 below shows a preliminary view of the relationship between the relative level of reserves and the MPI. This plot suggests that a slightly positive relationship between these two variables may prevail.

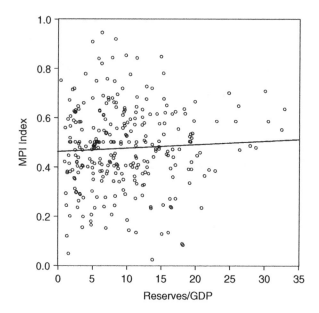

Figure 6.4   Monetary policy independence and reserves (1972–2014)

Modeling the Relationship

In sum, higher levels of reserves, through the channels outlined above, are assumed to contribute to the easing of the trilemma by promoting higher levels of each of its components. Using yearly data for the seven largest countries in the region for the 1972–2014 period,[11] this chapter empirically analyzes these potential relationships. Descriptive statistics of the variables employed in the analysis are presented in Appendix A. Augmented Dickey Fuller (ADF) tests were conducted to assess the stationarity properties of each individual variable, while lags for these tests were selected using the Schwarz information criterion (SIC). Stationarity results are presented in Appendix B.

As presented in the literature review section of this chapter, previous studies have only addressed the relationship between international reserves and the components of the trilemma indirectly. Moreover, most of these studies have relied on pooled panel data least squares regressions for their analysis. While useful in providing some insights, the underlying trade-off implied by the trilemma as well as the possibility for contemporaneous determination suggested by the hypothesized relationship among the variables present us with a clear potential for simultaneity, and consequently biased estimators. To avoid this issue, and to benefit from the richness in the analysis from recursive effects, the empirical analysis used here is based on individual country vector autoregressive (VAR) models, each of the form:

$$y_t = A_1 y_{t-1} + \ldots + A_p y_{t-p} + \varepsilon_t,$$

where y_t accounts for the vector of the respective endogenous variables considered, $A_1, \ldots, A_p$ represent the matrices of coefficients to be calculated and ε_t corresponds to a vector of innovations that are uncorrelated with their own lagged values and those of the right-hand-side variables. Moreover, to determine the appropriate number of lags to be included in the analysis we use the Hannan-Quinn (HQ) information criterion (refer to Appendix C).

All index values used in this chapter are obtained from the Aizenman et al. (2013) database. RESGDP is calculated as the ratio of total international reserves minus gold and the annual nominal GDP for each country. Data for reserves and GDP were gathered from the International Monetary Fund's IFS database.

A useful alternative to interpret the VAR estimates is using impulse response functions. The following section of this chapter presents impulse-response function graphs based on shocks of one standard deviation of the residuals using the inverse of the Cholesky factor of the residual covariance matrix with an adjustment for degrees of freedom.[12] Based on these findings, it is possible to narrow down our analysis to account for the effects of shocks to the indices of interest as a result of changes in the relative level of reserves.

RESULTS

The preliminary evidence presented in the previous section suggests a role for international reserve accumulation in advancing the main goals of the traditional trilemma of international finance. This section presents the results from the more exhaustive, disaggregated VAR analysis outlined above. Data availability differed across countries, and is reflected in the respective figures.

Exchange Rate Stability and Reserves

Figure 6.5a presents the impulse responses of the ERS index to one standard deviation shock in ΔRESGDP for each of the individual countries. Contrary to expectations, our VAR analysis provides limited statistical

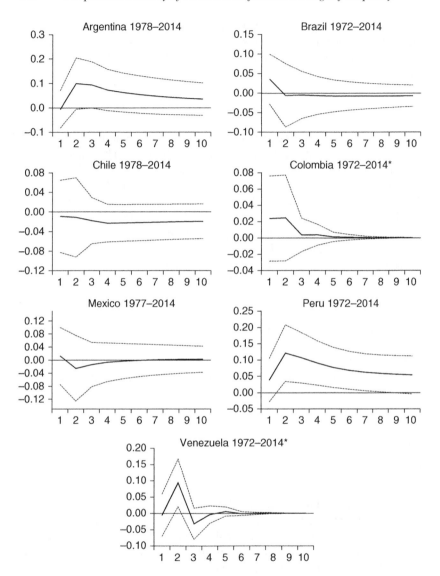

Note: The solid lines represent the impulse response to a Cholesky one-standard deviation shock in ΔRESGDP; the dashed lines show ±2 S.E. confidence intervals; * = response of ΔERS.

Figure 6.5a   Impulse responses of exchange rate stability to shocks in reserves/GDP

support for the presumed positive relationship between international reserves and the stability of a country's exchange rate. Based on these findings, it appears that countries that see reserve accumulation as a way out of the trilemma by trying to sustain stable exchange rates – while simultaneously being committed to liberalized capital accounts and independent monetary policy – are bound to see their attempts fail. This finding is in line with the recent literature on "the fear of reserve loss," under which most emerging countries (including those in Latin America) despite having unprecedented levels of reserves during the 2007–09 Global Financial Crisis, experienced significant depreciations of their currencies (Aizenman and Hutchison, 2012).

Of the seven countries considered, only two appear to have statistically significant responses to changes in the relative level of reserves: Peru and Venezuela. Potential implications of this finding for Peru will be addressed in the following section. In the case of Venezuela (and to a lesser degree Argentina),[13] increases in relative reserves appear to have a delayed and short-lived positive effect on its exchange rate stability index. This is of particular interest given the prominent role that fixed exchange rate regimes have played in these two countries during parts of the period used in our analysis. The impulse response of ERS to a shock in ΔRESGDP is especially large and statistically significant in Venezuela. A closer look at the Venezuelan case is merited.

Venezuela's currency pegs
After a prolonged history of fixed exchange rates, Venezuela's exchange rate was allowed to fluctuate from February 1989 until February 2003. On February 5, 2003, President Hugo Chavez – in an effort to offset some of the economic and exchange rate pressures surrounding an earlier coup attempt by the opposition – announced the reinstatement of an official peg of the Venezuelan bolivar to the US dollar. While characterized by some periods of devaluation, this peg remains in effect and stands in contrast to the rest of countries in the region, who have embraced managed flexible exchange rate regimes over the last couple of decades. Aside from Argentina's 1991–2002 currency board, Venezuela's currency pegs represent the only long-term binding fixed exchange rate regime in the region during the period considered in this study. The traditional theory on reserve accumulation holds that countries with fixed exchange rate regimes require higher levels of reserves relative to flexible exchange rate arrangements (Haberler, 1977). Thus, it follows that of all the Latin American countries considered, Venezuela presents the only consistently significant evidence in favor of the role of reserves in supporting exchange rate stability. Moreover, it is important to note that, as shown in Table 6.1, Venezuela

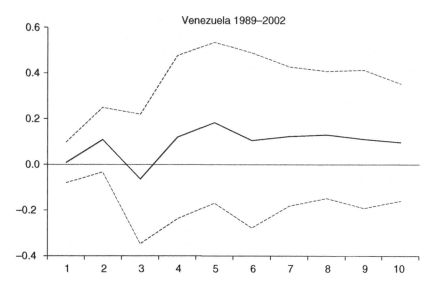

Figure 6.5b   *Venezuela's floating exchange rate period: Impulse responses of exchange rate stability to shocks in international reserves*

was also the only country in our sample that relied entirely on foreign reserve reductions to absorb the exchange market pressure associated with the Global Financial Crisis.

This effect is further illustrated by the fact that this relationship becomes statistically insignificant when we conduct a VAR analysis of the sub-sample of the floating exchange period in Venezuela (1989–2002). Figure 6.5b shows the response of ERS to a one-standard deviation shock to RESGDP for this period. As can be seen from this graph, once Venezuela allowed its exchange rate to float the relationship between changes in reserves and the stability of the exchange rate is no longer statistically significant, and therefore appears to reflect the experience of the other countries in the region.

Taken together, this evidence suggests that foreign reserves play a role in promoting exchange rate stability only in instances of fixed exchange rate regimes – such as that of the periods pre-1989 and post-2002 in Venezuela. For other countries with managed flexible exchange rates, or even softer pegs (e.g., Brazil 1994–98) there is no evidence of higher exchange rate stability associated with larger changes in the level of relative reserves.

Capital Account Openness, Monetary Policy Independence, and Reserves

Similar to the findings for the relationship of reserves and ERS, the impulse-response analyses for the effect of changes in relative reserves on capital account liberalization and monetary policy independence provide little statistically significant support for the expected positive relationships. Figures 6.6 and 6.7 present the responses of ΔKAO and MPI to a Cholesky one-standard deviation shock to ΔRESGDP. Here again, all countries, with the exception of Peru in the case of MPI, show no evidence of experiencing gains in either capital account openness and/or monetary policy independence due to rising changes in the relative level of reserves.

Peru: An exception to the rule?
In addition to showing little evidence for the expected gains in exchange rate stability, capital account openness and monetary policy independence associated with reserve accumulation, the previous figures highlight the stark difference between the responses by ERS and MPI in Peru and those in the other countries considered. Based on these results it appears that reserve accumulation "works" for Peru in terms of encouraging higher levels of exchange rate stability and monetary policy independence, and thus easing the trilemma. This raises an interesting question: why does reserve accumulation benefit Peru, but not other countries?

Further analysis shows that Peru is an exception to the rule only in the sense that it is uniquely positioned (in the region) to benefit from reserve accumulation. That is, unlike its neighbors, Peru has maintained exceptionally high levels of international reserves relative to their GDP. Figure 6.8 shows Peru's reserve position relative to the rest of the region.[14] For most of the period under consideration, Peru has maintained significantly higher levels of international reserves as a share of GDP. Indeed, in recent years that level has exceeded 20 percent of its GDP, and since 2007, the country's relative reserves have been nearly 2–2.5 times larger than the regional average. This observation is significant when put in the context of previous findings by others in the literature, who have argued that only at high levels of relative reserves are countries able to escape the trilemma. For instance, Aizenman et al. (2010) finds that high levels of relative reserves (exceeding a 21 percent of GDP threshold) allow countries to relax the trilemma. Once this observation is taken into account, it appears that the evidence found in this chapter supports their assertion that reserve accumulation "works" only for those countries with already high pre-existing levels of relative reserves. As of today, of all the large emerging Latin American countries, only Peru meets this threshold.

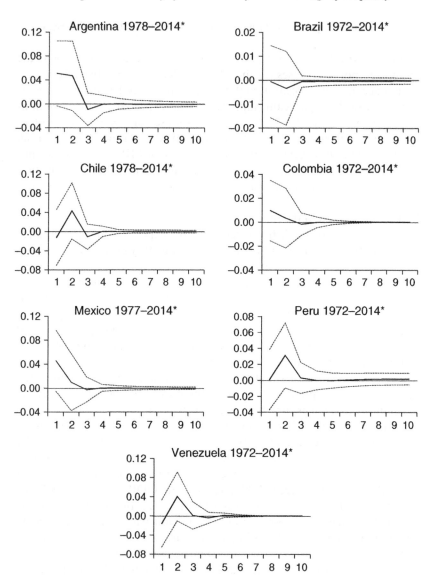

Note: The solid lines represent the impulse response to a Cholesky one-standard deviation shock in ΔRESGDP; the dashed lines show ±2 S.E. confidence intervals; * = response of ΔKAO.

Figure 6.6   Impulse responses of capital account openness to shocks in international reserves

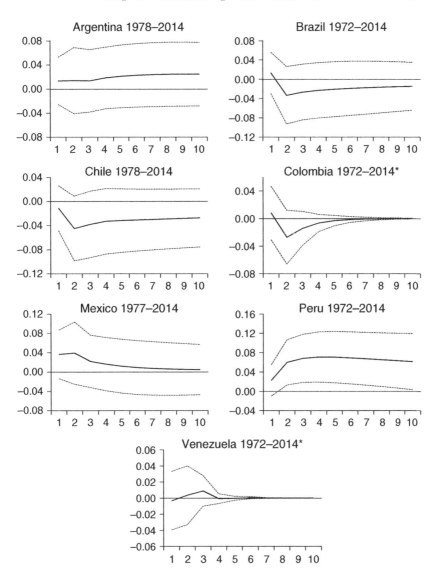

Note: The solid lines represent the impulse response to a Cholesky one-standard deviation shock in ΔRESGDP; the dashed lines show ±2 S.E. confidence intervals; * = response of ΔMPI.

Figure 6.7   Impulse responses of monetary policy independence to shocks in international reserves

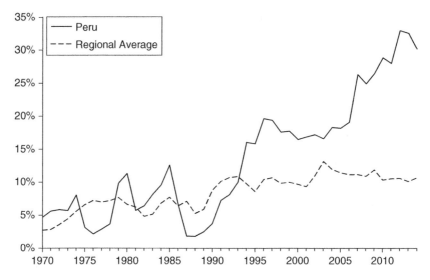

*Figure 6.8   Peru's foreign reserve accumulation in perspective (1970–
2014): Non-gold reserves/GDP*

CONCLUSION

Latin American countries, like the majority of emerging markets across the globe, have embarked in an unprecedented process of international reserve accumulation. These reserves, however, do not come free. Therefore, it is critical to assess the degree to which reserves are actually serving their desired purpose, and to what degree could these purposes be achieved in a more cost-efficient manner. This chapter builds on the limited (and some-what ambiguous) existing evidence by directly delving into the question of the effectiveness of international reserves in enhancing any of the policy goals considered under the traditional trilemma of international finance.

Contrary to most traditional expectations, the VAR analysis carried out in this chapter finds little evidence in support of the effectiveness of reserves in helping the holding countries ease the trilemma. With a few exceptions, increases in the level of reserves relative to GDP do not appear to be associated with changes in any of the three trilemma goals at a reasonable level of statistical significance. In other words, reserve accumulation does not appear to be working – at least in terms of helping the holding countries ease the trilemma.

However, two notable exceptions to this general conclusion reinforce some of the previous findings in the literature. First, only one country with a long history of a fixed exchange rate regime in the area (Venezuela) showed evidence of gains in exchange rate stability associated with increases in relative reserves. A closer look at the Venezuelan case suggested that in line with the traditional optimal reserve demand literature, gains in exchange stability from accumulating reserves accrue mostly in instances of hard pegs. Second, our findings suggest that only countries with high levels of reserves obtain benefits in terms of their exchange rate stability and monetary policy independence as a result of increases in holdings of foreign reserves. For instance, Peru – the only country in the region with reserves in excess of 21 percent of its GDP – is also the only country in our sample that appears to experience statistically significant increases in both indices as a result of an increase in relative reserves. This finding is in line with the evidence presented in Aizenman et al. (2010), which claims that only in countries with reserves exceeding 21 percent of GDP do these reserves ease the trilemma.

Rather than definitively answering the question of whether reserves "work" or not, the findings presented in this chapter raise important questions for policymakers in terms of the appropriateness of reserve hoarding. While not conclusive, these findings do provide some evidence in support of the idea that reserve accumulation contributes to easing the trilemma *only* in instances when reserves are significantly large. For countries holding a more moderate level, reserves appear to provide little to no benefit, except in cases of hard pegs of their exchange rate. Policymakers must consider the opportunity cost as well as their country's ability and willingness to accumulate the high levels of reserves necessary to significantly ease the trilemma. Moreover, and in light of the findings presented in Rosero (2015), it provides further impetus for the creation of mechanisms of regional support, such as reserve pools, which might allow countries to have access to larger stocks of reserves and hence collectively surpass the apparent threshold of reserve effectiveness.

NOTES

1. Data obtained from UNCTADstat.
2. Their model estimates expected reserve-to-GDP ratios by accounting for financial openness, the prevailing exchange rate regime, and monetary depth, as captured by M2.
3. Specifications of reserves include reserves/GDP; reserves as a percentage of external debt; reserves in months of imports; M2/reserves; and short-term debt as a percentage of reserves.
4. These results are, however, at odds with the data that show that many emerging markets did not rely on meaningful drawdowns of their reserves during the last crisis, but rather responded by allowing their currencies to depreciate. Moreover, while the coefficient is

lower for the high-reserve subsample, the significance of the other coefficient changes, which hints at the possibility of biased estimates. The size of the resulting coefficient of reserves is unrealistically high, and thus lacks economic significance.

5. As presented in Calvo and Reinhart (2002).
6. With a fixed or quasi-fixed exchange rate regime, the rise of reserves leads to exchange rate appreciation, which can be combated with sterilization of these inflows. The net result is the growth of the money supply, as well as growing upward pressure on the price level. As inflation and M2 increase, it becomes more difficult to justify the trade-off between inflation and a stable exchange rate.
7. All index values used in this chapter are obtained from the Aizenman et al. (2013) database.
8. While a small number of emerging market countries do opt for complete exchange rate flexibility, free floats by their own nature imply instability through exchange rate risk. This is particularly of concern in the context of relatively small emerging economies like those of Latin America (see Devlin et al., 2001)
9. Further descriptions of this and the remaining indices are available from Aizenman et al. (2013).
10. Edison et al. (2004) provides a comprehensive survey of the literature in this regard. However, it is important to note that while it is a component of the traditional trilemma framework, complete capital account openness should not necessarily be a desirable goal under all conditions. This is, for instance, illustrated in the evolving view of capital controls by institutions like the International Monetary Fund, which in November 2012 partially reversed its traditional institutional view and concluded that capital controls, under certain conditions, "can be useful for supporting macroeconomic policy adjustment and safeguarding financial system stability" (IMF, 2012).
11. Dates vary slightly due to data availability.
12. The degrees of freedom correction are calculated such that the (i,j)th element of the residual covariance matrix is given by $\Sigma_t e_{i,t} e_{j,t}/(T-p)$ where p is the number of parameters per equation in the VAR. RESGDP is used as the leading variable in the VAR system.
13. In an attempt to rein in the hyperinflation that prevailed at the end of the 1980s, Argentina opted for the establishment of a currency board on April 1, 1991. Under this arrangement the Argentinean peso was tied to the US dollar at a 1-to-1 rate until its collapse in January 6, 2002.
14. This regional average corresponds to the average of the remaining six countries considered in this chapter.

REFERENCES

Aizenman, J. (2009), "On the paradox of prudential regulations in the globalized economy: International reserves and the crisis a reassessment," *NBER Working Paper Series, No. 14779*, accessed July 18, 2018 at http://www.nber.org/papers/w14779.pdf.

Aizenman, J. and M. Hutchison (2012), "Exchange market pressure and absorption by international reserves: Emerging markets and fear of reserve loss during the 2008–09 crisis," *Journal of International Money and Finance*, **31**(5), 1076–91.

Aizenman, J. and J. Lee (2007), "International reserves: Precautionary versus mercantilist views, theory and evidence," *Open Economies Review*, **18**(2), 191–214.

Aizenman, J., M. Chinn and H. Ito (2010), "The emerging global financial architecture: Tracing and evaluating new patterns of the trilemma configuration," *Journal of International Money and Finance*, **29**(4), 615–41.

Aizenman, J., M. Chinn and H. Ito (2013), "The 'impossible trinity' hypothesis in an era of global imbalances: Measurement and testing," *Review of International Economics*, **21**(3), 447–58.

Alberola, E., A. Erce and J.M. Serena (2016), "International reserves and gross capital flows dynamics," *Journal of International Money and Finance*, **60**, 151–71.

Artus, P. (2009), "A quoi ont servi les réserves de change très importantes?" [What was the use of the very important foreign exchange reserves?], *Revue d'Economie Financière*, **95**, 259–74.

Baqir, R., M. Chivakul and G. Gray et al. (2010), *How did Emerging Markets Cope in the Crisis?*, Washington, DC: International Monetary Fund.

Blanchard, O., H. Faruqee and V. Klyuev (2009), "Did foreign reserves help weather the crisis?," *IMF News*, 8 October, accessed 18 July, 2018 at https://www.imf.org/en/News/Articles/2015/09/28/04/53/sonum100809a.

Calvo, G. and C. Reinhart (2002), "Fear of floating," *Quarterly Journal of Economics*, **107**(2), 379–408.

Devlin, R., A. Estevadeordal and P. Giordano et al. (2001), "Estabilidad macroeconómica, comercio e integración" [Macroeconomic stability, trade and integration], *Integración & Comercio*, **5**(13), 35–96.

Dominguez, K., Y. Hashimoto and I. Takatoshi (2012), "International reserves and the Global Financial Crisis," *Journal of International Economics*, **88**(2), 388–406.

Dooley, M., D. Folkerts-Landau and P. Garber (2005), *International Financial Stability: Asia, Interest Rates, and the Dollar*, New York: Deutsche Bank.

Edison, H.J., M.W. Klein, L.A. Ricci and T. Slok (2004), "Capital account liberalization and economic performance: Survey and synthesis," *IMF Staff Papers*, **51**(2), 220–56.

Feldstein, M. (1999), "Self-protection for emerging market economies," *NBER Working Paper Series, No. 6907*, accessed July 18, 2018 at http://www.nber.org/papers/w6907.

Fleming, J.M. (1962), "Domestic financial policies under fixed and under floating exchange rates," *International Monetary Fund Staff Papers*, **9**(3), 369–80.

Frankel, J. and G. Saravelos (2012), "Can leading indicators assess country vulnerability? Evidence from the 2008–09 Global Financial Crisis," *Journal of International Economics*, **87**(2), 216–31.

Glick, R. and M. Hutchison (2009), "Navigating the trilemma: Capital flows and monetary policy in China," *Journal of Asian Economics*, **20**(3), 205–24.

Haberler, G. (1977), "How important is control over international reserves?," in R.A. Mundell and J.J. Polack (eds), *The New International Monetary System*, New York: Columbia University Press.

Heller, H.R. (1966), "Optimal international reserves," *The Economic Journal*, **76**(302), 296–311.

IMF (2012), *The Liberalization and Management of Capital Flows: An Institutional View*, Washington, DC: International Monetary Fund.

Kletzer, K. (2000), "The effectiveness of self-protection policies for safeguarding emerging market economies from crises," *ZEI Working Papers B 08-2000*, ZEI – Center for European Integration Studies, University of Bonn, accessed July 18, 2018 at https://www.zei.uni-bonn.de/dateien/working-papaer/B00-08.pdf.

Machlup, F. (1966), "The need for monetary international reserves," *Banca Nazionale del Lavoro Quarterly Review*, **19**(78), 175–220.

Mundell, R.A. (1963), "Capital mobility and stabilization policy under fixed and flexible exchange rates," *Canadian Journal of Economic and Political Science*, **29**(4), 475–85.

Obstfeld, M., J.C. Shambaugh and A. Taylor (2005), "The trilemma in history: Tradeoffs among exchange rates, monetary policies, and capital mobility," *The Review of Economics and Statistics*, **8**(3), 423–38.

Obstfeld, M., J.C. Shambaugh and A. Taylor (2009), "Financial instability, reserves and central bank swap lines in the panic of 2008," *American Economic Review*, **99**(2), 480–86.

Rodrik, D. (2006), "The social cost of foreign exchange reserves," *International Economic Journal*, **20**(3), 253–66.

Rosero, L.D. (2015), "Insuring against neighboring crises: International reserves in Latin America," *Journal of Economic Integration*, **30**(3), 467–500.

Triffin, R. (1963), "After the gold exchange standard?," in H.G. Grubel (ed.), *World Monetary Reform: Plans and Issues*, Stanford, CA: Stanford University Press, pp. 422–39.

APPENDIX A

Table 6.A.1 Descriptive statistics

	Argentina				Brazil				Chile				Colombia			
	ERS	KAO	MPI	RESGDP	ERS	KAO	MPI	RESGDP	ERS	KAO	MPI	RESGDP	ERS	KAO	MPI	RESGDP
Mean	0.49	0.35	0.43	6.37	0.33	0.15	0.51	6.83	0.38	0.39	0.50	15.17	0.54	0.15	0.51	8.03
Median	0.42	0.25	0.42	5.19	0.24	0.00	0.50	6.35	0.35	0.41	0.52	14.76	0.51	0.16	0.50	8.43
Maximum	1.00	0.94	0.68	15.42	0.92	0.53	0.94	14.99	1.00	1.00	0.85	22.91	0.98	0.70	0.84	12.53
Minimum	0.02	0.00	0.13	0.98	0.05	0.00	0.15	1.66	0.06	0.00	0.02	6.66	0.15	0.00	0.14	2.46
Std. dev.	0.37	0.27	0.12	4.05	0.23	0.21	0.20	3.80	0.20	0.40	0.16	4.44	0.28	0.19	0.14	2.92
Skewness	0.25	0.88	−0.25	0.61	0.93	0.80	0.12	0.82	1.58	0.29	−0.65	−0.11	0.02	0.94	−0.05	−0.55
Kurtosis	1.56	2.52	3.14	2.32	3.09	1.85	2.60	2.73	6.20	1.40	4.17	1.92	1.37	2.87	3.10	2.25
Jarque-Bera	3.59	5.14	0.41	3.02	6.20	6.91	0.40	4.90	31.26	4.44	4.70	1.88	4.78	6.42	0.03	3.15
Probability	0.17	0.08	0.81	0.22	0.05	0.03	0.82	0.09	0.00	0.11	0.10	0.39	0.09	0.04	0.98	0.21
Sum	18.30	13.06	15.91	235.58	14.04	6.63	22.02	293.49	14.04	14.39	18.46	561.40	23.28	6.64	21.77	345.11
Sum sq. dev.	4.91	2.70	0.52	589.13	2.26	1.87	1.60	605.89	1.39	5.67	0.95	709.62	3.37	1.46	0.81	359.08
Observations	37	37	37	37	43	43	43	43	37	37	37	37	43	43	43	43
Time period	1978–2014				1972–2014				1978–2014				1972–2014			

Table 6.A.1 (continued)

	Mexico				Peru				Venezuela			
	ERS	KAO	MPI	RESGDP	ERS	KAO	MPI	RESGDP	ERS	KAO	MPI	RESGDP
Mean	0.43	0.59	0.47	5.96	0.44	0.59	0.44	13.82	0.78	0.44	0.48	12.83
Median	0.32	0.70	0.45	5.26	0.46	0.70	0.47	12.55	1.00	0.41	0.49	12.53
Maximum	0.93	1.00	0.92	14.70	1.00	1.00	0.71	32.96	1.00	1.00	0.78	30.59
Minimum	0.04	0.00	0.05	0.42	0.02	0.00	0.08	1.75	0.04	0.00	0.13	1.55
Std. dev.	0.27	0.27	0.22	3.87	0.27	0.42	0.14	9.19	0.35	0.33	0.15	6.28
Skewness	0.59	−0.45	0.12	0.63	0.43	−0.32	−0.51	0.48	−1.14	0.24	−0.11	0.37
Kurtosis	1.93	2.40	2.06	2.56	2.75	1.39	3.11	2.18	2.59	1.62	2.53	3.41
Jarque-Bera	4.02	1.87	1.49	2.79	1.44	5.35	1.87	2.89	9.60	3.82	0.48	1.27
Probability	0.13	0.39	0.48	0.25	0.49	0.07	0.39	0.24	0.01	0.15	0.79	0.53
Sum	16.18	22.26	17.90	226.32	19.10	25.50	18.83	594.36	33.37	18.97	20.72	551.71
Sum sq. dev.	2.61	2.77	1.86	553.67	3.00	7.28	0.88	3550.92	5.29	4.57	0.94	1656.63
Observations	38	38	38	38	43	43	43	43	43	43	43	43
Time period	1977–2014				1972–2014				1972–2014			

APPENDIX B

Table 6.A.2   Stationarity tests (augmented Dickey-Fuller)

Variables	Argentina	Brazil	Chile	Colombia	Mexico	Peru	Venezuela
ERS	−3.1838	−3.6385	−4.125	−2.1291	−3.7565	−3.5659	−2.3910
	0.0277	0.0088	0.0024	0.2347	0.0064	0.0106	0.1500
ΔERS	−	−	−	−9.0083	−	−	−8.8068
				0.0000			0.0000
KAO	−2.2144	−0.37652	−1.4364	−1.2599	−1.8506	−0.8852	−1.4317
	0.2042	0.9043	0.5559	0.6397	0.3519	0.7837	0.5582
ΔKAO	−6.6258	−6.1888	−7.4987	−8.5551	−6.1197	−5.4195	−5.8769
	0.0000	0.0000	0.0000	0.0000	0.0000	0.0000	0.0000
MPI	−3.3257	−4.7682	−4.1541	−2.3758	−3.2477	−3.8085	−2.436
	0.0208	0.004	0.0025	0.1546	0.0255	0.0056	0.1385
ΔMPI	−	−	−	−5.2977	−	−	−7.0763
				0.0001			0.0000
RESGDP	−1.4928	−1.1129	−1.5186	−2.0942	0.4286	−0.3903	−2.2864
	0.5279	0.7025	0.5150	0.2479	0.9820	0.9019	0.1807
ΔRESGDP	−6.8584	−6.4121	−6.6935	−4.8557	−8.8978	−6.2157	−5.9166
	0.0000	0.0000	0.0000	0.0003	0.0000	0.0000	0.0000

Note: Augmented Dickey-Fuller test statistic, *p*-value, and lag length are presented in that respective order.

APPENDIX C

Table 6.A.3   Hannan-Quinn criterion (HQC) for lag order selection

Lag	Argentina	Brazil	Chile	Colombia	Mexico	Peru	Venezuela
1	2.2342*	0.0531*	2.7812*	−0.2418*	2.5401*	2.4085*	3.84*
2	2.7923	0.5661	3.3436	−0.1133	2.9014	2.7434	4.5314

Note: * Corresponds to the lag order selected by the criterion.

7. The costs of foreign exchange intervention: Trends and implications

Devika Dutt

INTRODUCTION

Central banks regularly intervene in the foreign exchange markets. One of the most common forms of foreign exchange intervention is sterilized sale or purchase of international reserves by central banks. There is evidence to suggest that interventions increasingly take the form of purchases of foreign exchange reserves (Fratzscher et al., 2017; Yeyati, 2008).

For instance, Fratzscher et al. (2017) find that, in the 33 countries examined, central banks intervened in the foreign exchange market on 19.1 percent of the trading days between 1995 and 2011; of these, interventions took the form of purchases of foreign currency on 76.1 percent of the trading days. Their findings are consistent with other studies that document extensive central bank activity in the foreign exchange markets (Dominguez and Frankel, 1993; Menkhoff, 2013).

The trilemma of international economics states that it is only possible to maintain two of the following three policy objectives in an economy: fixed exchange rates, open capital account, and independent monetary policy. However, holding foreign exchange reserves allows central banks to weaken the constraints of the policy trilemma. As is described above, holding reserves can be used to act against undesirable movements of the exchange rate and cushion against the effects of volatile capital flows, among other things. Therefore, reserve holdings allow countries to lean against the trilemma (Ilzetzki, Reinhart and Rogoff, 2017; Steiner, 2017).

Foreign exchange intervention has led to an unprecedented increase in the accumulation of foreign exchange reserves in central banks around the world. Moreover, this accumulation is especially pronounced in developing countries and emerging market economies (EMEs). However, as is demonstrated in this chapter, the cost of maintaining foreign exchange positions is significant. This chapter measures the cost of maintaining foreign exchange reserves by central banks, and documents its variation across countries. It also discusses the determinants of this variation across countries.

This chapter shows that reserve accumulation resulting from foreign exchange interventions has increased substantially since the 1990s. The costs associated with these interventions have fluctuated, but have increased to large and significant magnitudes in recent years. This chapter also presents evidence that suggests that, on average, developing and emerging economies incur a higher cost than advanced economies. Moreover, countries with more open capital accounts incur a higher cost compared to countries with less open capital accounts. However, this relationship is more pronounced for developing and emerging economies, while advanced countries are able to maintain more open capital accounts, hold fewer reserves, and incur a lower cost. The chapter then discusses the role played by access to an institutional network of emergency liquidity assistance from a de facto international lender of last resort (ILOLR) in mitigating the cost of foreign exchange intervention.

The rest of this chapter is organized as follows. The next section briefly reviews the existing literature on reasons for reserve accumulation, extent and determinants of reserve accumulation, and cost of reserve accumulation and foreign exchange intervention. The third section lays out the definition of cost on which the analysis is based. The fourth outlines the data used. The fifth documents the extent of reserve accumulation and estimates the cost of foreign exchange intervention, while the sixth section discusses the determinants of these costs. The seventh section concludes, and outlines avenues for future research.

LITERATURE REVIEW

In the heyday of neoliberal restructuring all over the world, especially since the 1990s, openness of the external account was considered the order of the day. Governments were expected to reduce their intervention in markets and allow the market determination of all prices, including the exchange rate. Capital controls were considered an impediment to market discovery and a hurdle that needed to be overcome to achieve financial and economic development. Therefore, intervention in the foreign exchange market by central banks was considered an inefficient, ineffective tool of maintaining undervalued exchange rates for the purposes of export promotion or the pursuit of mercantilist objectives. The established wisdom was that market fundamentals would eventually make foreign exchange interventions unsustainable in the long run, and anticipating this, market forces would make it ineffective in the short run. The skepticism regarding foreign exchange intervention also stems from the sheer size of the foreign exchange market: it is the largest financial market in the world (Fratzscher et al., 2017). Therefore, the size of interventions is dwarfed by the volume and size of transactions that take place in a particular currency in the foreign exchange market.

Despite this skepticism, however, evidence suggests that foreign exchange interventions by central banks can be highly effective. For instance, Dominguez and Frankel (1993) find that intervention by the Federal Reserve and the Bundesbank was effective in moving the exchange rate in the desired direction in the mid-1980s. Adler and Mora (2011) focus on Latin American economies and find that interventions can slow the pace of appreciation of the exchange rate. However, these effects decrease with the degree of capital account openness and are more effective in the context of already overvalued exchange rates. Fatum and Hutchison (2003) provide evidence that sterilized intervention affects the exchange rate in the short run. Menkhoff (2013) surveys the literature on exchange rate interventions and argues that foreign exchange intervention often has an impact on exchange rate level and volatility in EMEs. Fratzscher et al. (2017) argue that intervention has been an effective tool for smoothing the path of exchange rates and in stabilizing the exchange rate in countries with narrow band regimes. It is also effective in affecting the level of the exchange rate in flexible exchange rate regimes when interventions are large and have been publicly announced. Blanchard and Adler (2015) find that official reserve intervention can stem pressures of currency appreciation in the face of capital inflows in EMEs. Therefore, the current consensus in the intervention literature seems to be that foreign exchange interventions can be effective for a variety of exchange rate–related policy objectives.

In addition, official reserve holdings can provide a buffer against a freely falling currency in the event of a sudden stop or reversal in capital flows. Bussière et al. (2015) find that pre-crisis levels of reserves and capital controls are associated with higher economic growth as they are both used to buffer against external shocks. Holding of international reserves equal to at least the value of short-term external debt reduces the annual probability of a country experiencing a share reversal in capital flows, which can precipitate an external debt and/or currency crisis, by ten percentage points (Rodrik, 2006). Moreover, a rise in reserve holdings often lowers the cost of private debt and equity capital (Feldstein, 1999). To some extent, reserve holdings have substituted for capital controls (Ilzetzki et al., 2017). Reserve accumulation is considered a by-product of a shift to the trilemma configuration towards greater capital mobility (Steiner, 2017) engendered by financial globalization. Therefore, reserve

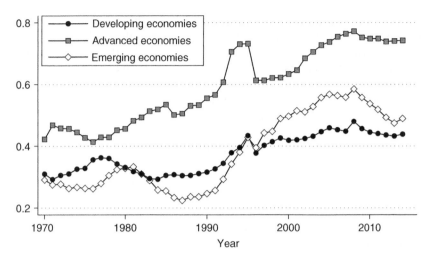

Source: Author's calculations based on Chinn and Ito (2006).

Figure 7.1   Capital account openness (Chinn-Ito index) over time

holding can be considered insurance against the costs of sudden stops and reversals in capital flows.

Perhaps unsurprisingly, accumulation of reserves has increased substantially with the increasing liberalization of the capital account around the world since the 1990s (Rodrik, 2006) and the East Asian crisis in 1997 (Aizenman, Chinn and Ito, 2010; Aizenman and Lee, 2007). Capital account openness as measured by the Chinn-Ito index has increased for all groups of countries examined (Figure 7.1).[1]

Some explanations for the trends in reserve accumulation can be found in the literature. Cheung and Ito (2009) find that accumulation of reserves has been pronounced in Asian economies since the Asian financial crisis. For instance, between 2000 and 2004, China, Japan, Korea, Malaysia, and Taiwan increased their holding of international reserves by 262 percent, 133 percent, 107 percent, 124 percent, and 126 percent, respectively. Similarly, Bussière et al. (2015) argue that the rate of reserve accumulation has partly been a response to crisis experienced in EMEs in the recent past. Countries that used more reserves in foreign exchange interventions and decumulated reserves in the past, during crises, rebuilt their reserve pool at a faster rate compared to others in the aftermath of crises, with the rate of accumulation eventually slowing down. Bussière et al. (2015) attribute the decline in the rate of reserve accumulation to the decline in the rate of increase of short-term external debt (ibid.). Cheung and Ito (2009) show that the explanatory power for traditional trade-related variables in explaining reserve accumulation is decreasing over time, while that of financial variables related to external financing has increased. They also show that, *ceteris paribus*, developed economies can afford to hold fewer reserve assets compared to developing economies if faced with the same conditions. Obstfeld, Shambaugh and Taylor (2010) argue that reserve accumulation is a key tool for managing financial stability in a globalized world and show that reserve growth in a broad panel of developing and developed economies is correlated with financial openness, financial development, and exchange rate policy. Dominguez (2012) shows that, during the Global Financial Crisis, reserve accumulation was higher in countries with sovereign wealth funds, lower for countries that drew on Federal Reserve swap lines, higher in countries with higher short-term external debt as a proportion of gross domestic product (GDP), higher for countries that experienced higher export growth, and lower for countries with a higher interest rate differential.

While the literature documenting the extent of reserve accumulation, and the reasons for it are extensive, the literature on the cost associated with it is quite limited, perhaps due to the perception that these costs are marginal and of second-order importance (Adler and Mano, 2016). Nonetheless, Rodrik (2006) approximates this cost for different country groups (developed, developing, and emerging) assuming different spread levels (0.03, 0.05, 0.07), and finds that the social opportunity cost of excess reserves stood at about 1 percent of GDP (for the assumed spread level of 0.05) of developing economies as of 2004. However, Rodrik (2006) does not use actual spreads for calculating costs and does not account for currency depreciation. Yeyati (2008) argues that the literature on the cost of reserve accumulation overestimates the cost as it does not consider the benefits of reserve accumulation in the form of the reduced probability of crisis and the reduced borrowing costs. Therefore, Yeyati (2008) argues that the marginal cost of reserve accumulation is typically overestimated by about 50 percent. Nonetheless, Yeyati (2008) also does not calculate the total costs being incurred ex post given the levels and accumulation of reserves across countries.

Adler and Mano (2016) is, to the author's knowledge, the only study that systematically estimates the marginal and total costs of reserve accumulation for a set of 73 developed and developing economies during 2012–13, and finds that ex ante marginal cost incurred by the median emerging market economy was in the interquartile range of 2–5.5 percent per year, and total costs in the range of 0.3–0.9 percent of GDP per year. Moreover, about 20 percent of the countries in their sample incurred greater than 1 percent of their GDP in sustaining foreign exchange reserve assets per year over the sample period. This chapter follows their method, and extends the period and sample of analysis.

DEFINITION OF COST

Foreign exchange reserves are typically held in the form of highly liquid safe assets, such as sovereign bonds of some developed nations, especially short-term US Treasury securities. However, the cost of acquiring these reserves is typically much higher than the return on these safe assets. Therefore, the cost of foreign exchange intervention is the cost of maintaining a given foreign exchange reserve position.

To consider operations that are strictly foreign exchange transactions and not monetary policy actions, the literature on foreign exchange interventions typically consider sterilized interventions by the central bank. A sterilized foreign exchange intervention is one in which the central bank substitutes between foreign and domestic assets on its balance sheet. Therefore, if the central bank purchases (sells) foreign exchange, it typically also sells (purchases) domestic assets such as government bonds through open market operations, to leave the monetary base and monetary policy rate unchanged.

Formally, the change in a central bank's net foreign asset position, ΔNFA due to a foreign exchange operation is:

$$\Delta NFA = \Delta MB - \Delta NDA,$$

where ΔMB is the change in the monetary base and ΔNDA is the net domestic asset position of the central bank (Adler and Mano, 2016). If the intervention is fully sterilized:

$$\Delta NFA = -\Delta NDA. \tag{7.1}$$

Adler and Mano (2016) argue that the extent of sterilization of the official reserve operation is irrelevant from the perspective of the opportunity cost of foreign exchange intervention. For instance, in the case of a reserve purchase, the extent of the operation that is unsterilized results in an expansion of the monetary base. However, this expansion could have been carried out by expanding the size of the central bank balance sheet with higher-yielding domestic government assets. Therefore, insofar as a monetary expansion is brought about from purchasing foreign reserve assets that is not sterilized by the sale of domestic government assets, an opportunity cost is still created. This is because this monetary expansion could, alternatively, have been created by purchasing higher-yielding domestic government assets. Therefore, the marginal cost of the operation would be the opportunity cost of increasing the foreign exchange reserve asset position of the central bank. The cost of maintaining this foreign exchange reserve asset position, measured by deviations from uncovered interest parity is:

$$MC_{k,t+1} = \frac{1 + i_{k,t}}{1 + i_t^*} * \frac{S_{k,t+1}}{S_{k,t}} - 1, \tag{7.2}$$

where $i_{k,t}$ is the nominal interest rate on the domestic government assets, i_t^* is the nominal interest rate on the reserve asset, and $S_{k,t}$ is the exchange rate expressed as the units of local currency per unit of foreign currency. The uncovered interest parity condition, in this context, is the condition under which there is no incentive to hold domestic government assets over reserve assets, as there is no arbitrage opportunity. Therefore, ex post, deviations from this condition measures the cost of holding the reserve asset as opposed to the domestic government asset.

Two things should be noted as regards the definition of the costs of intervention. First, the cost as it is being measured is not necessarily the *book cost* of intervention, that is, it is not the cost that is reflected in the central bank's balance sheet. The book cost would depend on the degree of sterilization of the foreign exchange intervention. The cost that is being considered here is the *opportunity cost*, based on the next best alternative to foreign reserve assets on the central bank's balance sheet. Second, the cost being measured here is the quasi-fiscal opportunity cost incurred by the central bank. Some literature, notably Rodrik (2006), measures opportunity cost to the economy as a whole, by considering the spread between private borrowing costs in the economy and the return on the foreign reserve assets. This formulation is likely to result in the measurement of a higher cost of intervention, as private borrowing costs in any economy are typically higher than the borrowing costs of the sovereign, or the nominal interest rate on domestic government assets ($i_{k,t}$ in equation 7.2) of a comparable term. However, this formulation of opportunity cost is unsatisfactory as foreign exchange interventions are not typically undertaken through the sale and purchase of private borrowers in an economy.[2] Moreover, it is not clear, in this formulation, which actors in the economy are bearing this cost of intervention.

Taking logarithms on both sides of equation 7.2:

$$mc_{k,t+1} = \ln(1 + MC_{k,t+1}) = \ln(1 + i_{k,t}) - \ln(1 + i_t^*)$$

$$+ \ln S_{k,t+1} - \ln S_{k,t} \cong (i_{k,t} - i_t^*) - \Delta S_{k,t+1}, \tag{7.3}$$

where $\Delta S_{k,t+1}$ is the log change in exchange rate from time t to $t + 1$.
The total cost of foreign exchange intervention is thus:

$$TC_{k,t+1} = MC_{k,t+1} * NFA_{k,t}. \tag{7.4}$$

Since most central banks are quasi-government bodies that typically transfer their surpluses to the government, this total cost is the quasi-fiscal cost of foreign exchange intervention. Therefore, this is a direct loss to the government surplus, and a diversion of government budgetary resources away from other uses of fiscal resources. Moreover, it directly increases the size of the government budget deficit.

DATA

The data related to reserve holdings and external debt is from the International Financial Statistics produced by the IMF, World Development Indicators produced by the World Bank, and OECDstat. In addition, data on capital account openness are based on the index created by Chinn and Ito (2006). This index is a composite of a variety of factors that determine the degree of capital account openness based on the IMF's *Annual Report on Exchange Arrangements and Exchange Restrictions.*

The classification of countries into advanced and developing is based on the classification of the United Nations Conference on Trade and Development (UNCTAD). The classification of countries into emerging markets is slightly trickier as UNCTAD and other multilateral organizations do not classify countries as EMEs. It seems more to be a matter of convention and varies from study to study. For the purposes of this chapter, the classification of Chinn and Ito (2006) is used.

EXTENT AND COST OF FOREIGN EXCHANGE INTERVENTION

Based on the definition of quasi-fiscal costs above, the trends in the costs of foreign exchange intervention can be observed in Figure 7.2. As mentioned previously, the cost of foreign exchange intervention has been estimated as the deviations from uncovered interest parity. This quasi-fiscal cost of holding reserves is calculated based on the spread between short-term sovereign bonds and US Treasury securities. Since no interest is received on reserves held in the form of gold, these are excluded in the calculation of costs of holding reserves.[3]

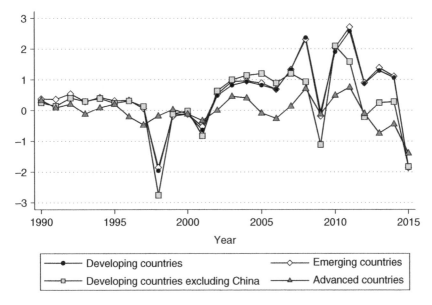

Source: Author's calculations.

Figure 7.2 Quasi-fiscal cost of reserves (% of GDP)

It is evident from Figure 7.2 that, while there is significant variation in the cost incurred by these country groups over time, the average cost incurred by advanced countries is lower than the average cost incurred by developing and emerging economies. The cost incurred by all countries peaked in 2011; however, the emerging economies incurred an average cost of nearly 3 percent of the GDP, while advanced economies incurred an average cost of less than 1 percent of GDP. This trend is also reflected in the trends in reserve accumulation, which are shown in Figure 7.3. The dramatic decline in costs in 2015 are likely to be due to an appreciating dollar, as even though reserve accumulation has reduced, it has not dramatically collapsed.

Table 7.1 shows the summary statistics of the costs incurred by year by developing countries. The average understates the magnitude of the costs incurred by some countries; therefore, Table 7.1 also lists the maximum cost incurred in any given year after 1990 and the country incurring it.

The magnitudes of the costs are not insignificant. For instance, in 2000, the government of Ghana spent 1.5 percent of its GDP on healthcare, but incurred nearly 4.3 percent of its GDP in conducting foreign exchange intervention. In 2010, government expenditure on education in Lebanon

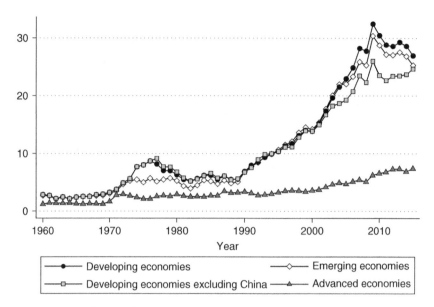

Source: Author's calculations.

Figure 7.3   Foreign exchange reserves (excluding gold) as a share of GDP

was 5.5 percent, which is comparable to the cost it incurred on foreign exchange intervention reserves (4.3 percent). In the middle of a severe financial crisis, the Icelandic economy spent 4.5 percent of its GDP on foreign exchange intervention.

As a rule of thumb, it is considered good practice for central banks to maintain reserves worth three months of imports (this is the Guidotti-Greenspan-IMF rule; Rodrik, 2006), as maintaining liquidity is considered to be the "key to financial self-help." Countries that hold substantial internationally liquid foreign currency reserves and/or a ready source of foreign currency loans are considered to be less likely to experience a speculative currency attack (Feldstein, 1999). However, central banks have been holding reserves far in excess of the three-month convention. Interestingly, the level of reserves in terms of months of imports has remained quite stable around the three-month mark for advanced countries.

Table 7.1   Summary statistics – quasi-fiscal cost of foreign exchange reserves of developing countries

Year	Mean	Standard Deviation	Maximum	Country incurring Maximum Cost
1990	0.166	0.903	4.282	Zambia
1991	0.071	0.582	2.944	Jamaica
1992	–0.005	0.647	1.838	Nigeria
1993	–0.176	0.739	1.766	Guyana
1994	0.002	0.639	2.809	Malawi
1995	–0.051	0.778	1.526	Hungary
1996	–0.229	0.996	1.381	Guyana
1997	–0.096	0.482	0.832	Lesotho
1998	–0.229	1.089	1.589	Lao
1999	0.017	0.812	4.502	Indonesia
2000	0.010	0.562	2.634	Ghana
2001	–0.084	0.574	1.229	Turkey
2002	0.163	0.745	2.795	Czech Republic
2003	0.249	1.342	4.621	Malta
2004	0.159	0.845	2.057	Albania
2005	0.106	0.558	2.051	Yemen
2006	0.127	0.464	2.203	Yemen
2007	0.469	1.240	9.321	Iraq
2008	0.489	1.404	6.568	Iraq
2009	–0.142	1.467	2.863	Lebanon
2010	0.480	0.963	4.075	Lesotho
2011	0.621	1.058	4.399	Iceland
2012	0.072	0.897	2.849	Lebanon
2013	0.169	0.809	2.771	Lebanon
2014	0.063	0.578	2.956	Lebanon
2015	–0.839	2.177	2.831	Lebanon
Total	0.083	1.004	9.321	Iraq

Source: Author's calculations.

FACTORS THAT DETERMINE RESERVE ACCUMULATION AND ITS COST

Country Group

In 2014, EMEs and developing economies incurred a cost of 1.16 percent and 1.12 percent of their GDP, respectively, for holding reserves. By contrast, advanced nations earned a return of 0.39 percent on their reserve

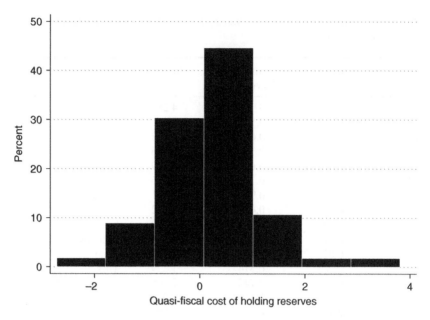

Source: Author's calculations.

Figure 7.4   Histogram of quasi-fiscal cost of developing countries in 2014

holdings in 2014. This is consistent with the results in Adler and Mano (2016). Figure 7.4 shows the histogram of the distribution of quasi-fiscal costs incurred by developing countries in 2014. Nearly 62 percent of developing countries incurred positive costs, and about 16 percent spent greater than 1 percent of their GDP in holding foreign exchange reserves in 2014.

Once again, it is interesting to note that advanced economies are on average incurring close to zero quasi-fiscal costs over the period under consideration. The average cost incurred by advanced nations has ranged between −1.09 percent of GDP and 0.83 percent of GDP since 1990. Clearly, advanced economies are able to incur lower average costs partly because central banks in these countries are holding a higher share of their reserves in the form of gold as opposed to foreign currency assets and partly because they simply do not hold significant reserves. However, these lower costs are interesting, especially since, on average, the advanced economies have more open capital accounts (see Figure 7.1).

Capital Account Openness

In addition to the disparity between the cost incurred by emerging and developing economies as a group and advanced economies as a group, there is also significant variation within these groups. In 2014, the reserves to GDP ratio varied from 2.56 percent in Zimbabwe to about 113 percent in Hong Kong. Official reserve interventions can be seen as a substitute for capital controls (Ilzetzki et al., 2017; Steiner, 2017). From Figures 7.5

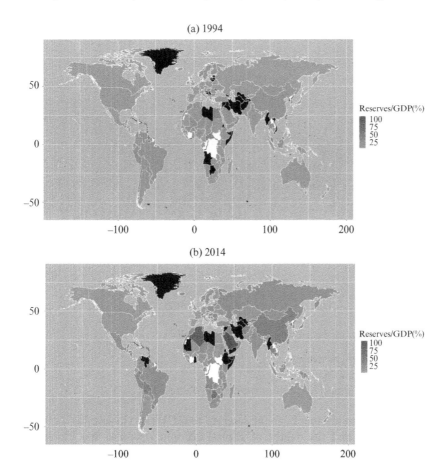

Note: Countries are shaded black if data were not available.

Source: Author's calculations.

Figure 7.5   Reserves to GDP ratio, 1994 and 2014

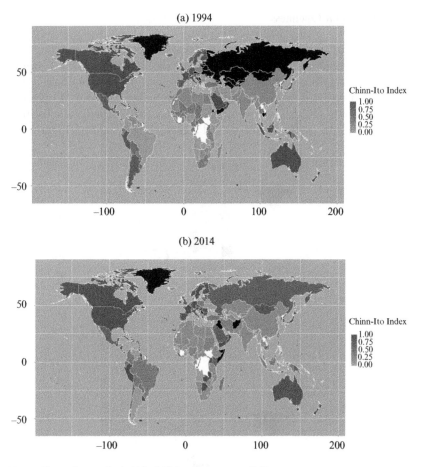

Note: Countries are shaded black if data were not available.

Source: Author's calculations.

Figure 7.6   Capital account openness, 1994 and 2014

and 7.6, we can see that both the reserves to GDP ratio in several countries in the world and the degree of capital account openness has increased between 1994 and 2014. The darker the shade in Figures 7.5 and 7.6, the higher is the reserve to GDP ratio and degree of capital account openness of the economy, respectively. However, it is not immediately apparent if countries with more open capital accounts have higher reserve accumulation and higher costs of foreign exchange intervention.

A different picture emerges if the correlation between cost incurred and

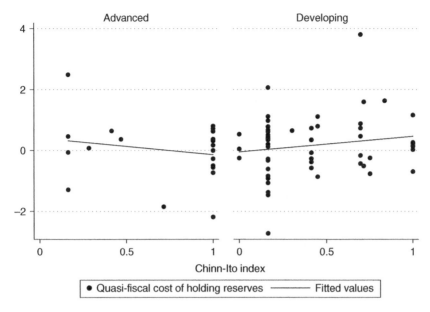

Source: Author's calculations.

*Figure 7.7   Scatterplot of quasi-fiscal cost and capital account openness in
2014*

capital account openness is analyzed for advanced countries and developing countries separately. Figure 7.7 shows the scatterplot between the cost
of foreign exchange intervention and capital account openness in 2014
separately for advanced countries and developing countries. The cost of
foreign exchange intervention and capital account openness (as measured
by the Chinn-Ito index) is negatively related to capital account openness,
that is, advanced nations that have more open capital accounts incur lower
costs. However, developing countries with more open capital accounts
incur higher costs. This relationship is also observed for the total period
under consideration (1990–2014).

Trade and Financial Variables

The size of a country's trade and exchange rate volatility is likely to affect
the extent of foreign exchange intervention. However, in their exploration
of the determinants of reserve holdings, Obstfeld et al. (2010) compare
whether trade-related or financial variables offer a better explanation
for the accumulation of reserves. They argue that financial motives have

always been an important motivation for the accumulation of reserves as an adverse shock to the balance of payments can arise from domestic deposit holders moving their assets abroad. In other words, in addition to sudden stops and share reversals of capital flows, capital flight is associated with domestic financial instability, and therefore domestic financial stability is an important consideration with regard to reserve accumulation. The central bank can stem the depreciation pressure in this event using its reserves. Obstfeld et al. (2010) argue that since the extent of the flight of capital out of domestic bank deposits depends on the size of M2 or the broad money supply, its size should play a role in determining the size of the reserve holdings of the central bank. Consequently, the size of M2 should play a role in determining the cost of foreign exchange intervention.

Additionally, the nature of the exchange rate regime is likely to have an impact on the size of reserve holdings. Having a pegged or de facto pegged exchange rate would require central banks to sell foreign exchange to stem pressures on the currency to depreciate and absorb foreign exchange to stem pressures on the currency to appreciate. Therefore, central banks in economies with pegged exchange rates are likely to hold higher reserves.

International Lender of Last Resort

It is striking that this system is consistently less expensive for advanced countries (see Figure 7.2). And this is despite the case that, on average, advanced economies are likely to have more open capital accounts than developing economies (see Figure 7.1). Why has this been the case? Feldstein (1999) argues that the only way to maintain private lending in an economy and increase credit is to ensure that lenders are reasonably sure of receiving a return on their investment. This can be done through ensuring the availability of some form of collateral. International reserves provide one form of collateral. However, a credible international lender of last resort (ILOLR) to which borrowers could turn to in the event of financial distress eliminates the need for such collateral. While some institutions have historically functioned as ILOLR at specific historical moments, in general there is no such consistent ILOLR. However, there are several institutional mechanisms through which the provision of an ILOLR is mimicked in times of financial distress. One such institutional arrangement is swap lines between central banks of several advanced economies. The role of these swap lines was exceptionally important during the recent financial crisis. However, not all countries have, historically, had access to the ILOLR in this form. This is particularly noteworthy since multilateral organizations such as the International Monetary Fund have not been very effective in playing the role of the ILOLR.

In the context of the British banking system in the nineteenth century, Bagehot (1873) argues that, to avoid a financial crisis in the face of a bank run and prevent a shortage of liquidity, the lender of last resort or the monetary authority should provide unlimited and automatic credit to any party with good collateral (McDowell, 2017). However, in general, no individual central bank can serve as central bank for the global financial system. McDowell (2017, p. 4) defines the ILOLR as "an actor that is prepared to respond to international financial crises by providing credit to illiquid institutions in foreign jurisdictions when no other actor is willing or able". In lender-of-last-resort operations, time is of the essence, as, in the absence of a timely injection of liquidity, a liquidity crisis can quickly morph into a solvency crisis. In this regard, the IMF has been inadequate as an ILOLR as it moves slowly, and often provides inadequate liquidity to financial systems in distress. However, in several instances, institutions in the United States have provided liquidity to foreign governments for the purposes of managing financial crises in the post-war period. Specifically, the Exchange Stabilization Fund of the US Treasury and the swap lines extended by the Federal Reserve have historically functioned as an ILOLR. Between 1980 and 2000, institutions in the United States effectively acted as the lender of last resort on 40 different occasions for about 20 countries (McDowell, 2017).

However, the United States has not provided the ILOLR facility uniformly. McDowell (2017) argues that the institutions that can function as the ILOLR in the United States, which are the Exchange Stabilization Fund of the US Treasury and the swap lines of the Federal Reserve in this analysis, have done so for foreign governments to prevent the collapse of their financial systems only insofar as the potential collapse of these financial systems jeopardizes the stability of the US financial system. This is not surprising since neither of these institutions has a mandate of stabilizing the global financial system. However, these institutions, specifically the Federal Reserve, are likely to be the most effective stabilizer of the global financial system since they have the power to create the global reserve currency, that is, the US dollar. The literature indicates the importance of access to these institutions. For instance, Bordo, Humpage and Schwartz (2014), find that during the Bretton Woods era, the mere announcement of an increase in the available credit under a pre-existing swap line stemmed the speculative sales of a deficit country's currency, even if the increased credit line was not actually drawn upon.

Specifically, the ILOLR facility has mostly been extended to advanced nations. Insofar as some developing countries have been recipients of assistance from the institutions that can function as ILOLR, the assistance has been less robust compared to that received by advanced nations. The central bank swap lines provided to the central banks of advanced nations were very large: in most instances, the size of the swap exceeded 50 percent of actual reserves. In the case of the European Central Bank, the size of the swap was larger than the size of the reserves held. However, for developing economies, the size of the swap never exceeded more than 50 percent of the reserves held (Obstfeld, Shambaugh and Taylor, 2009).

Therefore, the quasi-fiscal costs of holding reserves can potentially be mitigated by the extension of these institutional arrangements to developing countries, or creation of parallel arrangements between developing countries. To this end, several developing countries and emerging economies have formed regional agreements and mechanisms such as the Chiang Mai Initiative Multilateralization (CMIM), the Latin American Reserve Fund (FLAR), Arab Monetary Fund (ArMF), and the New Development Bank and contingent reserve arrangements (CRAs) of the BRICS countries (Grabel, 2015).

Being excluded from this institutional network of lender-of-last-resort operations partly explains the large accumulation of reserves and the cost associated with it. This suggests that the trends described in the chapter are not inevitable and can be avoided by, among other things, including emerging markets and developing economies in the access to the lender-of-last-resort facility.

CONCLUSION

This chapter documents the cost incurred in fairly common policy decisions undertaken by central banks all over the world, namely the costs of foreign exchange intervention. It shows that reserve accumulation resulting from foreign exchange interventions has increased substantially since the 1990s. The costs associated with these interventions have fluctuated, but have increased to large and significant magnitudes in recent years. The average policy configuration has moved away from the use of capital controls to manage the external account towards the reserve accumulation through frequent foreign exchange intervention. This has become standard practice in the existing international monetary system. However, this specific policy configuration is an expensive proposition as there is a significant cost associated with it. This cost is of concern as it is typically considered of second-order importance, and therefore has not drawn significant and systematic scrutiny. However, this chapter shows that its magnitude is not insignificant. Government surpluses always have many competing uses, and this cost being incurred by the fisc (that is, the amount of resources the government has at its disposal to spend) necessarily means that these resources cannot be used for a competing purpose, such as expenditure on health, education, poverty alleviation programs, or subsidies for crucial manufacturing industries. This is not to say that the trade-off is not worth it, as there are many reasons why central banks should hold reserves. However, the size of the trade-off varies across countries, which suggests that it is not inevitable.

The chapter also hypothesizes the reasons for this variation. Specifically, evidence suggests that, on average, developing and emerging economies incur a higher cost than advanced economies. Moreover, countries with more open capital accounts incur a higher cost compared to countries with less open capital accounts, which is consistent with the hypothesis that reserve accumulation through foreign exchange interventions has substituted for capital controls to some extent. However, this relationship is more pronounced for developing and emerging economies, and advanced countries are able to maintain more open capital accounts, hold fewer reserves, and incur a lower cost. This may be due to a variety of trade and financial variables, such as the exchange rate regime. However, it is also likely that access to an institutional network of emergency liquidity assistance from a de facto ILOLR, access to which is more common for advanced economies, reduces the need for foreign exchange intervention and reserve accumulation. The extent of the importance of these factors, and other potential factors, will be examined systematically in future work.

NOTES

1. While the country classification into developing and advanced countries is based on the *World Economic Situation and Prospects* report of the UN, the classification as emerging economies is more ambiguous. Here, countries are classified based on the country classification used in Chinn and Ito (2006).
2. Unconventional monetary policy during the recent financial crisis in some countries, notwithstanding.
3. While appreciation in the price of gold can be considered a return on reserve holdings, it is excluded in the estimation of costs in Figure 7.2. This is unlikely to significantly affect the cost estimate since an increasing proportion of reserves is being held in the form of non-gold assets at least in developing and emerging economies. However, about 50 percent of reserves of advanced economies are held in the form of gold reserves.

REFERENCES

Adler, G. and R. Mano (2016), *The Cost of Foreign Exchange Intervention: Concepts and Measurement*, Washington, DC: International Monetary Fund.

Adler, G. and C.E.T. Mora (2011), "Foreign exchange intervention: A shield against appreciation winds?," *IMF Working Paper No. 11/165*.

Aizenman, J. and J. Lee (2007), "International reserves: Precautionary versus mercantilist views, theory and evidence," *Open Economies Review*, **18**(2), 191–214.

Aizenman, J., M.D. Chinn and H. Ito (2010), "The emerging global financial architecture: Tracing and evaluating new patterns of the trilemma configuration," *Journal of International Money and Finance*, **29**(4), 615–41.

Bagehot, W. (1873), *Lombard Street: A Description of the Money Market*, New York: Scribner, Armstrong & Company.

Blanchard, O. and G. Adler (2015), "Can foreign exchange intervention stem exchange rate pressures from global capital flow shocks?," *NBER Working Paper No. w21427*.

Bordo, M.D., O.F. Humpage and A.J. Schwartz (2014), "The evolution of the Federal Reserve swap lines since 1962," *IMF Economic Review*, **63**(2), 353–72.

Bussière, M., G. Cheng, M.D. Chinn and N. Lisack (2015), "For a few dollars more: Reserves and growth in times of crises," *Journal of International Money and Finance*, **52**, 127–45.

Cheung, Y.-W. and H. Ito (2009), "A cross-country empirical analysis of international reserves," *International Economic Journal*, **23**(4), 447–81.

Chinn, M.D. and H. Ito (2006), "What matters for financial development? Capital controls, institutions, and interactions," *Journal of Development Economics*, **81**(1), 163–92.

Dominguez, K.M. (2012), "Foreign reserve management during the Global Financial Crisis," *Journal of International Money and Finance*, **31**(8), 2017–37.

Dominguez, K.M. and J.A. Frankel (1993), "Does foreign-exchange intervention matter? The portfolio effect," *The American Economic Review*, **83**(5), 1356–69.

Fatum, R. and M.M. Hutchison (2003), "Is sterilized foreign exchange intervention effective after all? An event study approach," *The Economic Journal*, **113**(487), 390–411.

Feldstein, M. (1999), "A self-help guide for emerging markets," *Foreign Affairs*, **78**(2), 93–109.

Fratzscher, M., O. Gloede and L. Menkhoff et al. (2017), "When is foreign exchange intervention effective? Evidence from 33 countries," *CEPR Discussion Paper No. DP12510*.

Grabel, I. (2015), "Post-crisis experiments in development finance architectures: A Hirschmanian perspective on 'productive incoherence'," *Review of Social Economy*, **73**(4), 388–414.

Ilzetzki, E., C.M. Reinhart and K.S. Rogoff (2017), "Exchange arrangements entering the 21st century: Which anchor will hold?," *NBER Working Paper No. w23134*.

McDowell, D. (2017), *Brother, Can You Spare a Billion?: The United States, the IMF, and the International Lender of Last Resort*, Oxford: Oxford University Press.

Menkhoff, L. (2013), "Foreign exchange intervention in emerging markets: A survey of empirical studies," *The World Economy*, **36**(9), 1187–208.

Obstfeld, M., J.C. Shambaugh and A.M. Taylor (2009), "Financial instability, reserves, and central bank swap lines in the panic of 2008," *American Economic Review*, **99**(2), 480–86.

Obstfeld, M., J.C. Shambaugh and A.M. Taylor (2010), "Financial stability, the trilemma, and international reserves," *American Economic Journal: Macroeconomics*, **2**(2), 57–94.

Rodrik, D. (2006), "The social cost of foreign exchange reserves," *International Economic Journal*, **20**(3), 253–66.

Steiner, A. (2017), "Central banks and macroeconomic policy choices: Relaxing the trilemma," *Journal of Banking & Finance*, **77**, 283–99.

Yeyati, E.L. (2008), "The cost of reserves," *Economics Letters*, **100**(1), 39–42.

8. Monetary policy under financial dollarization: The case of the Eurasian Economic Union

Zhandos Ybrayev

INTRODUCTION

There is a growing trend among central banks in developing nations to start adopting inflation-targeting monetary policy. However, despite the general improvement in controlling price levels over the last two decades, a substantial number of the population in the developing world still save and borrow in major foreign currencies. This high level of financial dollarization can complicate the conduct of monetary policy in different ways: higher upward inflationary pressures, balance sheets effects in the banking sector, and exchange rate fluctuations causing changes in the composition of household savings. These persistent effects are in line with initial Latin American case studies documented by Ize and Yeyati (2003), where even an extended period of macroeconomic stability did not contribute to a decline in the level of foreign-denominated financial assets in those economies.

Earlier literature on dollarization, for example, Freeman and Kydland (2000) and Calvo (2002), largely addressed the issue of currency substitution, or foreign currency primarily used as a means of payment and a unit of account, but not as a store of value. Therefore, previous investigations dealt with network externalities and the costs of switching the currency of denomination. However, prior debates did not establish theoretical justifications for changes in factors affecting the choice of currency of financial assets and corresponding inflation-level dynamics. At the same time, there are reasons to believe that a high degree of financial dollarization (holdings by a country's residents of financial assets and liabilities denominated in a foreign currency) might impose difficulties in both the transmission capacity of monetary policy and the overall functioning of the financial sector. In a standard emerging market economy, for example, where external debts of domestic firms are predominantly dominated in foreign currency, but which heavily rely on earnings in domestic currency, this potentially increases the fragility of the domestic banking sector due to well-documented issues of currency mismatches. This vulnerability, in turn, amplifies exchange rates risks, which in part is a consequence of a monetary policy that is concerned only with inflation and not with exchange rates.

The aim of this chapter is to investigate whether highly financially dollarized economies experience sufficiently lower inflation; to look at the effects of high levels of financial dollarization on the financial industry; and finally, formulate some relevant policy recommendations to reduce the potentially dangerous effects of a very high degree of financial dollarization. The chapter is organized as follows. The next section defines and provides a theoretical background on the phenomenon of financial dollarization. The third section presents the key sources of financial dollarization. The fourth discusses the transmission channels between financial dollarization and inflation, and describes the main obstacles these channels present to inflation-targeting monetary policy. The fifth demonstrates key findings from regression analysis based on a sample of Eurasian Economic Union member-states that have already adopted inflation-targeting monetary policies: Russia, Kazakhstan, and Armenia. The last section concludes with a number of policy suggestions derived from successful de-dollarization practices of different countries.

WHAT IS FINANCIAL DOLLARIZATION?

The first general use of the term dollarization refers to 1970s' currency-substitution cases in Latin America. These cases – in Peru, Mexico, Argentina, Chile, and Ecuador – represent the first attempts to analyze the consequences of abandoning local currency in favor of the US dollar and its effects on domestic monetary policy (Licandro and Licandro, 2003; Morón and Castro, 2003; Mishkin, 2011). Today, the term dollarization encompasses a number of economic phenomena related to the use of foreign currency within a country. Official or full dollarization is the case where the foreign currency is given (exclusively) legal tender status. Unofficial dollarization (also known as partial dollarization) broadly indicates the use of a foreign currency alongside the national currency when the former is not legal tender (Ize and Yeyati, 2003). Also, within partial dollarization is a distinction based on the different functions of money: the currency substitution effect refers to the use of a foreign currency as a medium of exchange, and the asset substitution effect refers to the use of a foreign currency as a store of value. According to Calvo

(2002), definitional distinctions also reveal differences in function. Thus, the concept of official dollarization implies that the nominal interest rate differential of financial assets should eventually bring about no difference in real returns, and consequently, will lead to the exclusion of any inflation-related risks. Therefore, a measure of dollar share of bank deposits, for instance, reflects the composition of financial assets, which is primarily an asset substitution case. While asset substitution mainly relates to the asset side of banks' balance sheets and thus the people's savings, the other side of this concept concentrates on liability dollarization, analyzing the foreign currency-denominated debt as a source of greater financial instability and issues with currency mismatches. As a result, the overall term financial dollarization refers specifically to the holdings by a country's residents of financial assets and liabilities denominated in a foreign currency. It also involves the fact that observed dollarization reflects both the demand and the supply of dollar assets, which further conveys an analysis of both sides of banks' balance sheets. The chapter next explores the main sources of financial dollarization and its relation to inflation dynamics in each country using the available records on Kazakhstan, Russia, and Armenia.

WHAT ARE THE SOURCES OF FINANCIAL DOLLARIZATION?

One of the early literatures on dollarization tackles the currency substitution effect (Calvo, 2002) and explores the holding of foreign money balances to hedge against expected risks and returns between different currencies. The consensus view presented in this literature is that monetary policy inefficiency is due to perfect substitutability between local and foreign currencies, which also means that the elasticity of this substitution is expected to rise in times of high exchange rate fluctuations. This view directly opposes the notion of adopting a floating exchange rate regime and having greater monetary policy autonomy. The last decade has been viewed as a reversal toward the new monetary policy methods and macroeconomic governance within the countries of the Eurasian Economic Union (Blockmans, Vorobiev and Kostanyan, 2012). In particular, Russia, Armenia and Kazakhstan have already announced the adoption of new monetary policy goals and switched to the flexible exchange rate regime.

The substitution approach suggests that the ratio between national and foreign currency holdings is a function of the interest rate differential between domestic and foreign interest rates. Thus, assuming perfect capital mobility and interest rate parity holds, domestic interest rates depend on the expected rate of depreciation, and thus, on the effect on expected inflation. Therefore, domestic residents have a strong preference to diversify the portfolio composition of their currency funds. Nevertheless, the persistence of a high level of dollarization in the 1990s in Latin America, at the same time as the domestic inflation rates in those countries of the region were significantly reduced, contradicts this view. According to Savastano (1996), however, the persistence of a high level of financial dollarization and the currency substitution effect after a period of stability is due to what they call past inflation memory, which provokes high inflation expectations even after a continuous favorable macroeconomic environment. The remedy they propose to counter this "memory" is to provide the economy with a long period of appreciation combined with low inflation to revert the system, which also reiterates the point that dollarization is mostly a response to past inflation.

In 2000, Freeman and Kydland updated the study of the currency substitution concept by examining the substitution between foreign currency and the less liquid components of domestic currency (e.g., time deposits) instead of between two types of currencies. According to Freeman and Kydland's analysis, foreign currency performs the role of a financial asset that is prone to future inflationary pressures and is also less liquid than the domestic currency. This analysis, verified by a large set of empirical tests, mainly contributes to a more realistic modeling of the currency substitution hypothesis, which also helps to formulate stronger results on the implications of welfare economics (i.e., real returns on domestic financial assets, for example). The workings of the model resonate with previous research that views the use of foreign currency mainly as a medium of exchange. Therefore, when the inflation rate is low, the use of foreign currency is minimal. Furthermore, some moderate level of inflation leads to the incorporation of a store-of-value function of foreign exchange, but still limited for the purchase of big-ticket items. At the time of rapid and high inflation, residents start to use foreign currency in transactions for a greater set of goods and services. Overall, the study advocates that a high level of financial dollarization enhances the welfare of households at extremely high levels of inflation, but reduces it when inflation stabilizes at rates lower than some minimal threshold level.

Ize and Yeyati (2003) propose another approach to identifying the drivers of dollarization – the minimum variance portfolio (MVP) allocation method. Because the currency composition comes from both sides of a bank's balance sheets, deposit and loan dollarization is highly correlated with key interest rates in the economy. Consequently, according to the MVP method, the degree of dollarization can be explained by inflation and real exchange rate depreciation rather than expected inflation and nominal depreciation, as in the case of currency substitution models. In other words, whereas the real return of national currency depends on changes in inflation, the real return on foreign currency depends on changes in the real exchange rate. As a result, stabilization-oriented monetary policy without the real exchange rate target may contribute towards the de-dollarization processes. This approach serves as an alternative way to explain dollarization hysteresis (a persistent high level of dollarization despite efforts to bring it down) without reference to past inflation memory. Accordingly, high levels of dollarization may still occur when the memory of previous macroeconomic discrepancies is not an issue and volatility of inflation stays high relative to the real exchange rate. The main conclusion from Ize and Yeyati (2003) is that inflation-targeting policy, which is usually combined with a free-floating exchange rate regime should lead to a decrease in the dollarization level because of an increased variability of the real exchange rate. It is important to note, however, that their observation is subject to a moderate degree of real dollarization when prices and wages are denominated in foreign currency.

It is argued that additional important sources of dollarization are due to a set of institutional factors. There are different ways in which the quality of institutions may provoke the beginning of a dollarization process within the country. For instance, according to De Nicolo and Zepharin et al. (2003), weak institutions may detract from the credibility of a commitment not to bail out foreign-denominated debt in the aftermath of a sudden devaluation, which can lead to a mispriced link to implicit government guarantees. Moreover, weak institutions may undermine the credibility of domestic monetary policies, as residents fear that their governments will erode the value of financial assets by generating unexpected future inflation. Levy Yeyati (2006) includes an index for restrictions against the holding of foreign currency-denominated deposits by residents (restrictions against dollarization) as well as other proxy variables to indicate the quality of institutions. In general, his results demonstrate a negative relationship between the level of dollarization and restrictions on dollarization. Thus, the fear that the policy may change in the future leads to dollarization even in a low-inflation setting. As a result, improvement in the quality of institutions is a major requirement for emerging market economies to reduce their vulnerability to extensive depreciation.

MONETARY POLICY UNDER A HIGH DEGREE OF FINANCIAL DOLLARIZATION

Standard, small, open-economy inflation-targeting models identify a central role for the exchange rate in the transmission mechanisms from monetary policy to inflation (Leiderman, Maino and Parrado, 2006). In addition, the high level of dollarization in a country has immediate effects on exchange rate flexibility. Thus, this chapter argues that high levels of dollarization reduce the effectiveness of monetary policy through banks' balance sheet effects and changes in deposit composition. Hence, a rise in the key domestic interest rate with the long-term purpose of combatting inflation typically causes short-term nominal and real exchange rate appreciation, which finally helps to reduce initial inflationary pressures through both direct and indirect transmission channels. The direct effect comes through the change in tradable goods due to a change in the exchange rate, and the indirect effect works through the contractionary impact on aggregate demand, output, and prices. When analyzing highly financially dollarized economies, it is important to stress the fact that a substantial share of deposits and thus loans in the banking sector are denominated in foreign currency (Licandro and Licandro, 2003). Immediately, therefore, the exchange rate takes on an even greater anchoring role compared to less dollarized countries, potentially inducing a higher exchange rate pass-through (elasticity of domestic import prices with respect to exchange rate changes). In addition, large fluctuations in foreign exchange may also raise credibility issues. Potentially adverse effects of exchange rate oscillations are likely to induce fear of floating by monetary authorities and require that they closely target exchange rate stability. Implementation of foreign exchange interventions might help to maintain such policy, and can also be successful for inflation-targeting economies since large oscillations of the exchange rate prevent utilization of a store-of-value function of the dollar.

One of the main characteristics of inflation-targeting monetary policy is an actual free floating of the exchange rate, which principally makes the domestic inflation level the "nominal anchor" for the real economy. If economic agents do not have sufficient information about the average price level and its most likely future dynamic patterns, there is a greater risk that they will misallocate resources due to incorrect observations of changes in relative prices. Thus, having a well-recognized and easily understandable anchor provides better communication with the public. In a system of fiat money, it is essential to put an additional constraint on monetary policy to limit the price level to a particular level at a specific period of time. As a result, an institutional commitment to long-run price stability is also an effective way to launch a nominal anchor. In addition, according to Mishkin, emerging market economies are often subject to disruptive effects of exchange rate fluctuations (2011). Too frequent and substantial interventions in the foreign exchange market might pose greater risks of turning the exchange rate into a nominal anchor. Therefore, it is very important to run a transparent monetary policy that will allow smoothing of short-run exchange rate volatility. Thus, a high level of financial dollarization would affect monetary policy through the exchange rate and would imply three outcomes: upward inflationary pressures, balance sheet effects of banks (change in deposit compositions), and a potential higher impact of exchange rate pass-through.

The actual circulation of a foreign currency alongside the local currency in a given economy certainly affects the conduct of domestic monetary policy and its ultimate goal – the level of inflation. Therefore, the earlier literature on this subject reiterated the fact that dollarization, by reducing the costs of switching to foreign currency to mitigate the negative effects of rapid inflationary pressures, also increases people's mistrust in their own domestic currency, which may increase the uncertainty in money demand accounting mechanisms, thus also impacting the capacity of the central bank to conduct monetary policy. While the very roots of this argument come from the currency substitution aspect of dollarization, it is still useful to link that type of reasoning to the dollarization of domestic savings accounts (Cowan and Do, 2003).

An additional fundamental concern related to financial dollarization is its potential to increase the degree to which the financial sector is prone to default (i.e., financial fragility). For instance, De Nicolo, Honohan and Ize (2003) recently demonstrated empirically that a dollarized banking sector is characterized by higher insolvency risk and higher deposit volatility. Currency mismatches can affect banks' balance sheets directly or indirectly by undermining the quality of their dollar loan portfolio. Banks with massive domestic dollar liabilities must balance their foreign exchange positions by either extending dollar lending to local currency earners or holding dollar assets abroad. To maintain their profitability and satisfy demand for loans, banks end up lending a large share of their dollar deposits domestically, which effectively transfers exchange rate risks to their unhedged clients while banks retain the resulting credit risk. Thus, currency mismatches in the event of large depreciations can have devastating effects and generate broad macro-systemic negative effects, particularly regarding output losses. As a result, a high degree of financial dollarization significantly affects the ability to conduct sound inflation-targeting monetary policy, which implies the existence of only one nominal anchor: overall price stability instead of popular alternatives to exchange rate- or real GDP-targeting regimes.

THE EURASIAN ECONOMIC UNION

After the collapse of the Soviet Union, newly created independent states began economic integration processes to strengthen their former economic ties. Among different attempts to build an effective alliance, the one between Kazakhstan, Russia, and Belorussia has been most successful. In 2012, the three countries transformed their customs union into a single economic space. They later signed an agreement to create the EEU (Treaty), and on January 1, 2015, the EEU was officially created. Armenia and the Kyrgyz Republic joined the Union later that year. The Eurasian Economic Union is an international organization for regional economic integration with an international legal personality established by the Treaty on the EEU. It provides free movement of goods and services, capital and labor, and pursues a coordinated single policy in the sectors designated by the Treaty and international agreements within the Union. The Eurasian Economic Union has an integrated, single market of 183 million people and a combined gross domestic product (GDP) of over 4 trillion US dollars (Blockmans et al., 2012). The Union operates through supranational and intergovernmental institutions. In addition, provisions for an optimal currency space and greater macroeconomic policy cooperation are envisioned in the future. As a result, current official implementation of inflation targeting by most of its member-states is considered to be a harmonization phase of their monetary policies.

This chapter focuses on Armenia, Russia, and Kazakhstan as they already run an inflation-targeting monetary policy and are also characterized as having a high degree of financial dollarization. Hence, empirical testing is based on macroeconomic variables derived from the above-mentioned countries and is considered to be a main contribution to the study of highly dollarized economies and their monetary policy efficacy. Figure 8.1 demonstrates respective annual inflation growth rates of our sample countries. The series runs from 2007m1 to 2017m1 (that is, monthly data). All the data are derived from each country's respective central bank websites. From Figure 8.1, we can identify two major inflationary episodes. One of them occurred in the aftermath of the Global Financial Crisis of 2008 and the second occurred after the free floating of their exchange rates and a subsequent sharp decline in world oil prices in 2015, affecting both oil exporting countries in the region. This graph generally shows a high vulnerability of these states to externally generated shocks. It is worth mentioning that Armenia has recently experienced an actual disinflation period.

Figures 8.2 through 8.4 indicate corresponding foreign currency-denominated deposits ratios in Armenia, Russia and Kazakhstan. These

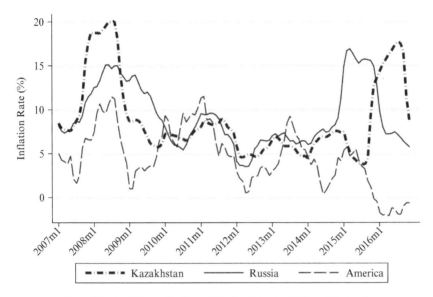

Sources: Central Bank of Armenia, Central Bank of Russia, National Bank of Kazakhstan.

Figure 8.1   Annual inflation rates in Kazakhstan, Russia, and Armenia

figures also demonstrate the overall dynamics of dollarized deposits to total deposits relative to inflation. As I mentioned above, the best technique to estimate the level of financial dollarization is to measure the share of foreign currency deposits over total deposits within a country. Also, it is important to mention that the highest level of financial dollarization is in Armenia, which is consistently around 70 percent. At the same time, the lowest level is in Russia and fluctuates steadily around 25–30 percent. Also, for the past several years, Kazakhstan has experienced a surge in its foreign currency deposits ratio with a recent ratio of dollarization between 50 and 60 percent.

EMPIRICAL TESTS

Based on data from the countries of Eurasian Economic Union over the period 2007–17, this chapter estimates two main channels through which a high level of financial dollarization can affect monetary policy. First, a current structural issue in all three countries is that banks have a comparatively large number of foreign exchange deposits on the liability

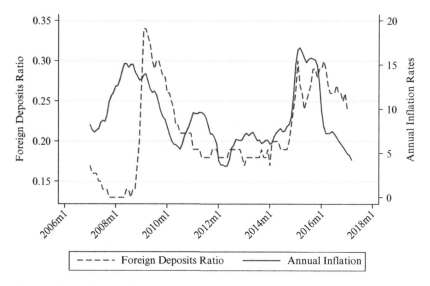

Source: Central Bank of Russia.

Figure 8.2   Foreign deposits ratio and inflation in Russia

side of their balance sheets. However, domestic payments are mainly made in their respective national currencies, which exposes banks to greater risks, especially in times of large depreciations. Thus, the first question we want to explore is how exchange rate fluctuations affect the composition of domestic savings. Taking into account the current underdevelopment of financial instruments to facilitate saving, bank deposits remain the most reliable indicator of household savings. At the same time, central banks in all three countries publish reports on domestic deposits both in domestic and foreign currencies. Therefore, financial dollarization is computed as the ratio of total foreign currency deposits to total domestic deposits at the end of each month.

We expect that the exchange rate fluctuations should affect deposit composition, suggesting that monetary policy itself stimulates economic agents to switch savings in foreign currency. In this model, the dependent variable is the first-differenced ratio of foreign currency deposits (ΔFD). We regress this variable on a set of independent variables: the first difference of the nominal exchange rate (Δer), consumer price inflation (CPI) annual rates ($\Delta \pi$), the logged difference of the money supply ($\Delta M2$), the first difference of the monthly-adjusted key interest rate (Δi), and the annual growth rate of the industrial production index (Δgdp) that

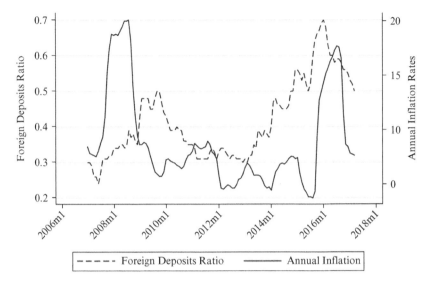

Source: National Bank of Kazakhstan.

Figure 8.3   Foreign deposits ratio and inflation in Kazakhstan

will serve us as proxy of real GDP over the given period. Then, we test whether our series contains unit roots by performing the augmented Dickey-Fuller (ADF) test. For all three cases, we cannot reject the null hypothesis of a unit root at standard levels. At the same time, first differences of our variables make them stationary, which implies that the series are I(1). Next, we repeat the same technique with the difference of total deposits ratio (ΔTD) as a dependent variable and compare the outcomes:

$$\Delta FD(t) = \alpha 0 + \beta 1 \Delta er + \beta 2 \Delta \pi + \beta 3 \Delta i + \beta 4 \Delta gdp + \varepsilon(t),$$

$$\Delta TD(t) = \alpha 0 + \beta 1 \Delta er + \beta 2 \Delta \pi + \beta 3 \Delta i + \beta 4 \Delta gdp + \varepsilon(t).$$

Table 8.1 presents regression results on both the total and foreign currency savings separately.

The results of the above regressions suggest that savers in Eurasian Economic Union member countries switch to foreign-denominated assets when the exchange rate depreciates in all three cases. The financial dollarization index, measured as the ratio of foreign deposits to total domestic deposits, responds twice as much to the exchange rate than to the total deposits ratio alone. The results are also statistically significant

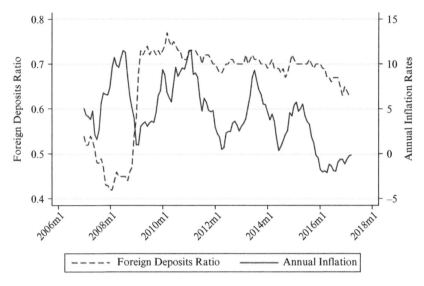

Source: Central Bank of Armenia.

Figure 8.4   Foreign deposits ratio and inflation in Armenia

at the 1 percent level, whereas other control variables do not demonstrate any significant explanatory power. Therefore, we conclude that exchange rate changes (controlling for inflation) mainly impact the composition of total saving and not the overall quantity. Since the historical data does not differentiate between various origins of the exchange rate shocks, based on estimated parameters a 10 percent depreciation would lead to at least a 10 percent increase in the foreign currency deposits ratio in all three countries. As a result, any concerns with increasing financial dollarization should address the issue of exchange rate stability.

The second question that we address is an implication of dollarization on domestic prices, and specifically, whether highly financially dollarized economies tend to exhibit higher inflation. To do this, I add specific structural change factors to test if the actual period after the introduction of an inflation-targeting monetary policy brings any significant changes in comparison to our benchmark model. I specify a structural break dummy into our model, which is the time period when an inflation-targeting monetary regime was introduced in each country separately. I do this to trace out the effects on inflation and discuss any potential exchange rate pass-through effects under the most common monetary policy in the region:

Table 8.1 Changes in deposit composition

Variables	(1) Δ Total Deposits Ratio (Kazakhstan)	(2) Δ Foreign Deposits Ratio (Kazakhstan)	(3) Δ Total Deposits Ratio (Russia)	(4) Δ Foreign Deposits Ratio (Russia)	(5) Δ Total Deposits Ratio (Armenia)	(6) Δ Foreign Deposits Ratio (Armenia)
Δ Exch. rate	0.00203***	0.00453***	0.00308***	0.01454***	0.00117***	0.00189***
	(0.00028)	(0.00083)	(0.00061)	(0.00204)	(0.00033)	(0.00052)
Δ Inflation	0.00013	0.00057	0.00032	0.00157	0.00074	0.00162
	(0.00041)	(0.00122)	(0.00040)	(0.00133)	(0.00081)	(0.00127)
Δ M2	0.58406***	0.00537	0.44614***	-0.33438**	0.23063***	-0.05296
	(0.05512)	(0.16324)	(0.04313)	(0.14510)	(0.06004)	(0.09409)
Δ Interest rate	-0.00719**	-0.01626**	-0.00306*	0.00756	-0.00274	-0.01189
	(0.00277)	(0.00820)	(0.00174)	(0.00586)	(0.00878)	(0.01376)
Δ GDP	0.00038	-0.00014	0.00000	-0.00177**	0.00015	-0.00096*
	(0.00049)	(0.00145)	(0.00025)	(0.00086)	(0.00037)	(0.00058)
Constant	0.00271	0.00821	0.00616	0.00677	0.01024**	0.01342*
	(0.00428)	(0.01268)	(0.00405)	(0.01364)	(0.00479)	(0.00751)
R-squared	0.60989	0.23582	0.54659	0.44693	0.16439	0.18112

Note: Standard errors in parentheses; *** $p < 0.01$, ** $p < 0.05$, * $p < 0.1$.

$$\Delta \pi(t) = \alpha 0 + \beta 1 \Delta FD + \beta 2 \Delta M2 + \beta 3 \Delta i + \beta 4 \Delta gdp$$
$$+ \beta 5 \Delta er + \beta 6 (Dt^* \Delta FD) + \varepsilon(t).$$

According to Table 8.2, in all three cases (Armenia, Russia and Kazakhstan), the results confirm the expectations that financial dollarization (ratio of foreign currency deposits to total deposits) is positively associated with a higher inflation response. In other words, an increase in dollar holdings by domestic agents will likely lead to an increase in general prices. However, though the financial dollarization coefficients exhibit large numbers, they are not statistically significant. Similarly, in most cases we have obtained the expected and correct positive correlation for interest rates, exchange rates (depreciation goes with positive sign), money supply growth. The most likely interpretation for the interest rate variable is an issue of reverse causation, since increases in dollarization levels push banks to raise interest rates on domestic deposits. We have also obtained different coefficients for real GDP. This might be because our industrial production index is an inadequate proxy for GDP. Alternatively, this result might be due to the fact that there are various sources of income in those countries that are difficult to capture

Table 8.2   Dollarization and inflation

Variables	(1) Δ Inflation (Kazakhstan)	(2) Δ Inflation (Russia)	(3) Δ Inflation (Armenia)
Δ FD ratio	3.43357	7.92874	8.87176
	(7.34820)	(6.69242)	(6.96464)
Δ M2 supply	12.69684	1.19748	−0.02662
	(12.59230)	(10.53788)	(6.96396)
Δ Interest rate	−0.34162	0.11428	4.42431***
	(0.64586)	(0.41852)	(0.93001)
Δ GDP	0.09225	−0.21859***	0.01283
	(0.11219)	(0.05844)	(0.04303)
Δ Exch. rate	−0.01331	0.02443	−0.07868*
	(0.07233)	(0.17503)	(0.04020)
Structural break	0.56904***	0.13112***	−0.12119**
	(0.07967)	(0.04999)	(0.05609)
Constant	3.43357	7.92874	4.46230***
	(7.34820)	(6.69242)	(0.37047)
R-squared	0.02564	0.16961	0.19548

Note: Standard errors in parentheses; *** $p < 0.01$, ** $p < 0.05$, * $p < 0.1$.

only through industrial production, for example, foreign remittances. However, the directly proportional link between financial dollarization and inflation (correlation between foreign currency deposit ratio and inflation rate) cannot be taken as a sign that monetary policy is less effective under a high degree of financial dollarization. In fact, a higher price response does not restrain the scope for monetary policy by the regional central banks. In particular, even if a response by a contractionary monetary policy to increase the interest rate differential eventually facilitates a decrease in foreign currency deposits, a set of regulatory policies are bound to be more effective to reduce the harmful effects of financial dollarization.

It is essential to note that this model is not intended to examine the short-run elasticity of inflation, but rather to test whether and to what extent financial dollarization affects our monetary variables of interest. Since Armenia is the only country in the sample that is experiencing inflation targeting for an extended period of time, we can clearly see that over time the change in inflation response fraction eventually turns negative, which implies that the inflation-targeting monetary policy might prove effective in reducing the adverse effects of deposit dollarization. Similarly, the case of Kazakhstan and Russia that switched to the new monetary agenda relatively recently, also verifies the fact that economic agents in an environment of immediate uncertainty prefer shifting their savings into foreign-denominated financial assets. Overall, according to our regression estimates, in the short run we can conclude that financially dollarized economies of the Eurasian Economic Union are associated with higher inflation rates.

Dollarization is one of the most distinct characteristics of developing nations in general and of the Eurasian Economic Union countries in particular. Negative effects of dollarization on macroeconomic dynamics at this early stage of development in sample countries mostly consist of a high degree of uncertainty and the implementation of money and credit policies. As mentioned above, our results also predict that higher inflation and higher inflation volatility lead to reallocation in agents' portfolios. Correspondingly, we can conjecture that in a high- and moderate-inflation background, financial dollarization results from a lack of trust in the national currency stemming from the belief that monetary authorities will not necessarily follow policies that will ensure long-run currency stability. As a result, improving the central bank's accountability and transparency along with the ability to actually achieve its main policy goals have proven to reduce the dollarization level since the public will no longer need to protect their wealth through the usage of financial dollarization. Overall, the results of these empirical tests suggest that financial dollarization would likely persist if the exchange rate fluctuations remain high, which in turn would create conditions for higher inflation environments.

DE-DOLLARIZATION STRATEGIES FOR THE EURASIAN ECONOMIC UNION

Since this chapter argues that the high level of dollarization is a serious obstacle to efficient monetary policy, we provide ways to combat high dollarization in this section. Our method is to draw upon successful examples around the world and isolate a set of tools that proved effective. First, prudential requirements must be stricter when dealing with a financial system that lends to an agent who receives its income in domestic currency. Liquidity requirements also must be higher in foreign currency transactions, reflecting the inability of central banks to perform their lender-of-last-resort role in foreign currency. Generally, the road to reducing dollarization should be based on discouraging the use of the dollar and enhancing the attractiveness of domestic currency as a medium of exchange. Therefore, measures are needed to ensure that hidden externalities are properly internalized through enhanced prudential settings. One of the major preconditions of de-dollarization is a credible commitment to price stability and sound monetary policy to finally gain a stable market share for domestic currency.

Reinhart, Rogoff and Savastano (2003) state that only a small number of countries managed to successfully de-dollarize their locally issued foreign currency obligations, either by amortizing the debt stock at the initial terms or by changing the currency denomination of the debt. In addition, authors searched for scenarios where the ratio of foreign deposits to broad money declined by 20 percent and then moved to a level below 20 percent immediately after the decline and remained there until the end of the sample period. As a result, they have identified only four countries out of 85 that met those initial conditions during the period 1980–2001. It is worth mentioning that when transition economies experienced a sharp decline in their foreign deposits ratio below 20 percent, including Russia, they usually followed up with an increase in dollarization ratio exceeding that initial level of 20 percent. However, in three of the four cases mentioned above, as soon as the monetary authorities imposed restrictions on the convertibility of dollar deposits, the reversal of a decline in dollarization had taken place. The authors conclude that only Israel and Poland appear to have experienced a large and lasting de-dollarization process, which was also supplemented by a successful disinflation program based around a strong exchange rate anchor and the introduction of various financial assets with alternative forms of returns.

Galindo and Leiderman (2005) analyze de-dollarization attempts by conducting a survey among central banks in Latin America. They report that one of the most useful strategies in the effort to de-dollarize is developing CPI-indexed domestic financial instruments during a time of high and volatile inflation. In addition, these authors suggest that the latest trend is to develop an independent and fully competitive market for domestic financial assets, where Chile and Peru are the best examples. Furthermore, in the case of Peru, Morón and Castro (2003) argue that the detrimental effects of financial dollarization are experienced through balance sheet effects that intensify the effect of external shocks on real macroeconomic variables. The authors find that regulatory tools that are based on encouraging residents toward the use of local currency-denominated assets may also lead to capital flight. Thus, an inflation-targeting regime is considered a useful strategy to combat dollarization. The experience of Uruguay in de-dollarization can be summarized by two main channels: the development of a market in national currency to generate a credible alternative to foreign currency; and the strengthening of the safety net through the regulatory identification of non-marketable risks. Finally, the unique example of Chile refers to policy measures such as strict capital controls, prudent fiscal policy, improved institutional design, and a combination of private and fully funded pension systems.

CONCLUSION

The aim of this chapter was to search for the links between financial dollarization and its effect on the conduct of monetary policy, and specifically of inflation targeting as a main policy strategy in developing countries. Therefore, key drivers of dollarization were identified first, and then a number of consequences were provided in relation to macroeconomic and financial variables. Due to the lack of empirical studies, there were a number of incomplete policy debates that do not take into account historical facts of particular regions.

Based on data from the Eurasian Economic Union countries, our empirical tests have shown that a high level of financial dollarization tends to increase upward inflationary pressures at least in the short run, and change the composition of total savings away from domestic currencies toward foreign ones, which potentially increases financial fragility in the banking sector. Thus, persistent high levels of financial dollarization imply

172   *The political economy of international finance in an age of inequality*

that monetary policy is significantly limited through a greater exposure of the banking sector to currency mismatches issues, which further increases demand for foreign assets.

As a result, important monetary concepts such as credibility and trust in domestic financial instruments take time to build, and even more time is necessary in already highly financially dollarized economies. As a result, the policy mix of inflation-targeting monetary policy and high level of financial dollarization leaves central banks with a small choice of instruments with which to respond to macroeconomic and financial challenges. It would be helpful to find more macroeconomic instruments to help achieve macroeconomic goals. Thus, any successful approach to reduce that excessive level of dollarization would include a set of macro-prudential regulations in the financial market.

REFERENCES

Blockmans, S., I. Vorobiev and H. Kostanyan (2012), "Towards a Eurasian Economic Union: The challenge of integration and unity," *CEPS Special Report No. 75*.

Calvo, G. (2002), "On dollarization," *Economics of Transition*, **10**(2), 393–403.

Cowan, K. and Q. Do (2003), "Financial dollarization and central bank credibility," *Policy Research Working Paper No. 3082*, Washington, DC: World Bank.

De Nicolo, G., P. Honohan and A. Ize (2003), "Dollarization of the banking system: Good or bad?," *IMF Working Paper No. 03/146*.

De Nicolo, G., M.G. Zepharin, P.F. Bartholomew and J. Zaman (2003), "Bank consolidation, conglomeration, and internationalization: Trends and implications for financial risk," *IMF Working Paper No. 03/158*.

Freeman, S. and F.E. Kydland (2000), "Monetary aggregates and output," *The American Economic Review*, **90**(5), 1125–35.

Galindo, A. and L. Leiderman (2005), "Living with dollarization and the route to dedollarization," *Inter-American Development Bank Working Paper No. 526*.

Ize, A. and E.L. Yeyati (2003), "Financial dollarization," *Journal of International Economics*, **59**, 323–47.

Leiderman, L., R. Maino and E. Parrado (2006), "Inflation targeting in dollarized economies," in A. Armas, A. Ize and E.L. Yeyati (eds), *Financial Dollarization: Procyclicality of Financial Systems in Asia*, London: Palgrave Macmillan, pp. 99–114.

Licandro, G. and J.A. Licandro (2003), "Building the dedollarization agenda: Lessons from the Uruguayan case," mimeo, Central Bank of Uruguay.

Mishkin, F. (2011), "Inflation targeting in emerging economies," *NBER Working Papers No. 7618*.

Morón, E. and J.F. Castro (2003), "De-dollarizing the Peruvian economy: A portfolio approach," *Discussion Paper No. 03/01*, Centro de Investigacion de la Universidad del Pacifico.

Reinhart C.M., K.S. Rogoff and M. Savastano (2003), "Addicted to dollars," *NBER Working Paper No. 10015*.

Savastano, M. (1996), "Dollarization in Latin America: Recent evidence and some policy issues," *IMF Working Paper No. 96/4*.

Yeyati, L. (2006), "Financial dollarization: Evaluating the consequences," *Economic Policy*, **21**(45), 61–118.

PART III

Power relations in the international financial system: Global and regional dimensions

9. The cost of a SWIFT kick: Estimating the cost of financial sanctions on Iran*

Mariam Majd

INTRODUCTION

The reality of one country (or city-state) sanctioning another has been in existence at least since the time of Ancient Greece when Pericles levied sanctions against nearby Megara in 432 BC (Hufbauer, Schott and Elliott, 1990). This reality has also since that time naturally generated an accompanying discussion as to sanctions' effectiveness – whether they had the desired impact, what negative externalities they occasioned, what costs were borne by sender countries, whether sanctions replaced or merely preceded war as an enforcement mechanism, and so on. Over time, it seems that the accompanying questions have not changed as much as the sanctions themselves. In 1997, Jonathan Kirshner identified trade sanctions (sanctions banning imports from or exports to a state) as being the type of sanction most commonly employed (Kirshner, 1997). But, by the 2000s, the United States was increasingly utilizing financial sanctions: sanctions focusing on the flow of funds to and from a target. The stated reason for this shift was that financial sanctions offered the ability to target a government elite (who usually had the resources to circumvent trade sanctions) and spare the civilian population, who usually suffered disproportionately under comprehensive trade sanctions (Normand, 1996; Lopez and Cortright, 1997).

In 2012, the United States imposed a unique financial sanctions package on Iran (hereafter referred to as the 2012 sanctions package): it required that the Islamic Republic be removed from the Society for Interbank Financial Telecommunication (SWIFT) payments platform, and it also sanctioned Iran's central bank. Despite the sanctions' seeming comprehensiveness, they were nevertheless touted as being "smart" or narrowly targeted to Iran's financial and governmental elite. Journalistic accounts emerging in and around 2012, however, began telling a different story as reports of food insecurity, medicine shortages, and rising levels of poverty among ordinary Iranians – the group allegedly most shielded from sanctions' per their design – were blamed on the 2012 sanctions package. Though formal analyses of the effect of sanctions on Iran's civilian population are few in number, those that have been conducted seem to confirm journalistic accounts of impacts on Iran's citizenry (Hosseini, 2013; Karimi and Haghpanah, 2014; Massoumi and Koduri, 2015; Setayesh and Mackey, 2016).

Even less forthcoming than formal assessments of impacts to ordinary Iranians are those analyzing impacts to Iran's real economy. Specifically, this author is unaware of any econometric analyses of the annual cost to Iranian gross domestic product (GDP) of the 2012 sanctions package. This analysis is useful to conduct, however, as it would not only add to our understanding of whether the 2012 sanctions package had its intended impact but would also allow us to compare the magnitude of impact across time and countries.

This chapter attempts to measure the annual cost to Iranian GDP of the 2012 sanctions package where cost is defined as the difference between what Iran's GDP would have been if the 2012 sanctions package had not been implemented and what Iran's GDP actually was. To determine what Iran's GDP would have been if the sanctions package had not been imposed in 2012, a time-series forecasting technique is utilized. I find that the cost of full implementation (2012–15) of these sanctions to Iranian GDP was, on average, approximately $60.4 billion per year, or about 16.2 percent of what actual GDP was during that time and 13.9 percent of what it would have been if the sanctions had not been imposed. Because, in theory, Iran's real economy was not supposed to be heavily impacted by the 2012 sanctions package, I suggest that the substantial cost to Iran's GDP challenges the notion that the 2012 sanctions package can be viewed as having been narrowly targeted.

The chapter is divided into several sections. The next section traces the evolution of the so-called "smart" or targeted, financial sanctions. The third section details the development of financial sanctions in the Islamic Republic of Iran and focuses on a special type of financial sanction: the 2012 SWIFT cut-off. The fourth section describes past efforts to measure the costs of sanctions and highlights the importance of measuring dollar costs to the real economy in the case of targeted financial sanctions. The fifth section presents a time-series forecasting model to estimate the cost to Iranian GDP of the 2012 sanctions package. The final section summarizes the chapter's central findings.

THE EVOLUTION OF "SMART" SANCTIONS

The concept of smart sanctions emerged in the 1990s as a response to the devastating impacts to the Iraqi civilian population of comprehensive sanctions imposed by the UN Security Council after Saddam Hussein's invasion of Kuwait. Though these comprehensive sanctions were viewed as a more humane alternative to outright war with Iraq, some researchers and policy-makers later argued that the sanctions' consequences were in some cases as "harmful as war itself" (Normand, 1996; Lopez and Cortright, 1997, p. 327). Not only, it was argued, did the comprehensive sanctions take the greatest toll on the civilian population while sparing government elites who had the means to work around them, but they also allowed the Iraqi government to play the hero in providing aid to its people and deprived opposition groups of crucial resources needed to mount a viable campaign (Lopez and Cortright, 1997).

The more "smart" and humane alternatives thus were claimed to reverse these effects. By focusing sanctions on financial realms, civilian populations and opposition groups allegedly would be spared while government elites would suffer. Smart financial sanctions – the methods of which included freezing financial assets, refusing debt rescheduling and funds (credit, loans, assistance, etc.), restricting activity of diplomats, and even boycotting sports and cultural events – accomplished the seemingly unachievable goal of being both more humane and successful, where success is defined by a change in the target's policies; indeed, Lopez and Cortright report the Institute for International Economics' empirical finding that the success rate of financial sanctions as compared to comprehensive trade sanctions was, at the time, 41 and 25 percent, respectively (Lopez and Cortright, 1997).

Policy-makers' support for the combined precision and success of financial sanctions remained into the first decade of the twenty-first century (Cortright and Lopez, 2002; Brzoska, 2003; Shagabutdinova and Berejikian, 2007), and following the events of September 11, 2001, they were utilized almost exclusively against targets. At the same time, the United States government was also expanding on its capacity to monitor and control global financial transactions. The issuance of Executive Order 13224, for instance, on September 23, 2001 by the US Office of the Coordinator for Counterterrorism, authorized the US government to designate and block the assets of foreign individuals or entities that had engaged or were at risk of engaging in terrorism or support of terrorism. Title III of the USA Patriot Act ("International Money Laundering Abatement and Anti-Terrorist Financing Act of 2001") passed by Congress in 2001 gave the Treasury Secretary broad discretion to subject banking and financial institutions (domestic and global) to increased scrutiny in the service of preventing international money laundering and financing of terrorism. The Financial Action Task Force (FATF) was expanded in 2001 to respond to threats of not only money laundering but also terrorist financing. Under its "Special Recommendations on Terrorist Financing" the FATF advised countries to freeze funds and assets of suspected terrorists and financiers of terrorism and to adopt measures making it easier for authorities to do so. The FATF also required countries to more closely monitor and evaluate the transactions of financial institutions. Finally, in 2006, the CIA, overseen by the Treasury department (headed by Juan Zarate), secretly subpoenaed and won access to the financial records database of the Society for Worldwide Interbank Financial Telecommunication (SWIFT).

SWIFT is an independent company based in Brussels that became operational in 1977 (Lichtblau and Risen, 2006). The company only provides a messenger service between banks and financial institutions; that is, it neither maintains deposit accounts nor transfers actual funds but rather simply delivers a standardized financial message. To get a more concrete sense of what SWIFT does, we can imagine three people residing in the same town of the United States – Robert, Sai, and Tasha – and suppose that Robert wants to send $10 to Tasha. Let us further suppose that instead of walking over to Tasha's house and handing her a $10 bill, Robert opts to employ the services of Sai. For a fee, Sai will go over to Robert's house and have him fill out a form for deposit (we might properly consider it to be a simple check) that she created in conjunction with Robert and Tasha's banks (in this way, her financial message is convenient to and therefore preferred by Robert and Tasha's banks). Once Robert fills out the form, Sai delivers it to Tasha's banking institution and upon its receipt, a process is put in motion whereby $10 is removed from Robert's banking account and deposited into Tasha's. In this simple example, Sai essentially performs the same function as SWIFT: she simply delivers a financial message (i.e., the form or check).

Given the ease with which two individuals residing in the same town can transact, Robert's use of a messenger service in the previous illustration is perhaps only justified by his own laziness. But with regard to global financial transactions, the movement of funds is naturally quite complex and so it is in this arena that SWIFT provides a crucial service, all the more because it is unique. That is, SWIFT is the *only* common infrastructure through which global financial institutions can interact directly that can be considered universal.[1] To continue use of our previous hypothetical scenario, we might imagine a circumstance whereby the *only* way Robert and Tasha's banks can interact is through Sai's form for deposit. In this case, Sai becomes not only a messenger but also a network since she possesses a unique platform through which people and funds are interconnected. In the same way, SWIFT is also a network (i.e., it is also a platform through which financial institutions communicate).

The ability to monitor SWIFT transactions represented a significant breakthrough in the government's capacity to monitor global financial transactions. When it was founded in the 1970s, SWIFT could claim as members 518 different institutions from 22 different countries and it processed roughly 10 million messages annually. Today, it claims 11 000 institutions from over 200 countries and processes approximately 26 million messages in *one day*, with the Europe, Middle East and Africa (EMEA) region generating the largest proportion of traffic[2] (SWIFT, 2016b). Further, it is believed that the dollar value of SWIFT transactions in 2001 was more than $7.7 trillion[3] annually (Scott and Zachariadis, 2014), or more than one-third of total world exports of goods and services in 2016.

FINANCIAL SANCTIONS IN IRAN

Until 2007, most sanctions against Iran were trade based and aimed at Iran's energy sector. In 2007, however, the Bush administration imposed its first targeted, financial sanction (i.e., "smart" sanction) against Iran.[4] Alleging that Iran's fourth largest bank at the time (Bank Sepah) had supported entities affiliated with Iran's nuclear program, the United States extended Executive Order (EO) 13382. True to the form of a "smart" sanction, EO 13382 was limited to the bank and its chairman: assets under US control were frozen and US entities were banned from engaging in business with the bank. The practice of targeted sanctions continued, though the bullseye began to widen: in October 2007, following the charge that Iran was funding terrorism, sanctions severed ties to the US financial system of more than 20 groups associated with Iran's armed forces (Iranian Revolutionary Guard Corps) and of three more of the largest Iranian banks (including its largest one, Bank Melli Iran). In 2008, the United Nations Security Council (UNSC) increased sanctions to monitor Iranian banks and extended asset freezes (Resolution 1803); further, in 2009, the 111th US Congress passed the "Comprehensive Iran Sanctions, Accountability, and Divestment Act of 2009" (CISADA 2009) whereby all of Iran's oil and gas industry was sanctioned.

In 2010, sanctions again intensified in response to the charge of the Islamic Republic's continued nuclear proliferation (as revealed in the May 31, 2010 International Atomic Energy Agency [IAEA] report). In addition to banning nuclear and missile investment, materials and activities, Resolution 1929 issued by the UNSC on June 9, 2010 also imposed a number of financial penalties on Iran: countries were required to prevent financial services to and banking relationships with the Islamic Republic if there was suspicion that they could be linked to nuclear proliferation. Additionally, the Resolution emphasized the need to monitor all Iranian banks including the Central Bank of Iran (The White House, 2010). On July 1, 2010, formal comprehensive sanctions on Iran were implemented by the US Congress with the "Comprehensive Iran Sanctions, Accountability, and Divestment Act of 2010" (CISADA 2010). Under CISADA 2010, the criminal penalty for violating sanctions was increased and a number of additional punitive measures and restrictions were developed: foreign companies that sold Iran materials relevant to its energy sector were sanctioned and enduring exemptions for imported goods into the United States from Iran were denied (this included banning items that had long been imported into the United States like Iranian carpets and pistachios); US banks were prohibited from conducting business with any foreign bank that also dealt with the Iranian Revolutionary Guard Corps (a branch of Iran's armed forces); Iran was banned from accessing US foreign exchange, the banking system, and property transactions (Fayazmanesh, 2013).

In 2012, Iran fell under the most comprehensive set of sanctions ever levied against the Islamic Republic, which focused on barring Iran from the global financial system (the 2012 sanctions package). By January, the efforts that would eventually culminate in Iran's removal from the SWIFT system had begun. United Against Nuclear Iran (UANI) – a private, non-profit lobbying group – began petitioning the United States government to block Iran's access to SWIFT; by February 1, 2012, the Johnson-Shelby Iran Sanctions, Accountability and Human Rights Act of 2012 was introduced into the Senate Banking Committee with an amendment by Senators Robert Menendez and Roger Wicker (the latter on behalf of Senator Mark Kirk) to sanction banks with executive members on the board of SWIFT if the messaging network did not disallow Iranian banks from using the transactions service (Rogin, 2012; and United Against Nuclear Iran website[5]). In March 2012, Iran was the first country to have ever been cut off from SWIFT. At roughly the same time, Executive Order 13599 had also been passed, which blocked Iran's central bank and entire body of financial institutions from the US financial system as well as froze its existing assets in the United States. Several months later in June, the 2012 National Defense Authorization Act gave the President power to sanction foreign banks that engaged in financial transactions with Iran's oil sectors. Finally, in July, a European Union (EU) Iranian oil embargo was coupled with a freeze of Iranian Central Bank assets in the EU and denial of service with US and EU insurers (securing insurance is a key component of the capacity to ship oil).

MEASURING THE COST OF "SMART" SANCTIONS

Despite the seeming comprehensiveness of the 2012 sanctions package and its immediate predecessors, all were advertised as being "smart" sanctions, or sanctions that were narrowly tailored to Iran's financial and governmental elite (Faucon, 2012; Hariyanto and Ismar, 2012; Gladstone, 2013). Beginning in January 2010, for instance, weeks before CISADA 2009 was passed, Hillary Clinton (then Secretary of State) remarked:

> It is clear that there is a relatively small group of decision makers inside Iran. . . They are in both political and commercial relationships, and if we can create a sanctions track that targets those who actually make the decisions, we think that is a smarter way to do sanctions. (Sahimi, 2010)[6]

Similarly, the Fact Sheet released by the White House on Resolution 1929 also emphasized a targeted approach (The White House, 2010) as did Barack Obama upon signing CISADA 2010 (Obama, 2010).

Similar claims were also made with regard to the SWIFT sanction: three months before Iran was officially removed from the SWIFT network, Mark Dubowitz – CEO of the Foundation for the Defense of Democracies and co-director of the Center on Sanctions & Illicit Finance (along with Zarate) – wrote an article in the *New York Times* bidding readers to continue believing in the efficacy of sanctions: "The truly crippling sanctions. . .would never be accepted by Western politicians, who are fearful. . .of being seen as too harsh on the Iranian people. But giving up on sanctions is not the answer. Instead, we have to make them smarter" (Gerecht and Dubowitz, 2011, p. A21). Further, David Cohen – Under Secretary for Terrorism and Financial Intelligence at the US Department of the Treasury – made a number of assurances that the SWIFT sanctions were targeted, allowed for the import of food and medicine, and minimized damage to the Iranian people (Faucon, 2012). He also made similar statements in more general remarks published by the Treasury:

> We have been able to move away from clunky and heavy-handed instruments of economic power. . . Sanctions that focus on bad actors within the financial sector are far more precise and far more effective than traditional trade sanctions. And the trade restrictions that we continue to employ today are also smarter and more surgical, targeting specific classes of products rather than cutting off entire economies. (US Department of the Treasury, 2014)

The Obama administration's National Security Strategy of 2015 also emphasized a narrowly tailored approach with regard to the US role in the "International Order":

> Targeted economic sanctions remain an effective tool for imposing costs
> on those irresponsible actors. . . Our sanctions will continue to be carefully
> designed and tailored to achieve clear aims while minimizing any unintended
> consequences for other economic actors, the global economy, and civilian
> populations. (The White House, 2015)

But, despite promises of narrow tailoring, in practice the 2012 sanctions package seemed to have heavily impacted Iran's real economy and civilian population.[7] Journalistic accounts document the scarcity of crucial medicines (Bozorgmehr, 2012; Borger and Dehghan, 2013), foodstuffs, and medical devices (Mohammed, 2012; Gladstone, 2013). Also reported were rising poverty levels owing to rising food prices, high inflation, and increasing unemployment (Warrick and Ball, 2012; Bozorgmehr, 2013; Nasseri and Motevalli, 2015). Though formal analyses of impacts of the recent sanctions are less easy to encounter, those that have been conducted confirm what has been reported in the news media. A number of researchers, for instance, confirm that medicines have become scarce and unaffordable for ordinary citizens (Hosseini, 2013; Karimi and Haghpanah, 2014; Massoumi and Koduri, 2015; Setayesh and Mackey, 2016). Of the 73 drugs that Setayesh and Mackey (2016) identify as in shortage because of the SWIFT sanctions, 44 percent are classified as essential medicines according to the World Health Organization.

Empirical analyses of the broader impacts to Iran's economy of the 2012 sanctions are scarce; accordingly, several researchers have noted the need to develop these analyses (Moret, 2015; Haidar, 2017). Specifically, the actual dollar cost of the 2012 sanctions package to the Iranian economy has not yet been empirically analyzed, though a visible decrease in Iranian GDP in 2012 is clear (Figure 9.1).

Figure 9.1 plots Iranian GDP in 2015 US dollars from 1980 to 2022, where 2016 and beyond are IMF estimates. The figure demonstrates that in 2012 there is a visible interruption to a strong upward trajectory in Iran's GDP that had existed ever since the end of the Iran–Iraq war. Though the years 2016 onward represent International Monetary Fund (IMF) forecasts of Iran's GDP, it is also clear that in 2015 (also the year of signing for the Joint Comprehensive Plan of Action adding Iran back to the SWIFT system) there is a sharp uptick in Iran's GDP, the slope of which matches the general slope of Iran's GDP prior to 2012. IMF forecasts also suggest that Iran's economy will grow at a rate close to that prior to the implementation of the 2012 sanctions package.

Empirically analyzing the cost of the 2012 sanctions package to Iran's GDP fulfills a number of functions. First, because the 2012 sanctions package was marketed as "smart" or narrowly targeted, its impact on the real economy (in the form of a negative shock to GDP) facilitates a

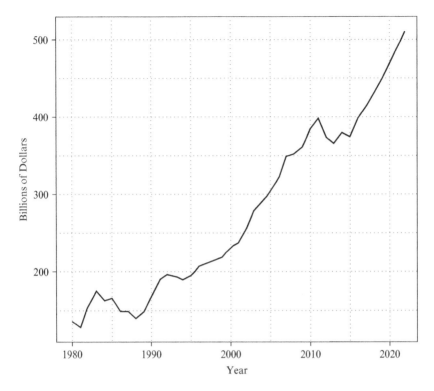

Source: IMF World Economic Outlook Database and author's calculations.

Figure 9.1   Iran's real GDP (1980–2022) in billions of 2015 dollars

specific understanding of the degree to which the sanction failed to meet
that stated objective. An empirical analysis also provides a way to compare
the magnitude of this failure to the impact of sanctions levied in other
countries. Additionally, because the SWIFT sanction is still a new enforcement tool in the international arena, having a baseline understanding of
the magnitude of its impact assists in anticipating the specific outcomes of
its potential future use.

ECONOMETRIC ANALYSIS

In this section, I measure the annual cost to Iran's real GDP of the 2012
sanctions package. I define annual costs to be the yearly difference between
Iran's potential GDP (Iran's GDP without the 2012 sanctions package)

and what Iran's GDP was in fact. To determine what Iran's potential GDP would have been without the imposition of the 2012 sanctions package, I employ a time-series forecasting technique: following the Box and Jenkins methodology (1976), an autoregressive integrated moving average (ARIMA) model is fitted to the data prior to SWIFT sanctions and projected forward to 2022. Cost estimates are obtained by differencing the projected forecasts and the actual performance of Iran's GDP (per IMF data and forecasts) over the time period to generate annual costs of the sanctions.

It should be highlighted, however, that in not simply forecasting Iran's GDP but also using it as a counterfactual, an implicit, though standard, assumption is being made (Atkinson, Luttrell and Rosenblum, 2013): trend growth in Iran's GDP would have continued if the 2012 sanctions package had not been imposed. The adoption of this assumption is based on two considerations: first are the complications inherent in using structural macroeconomic models (which are better suited to assessing causal impacts) in this complex case (discussed in detail below); and second is the clearly visible sharp drop-off and uptick in Iran's GDP corresponding with the imposition and lifting, respectively, of this unique set of sanctions on the Iranian economy.

Data

The data consists of time-series data on Iranian GDP during the period 1980–2022. They are taken from the IMF World Economic Outlook Database. During the period 2016–22, the IMF forecasts Iranian GDP. The data used was originally reported in billions of constant rials (Iran's national currency) and current US dollars. For use in this analysis, the data was converted to constant 2015 US dollars for ease of interpretation by using GDP in constant rials to produce an index that was then multiplied by Iran's GDP in 2015 current dollars to get GDP in constant 2015 dollars.

Methodology

A time-series forecasting model is used to determine what Iran's GDP would have been if the sanctions package had not been imposed in 2012. Students of econometrics will recall that a key assumption needed to develop estimators for a classical regression model is that there is no covariance between disturbances of different observations (i.e., the disturbances are non-autoregressive). Though violation of this assumption poses a distinct problem for regression analysis, the correlation between data can be harnessed in time-series analysis to make predictions. Applied to forecasting, time-series models use past data values to predict future values and so are unlike structural macroeconomic models that attempt to define a trend through causal relationships between variables that is informed by economic theory. Though they cannot explain causation, time-series forecasting techniques are particularly useful tools when the movement of values is thought to be influenced by a complex set of relationships. With regard to these complex dynamics (as naturally underlies movements in macroeconomic indicators), structural macroeconomic models are vulnerable to misspecification, endogeneity, and omitted variable bias, thus making time-series forecasting techniques an especially effective alternative (Marcellino et al., 2007; Xin, Xie and Li, 2008; Keck, Raubold and Truppia, 2009; Wang, 2016).

The dynamics that underlie movements in Iran's GDP are complex, indeed. The economy has operated under a host of sanctions since 1979 that are different in scope, effect, and duration. A significant literature exists theorizing the effect of sanctions on economies, governments, and citizen-ries, but there does not exist a wide-ranging consensus view on the effect of individual sanctions, much less on the dynamics of multiple and variable sanctions (Hufbauer et al., 2007; Eriksson, 2011; Sitt et al., 2010; Haidar, 2013). In short, the sanctions regime imposed on Iran since the Revolution makes it difficult to understand the dynamics of Iranian GDP in a way that would readily lend itself to forecasting using a structural macroeconomic model. Further complicating a causal analysis is the unconventional mon-etary policy adopted by Mahmoud Ahmadinejad during his presidency (Amuzegar, 2013; Ghorashi, 2016). Finally, the effort to model Iran's GDP using a structural macroeconomic model is complicated by a common prob-lem that is only exacerbated in the case of a pariah state: data availability (Valadkhani, 2003; Amuzegar, 2013; Alaedini and Ashrafzadeh, 2016).

I follow the Box and Jenkins methodology (1976) to fit an autoregressive integrated moving average (ARIMA (p, d, q)) model to forecast Iran's GDP during the time period 2012–22. The ARIMA model forecasts a variable based on the assumption that it is a linear combination of its past values and past errors; its general form is expressed as:

$$y_t = \phi_1 y_{t-1} + \phi_2 y_{t-2} + \ldots + \phi_p y_{t-p} + \varepsilon_t + \theta_1 \varepsilon_{t-1} + \theta_2 \varepsilon_{t-2} + \ldots \theta_q \varepsilon_{t-q}$$

where ϕ_i and θ_j are parameters and y_t is the forecasted value. Further, p identifies the number of lags of the dependent variable used in the model (also known as the auto regressive [AR] term), d identifies the number of times the data needed to be differenced to achieve stationarity (also known as the integrated [I] term), and q specifies the previous error terms used in the model (also known as the moving average [MA] term).

Table 9.1   ARIMA (0,2,1)

ARIMA (0,2,1)	Estimate
MA(1)	−0.84
	(0.11)
Obs.	32
Log-likelihood	−116.84
AIC	237.69
BIC	240.49

Note: Standard error in parenthesis.

Because fitting an ARIMA (p, d, q) model requires that the variability of the data is constant over time (i.e., stationarity), the data is second-differenced (d= 2) and an augmented Dickey-Fuller test – a standard formal test for stationarity – is used to confirm stationarity. The autocorrelation and partial autocorrelation functions[8] are used to determine the number of lags of the dependent variable (p) and the previous error terms (q) used in the model. An ARIMA (0,2,1) model (Table 9.1) is selected based on minimizing the Akaike and Bayesian information criteria and is substantiated after investigation of the model residuals.[9]

Results

Figure 9.2 displays the results of using the estimated model to forecast Iranian GDP for the period 2012–22.

The dashed black line above the noticeable plunge in Iran's GDP starting in 2012 is the forecasted value of GDP in 2015 dollars. That is, the dashed line represents what Iranian GDP *would have been* if the 2012 sanction package had not been imposed and GDP had continued to follow the pre-2012 sanctions trend.

Table 9.2 compares annual forecast values to actual GDP values (including IMF projections of actual GDP from 2016 onwards).

Using the average value of the lower and upper 95 percent confidence level as our forecasted GDP reveals that the cost of full implementation of the 2012 sanctions package (2012–15) to Iranian GDP was, on average, approximately $60.4 billion per year, or about 16.2 percent of what average annual real GDP actually was during that time and 13.9 percent of what average annual GDP would have been if the sanctions had not been imposed. In addition, by 2014, Iranian GDP was approximately 13.7 percent of what it would have been had the 2012 sanctions package not been imposed. If IMF projections are accepted, then the numbers also indicate

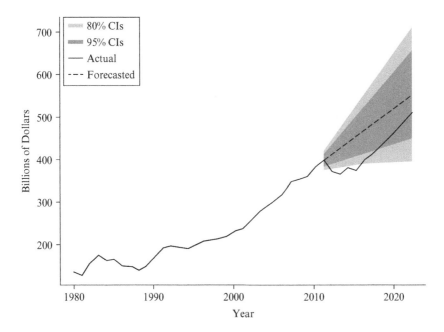

Source: Underlying data on Iran's GDP is sourced from the IMF World Economic
Outlook Database and subject to the author's calculations to obtain Iran's real GDP in 2015
dollars.

*Figure 9.2   Forecasts for Iran's real GDP (billions of 2015 dollars) from
ARIMA (0,2,1)*

that from 2016 onwards, the actual value of Iran's GDP was higher than
the lower limit of the 95 percent confidence interval for that year; that is,
from 2016 onwards, the value of Iran's actual GDP is not significantly
lower than the forecasted value, meaning that the effect of 2012 sanctions
package was significantly present only when it was in full implementation
(2012–15).

If costs are understood to be the difference between Iran's forecasted
and actual GDP, then the impact to Iran's GDP in the period 2012–15
when the sanctions package was fully implemented is sizeable. By 2015,
the aggregate cost of sanctions (the sum of annual costs during the period
2012–15) was approximately $241.73 billion, or 64.8 percent of Iran's
actual real GDP in 2012. For comparison, we might consider that the
cost of the most recent financial crisis (2007–09) is estimated to be 40–90
percent of US real GDP in 2007 (where cost is similarly measured as the
difference between forecasted and actual US GDP) (Atkinson et al., 2013).

Table 9.2   Annual costs to Iran's real GDP from SWIFT sanctions

Year	Actual GDP ($B)	Forecast GDP ($B)	Lo95 CI ($B)	Hi95 CI ($B)	Real Forecast ($B)
2012	372.76	412.72	377.10	448.33	39.96
2013	365.64	426.72	379.66	473.77	61.08
2014	380.44	440.72	382.36	499.08	60.28
2015	374.31	454.72	384.92	524.51	80.41
2016	398.80	468.72	387.24	550.20	69.92
2017	411.90	482.72	389.24	576.19	70.82
2018	429.48	496.72	390.91	602.52	67.24
2019	448.61	510.72	392.23	629.21	62.11
2020	468.64	524.72	393.20	656.25	56.08
2021	489.38	538.72	393.80	683.64	49.34
2022	510.81	552.72	394.04	711.40	41.91

Note: All entries are in billions of 2015 dollars. Forecasted GDP represents an average of the low and high 95% confidence interval values.

The statements made by policy-makers and state officials before, during, and after the 2012 sanctions package implementation characterize these sanctions as having been narrowly tailored to Iran's financial and governmental elite. Based on their advertisement, then, these sanctions should not have had a sizeable impact on Iran's real economy, particularly since the banking and financial sectors only make up approximately 2.5 percent of Iran's GDP (Babakhani, 2016). Thus, that the 2012 sanctions package did have a considerable impact to Iran's real GDP challenges the notion that these sanctions were narrowly targeted or "smart" and may add to considerations over whether and in what form they should be employed in the future.

CONCLUSION

The concept of a narrowly targeted or "smart" financial sanction is a response to a humanitarian crisis in Iraq triggered by comprehensive trade sanctions. After the deleterious effect of comprehensive sanctions to ordinary Iraqis had been revealed and popularized, policy-makers and government officials looked for ways to impose punitive measures on rogue states without harming their respective citizenries. "Smart" or narrowly targeted financial sanctions seemed to offer an answer: by focusing on the flow of funds instead of the realm of trade, sanctions were theorized to be a less blunt enforcement mechanism that would allow the civilian population of a targeted country to be spared from harm.

In 2012, a unique set of financial sanctions were levied against the Islamic Republic of Iran (where a financial sanction aims to decrease the flow of funds to and from a target). Among other punitive measures levied against the country in 2012, Iran was forced to comply with sanctions against its central bank and was the first country to have been removed from the Society for Worldwide Interbank Financial Telecommunications. Despite the seeming comprehensiveness of this set of sanctions, policy-makers and government officials alleged at the time (and would continue to contend later) that they were in fact narrowly targeted to Iran's governmental and financial elite (i.e., the sanctions were "smart").

Though the 2012 sanctions package was allegedly designed to prevent sizeable impacts to Iran's real economy or civilian population, journalistic accounts and academic analyses have reported on the sufferings of Iran's citizenry owing to the sanctions package. Formal analyses of the effects of the 2012 sanctions package on Iran's real economy have been less forthcoming than those on the effects to the average Iranian, however. Specifically, this author is unaware of any empirical analysis of the annual impact to Iran's GDP of the 2012 sanctions package, though this analysis would reveal the exact extent to which the sanctions package failed to meet its advertised objective of being narrowly targeted. Further, a formal analysis of the 2012 sanctions package impact to Iran's GDP assists in anticipating the specific outcomes of its potential future use.

In this chapter, I employ a time-series forecasting model to measure what Iran's GDP would have been if the sanctions package had not been imposed in 2012. By subtracting the actual value of Iran's GDP during the period after sanctions were imposed from forecasted values, I arrive at a measure of cost to Iran's GDP of the 2012 sanctions package. My results demonstrate that the cost of full implementation (during the period 2012–15) of these sanctions to Iranian GDP was, on average, approximately $60.4 billion dollars per year, or about 16.2 percent of what GDP actually was during that time and 13.9 percent of what it would have been if the sanctions had not been imposed. Further, by 2015, the aggregate cost of sanctions (the sum of annual costs during the period 2012–15) was approximately $241.73 billion, or 64.8 percent of Iran's actual real GDP in 2012. The 2012 sanctions package therefore made a considerable impact to Iran's real GDP, which belies the claim that these sanctions emulated their early-century predecessors in being narrowly targeted or "smart."

NOTES

*   I would like to thank Gerald Epstein, Deepankar Basu, Raphael Gouvea and the members of the International Finance Working Group for valuable feedback on this chapter. I also thank G. Reza Ghorashi for introducing me to the topic of financial sanctions on Iran and providing helpful guidance. Of course, I alone am responsible for all remaining errors.
1.   It should be noted that in response to the adoption of a SWIFT sanction tactic by the United States, a few alternatives to the SWIFT platform were initiated, though none can reasonably be said to compete with SWIFT. In 2014, when the United States and European Parliament considered banning Russia from SWIFT following its military intervention in Ukraine, Russia immediately began calling on its banks to create an alternative to the SWIFT system. By 2017, the Central Bank Governor claimed the alternative platform, the system for transfer of financial messages (SPFS), was complete. In practice, however, the SPFS system seemed to operate more like a bridge to the Russian financial system in the absence of a SWIFT link than a global alternative: only Russian banks were linked to SPFS and its function was to enable the receipt of SWIFT's financial messages even if it were to deny services (Reuters, 2017). Further, in 2015, China's Cross-Border Interbank Payment System (CIPS) became operational. CIPS, however, is a payment system that only settles cross-border renminbi payments and trade. Moreover, by 2016, China International Payment Service Corporation (CIPS Co.) had signed a "Memorandum of Understanding" with SWIFT whereby CIPS would be connected to the global network through SWIFT itself (SWIFT, 2016a). Readers may further be tempted to offer Fedwire (owned and operated by the Federal Reserve Banks) and the Clearing House Interbank Payments System (CHIPS) as counterexamples to SWIFT's uniqueness, but it should be noted that either one is a *payment* system and not a messaging system; moreover, Fedwire is limited to domestic US financial institutions while CHIPS is limited to financial institutions that have a domestic presence; in fact, in 2006, SWIFT originated 70 percent of the messages on the CHIPS system (US Department of the Treasury, 2006).
2.   Intra-EMEA, intra-Americas, and intra-Asia Pacific represent 47.6 percent, 11.5 percent, and 6.6 percent of all intra-regional and sent messages in 2016, respectively.
3.   SWIFT does not release data on the aggregate value of its message traffic and so a more updated figure of this amount is unavailable.
4.   Financial sanctions are defined as follows: "Financial sanctions focus on the flow of funds and other forms of value to and from a target country, corporation, individual, or other entity. These sanctions can have wide impact because they can not only freeze financial assets and prohibit or limit financial transactions, but they also impede trade by making it difficult to pay for the export or import of goods and services" (Carter and Farha, 2013, p. 904).
5.   Accessed July 20, 2018 at https://www.unitedagainstnucleariran.com/.
6.   Additional comments from state officials to this effect are reported in Sahimi (2010).
7.   It is important to note other researchers' work detailing the fact that the 2012 sanctions package did not work alone in occasioning adverse effects on the civilian population after 2012. Rather, these sanctions not only added to but also *exacerbated* inefficiencies that had already existed in the Iranian economy. For more on this point, see Ghorashi (2016).
8.   The autocorrelation function (ACF) plots the correlation between the variable being forecasted (here, GDP) and its past values. The partial autocorrelation function (PACF) plots the correlation between the variable being forecasted and its past values *that is not the result of previous correlations*.
9.   The Bayesian information criterion (BIC) offers one solution to the challenge of choosing parameter values for an ARIMA (p, d, q) model; the problem arises from the fact that if too high a value is chosen, forecasts may suffer from increased estimation error, whereas if too low a value is chosen, forecasts may ignore relevant information contained in past values. The BIC penalizes increases to the parameter values so that the true parameter values can be determined (Stock and Watson, 2012, p. 551).

REFERENCES

Alaedini, P. and H.R. Ashrafzadeh (eds) (2016), "Iran's post-revolutionary social justice agenda and its outcomes: Evolution and determinants of income distribution and middle-class size," in *Economic Welfare and Inequality in Iran*, New York: Palgrave Macmillan, pp. 15–45.

Amuzegar, J. (2013), "Ahmadinejad's legacy," *Middle East Policy*, **20**(4), 124–32.

Atkinson, T., D. Luttrell and H. Rosenblum (2013), "How bad was it? The costs and consequences of the 2007–09 financial crisis," *Federal Reserve Bank of Dallas Staff Papers*, July.

Babakhani, S., F. Kazemi, M. Jünemann and A. Jozi (2016), *Banking Industry Iran: Current Status, Opportunities and Threats*, ILIA Corporation.

Borger, J. and S.K. Dehghan (2013), "Iran unable to get life-saving drugs due to international sanction," *The Guardian*, 13.

Box, G.E.P. and G.M. Jenkins (1976), *Time Series Analysis: Forecasting and Control*, Revised Ed., Holden-Day.

Bozorgmehr, N. (2012), "In Iran, sanctions take toll on the sick," *Washington Post*, September 4, accessed July 20, 2018 at https://www.washingtonpost.com/world/middle_east/sanctions-take-toll-on-irans-sick/2012/09/04/ce07ee2c-f6b2-11e1-8253-3f495ae70650_story.html?utm_term=.f9d86e9d73de.

Bozorgmehr, N. (2013), "Inflation and weak rial squeeze Iran's middle," *Financial Times*, October, 26, 7.

Brzoska, M. (2003), "Review essay: From dumb to smart? Recent reforms of UN sanctions," **9**(4), 519–35.

Carter, B.E. and R.M. Farha (2013), "Overview and operation of US financial sanctions, including the example of Iran," *Georgetown Journal of International Law*, **44**, 903–13.

Cortright, D. and G.A. Lopez (eds) (2002), *Smart Sanctions: Targeting Economic Statecraft*, Lanham, MD: Rowman & Littlefield.

Eriksson, M. (2011), *Targeting Peace: Understanding UN and EU Targeted Sanctions*, London: Routledge.

Faucon, B. (2012), "In Iran, private sector feels squeeze of sanctions," *Wall Street Journal*, August 2.

Fayazmanesh, S. (2013), *Containing Iran: Obama's Policy of "Tough Diplomacy"*, Newcastle-upon-Tyne, UK: Cambridge Scholars Publishing.

Gerecht, R.M. and M. Dubowitz (2011), "Don't give up on sanctions," *New York Times*, November 19.

Ghorashi, G.R. (2016), "Iran's post-sanctions economic challenges," *American International Journal of Humanities and Social Science*, **2**(1), accessed July 20, 2018 at aijhss.cgrd.org/images/Vol2No1/3.pdf.

Gladstone, R. (2013), "Double-digit inflation worsens in Iran," *New York Times*, April 2.

Haidar, J. (2013), "Sanctions and trade diversion: Exporter-level evidence from Iran," *VOX*, April 9, accessed July 20, 2018 at voxeu.org/article/iran-sanctions-and-diverted-trade-exporter-level-evidence.

Haidar, J. (2017), "Sanctions and export deflection: Evidence from Iran," *Economic Policy*, **32**(90), 319–55.

Hariyanto, J. and A. Ismar (2012), "Iran's president says US pressure is unfair," *Wall Street Journal*, 8 November.

Hosseini, S.A. (2013), "Impact of sanctions on procurement of medicine and medical devices in Iran: A technical response," *Archives of Iranian Medicine (AIM)*, **16**(12), 736–8.

Hufbauer, G.C., J.J. Schott and K.A. Elliott (1990), *Economic Sanctions Reconsidered: History and Current Policy, Vol. 1*, Washington, DC: Peterson Institute.

Hufbauer, G.C., J.J. Schott, K.A. Elliott and B. Oegg (2007), *Economic Sanctions Reconsidered*, 3rd edition, Washington, DC: Peterson Institute.

Karimi, M. and S. Haghpanah (2016), "The effects of economic sanctions on disease specific clinical outcomes of patients with thalassemia and hemophilia in Iran," *Health Policy*, **119**(2), 239–43.

Keck, A., A. Raubold and A. Truppia (2009), "Forecasting international trade: A time series approach," *OECD Journal: Journal of Business Cycle Measurement and Analysis*, **2**, 157–76.

Kirshner, J. (1997), "The microfoundations of economic sanctions," *Security Studies*, **6**(3), 32–64.

Lichtblau, E. and J. Risen (2006), "Bank data is sifted by US in secret to block terror," *New York Times*, **23**, 66–205.

Lopez, G.A. and D. Cortright (1997), "Financial sanctions: The key to a 'smart' sanctions strategy," *Die Friedens-Warte*, **22**(4), 327–36.

Marcellino, M., F. Diebold, R. Clark and M. Watson (2007), "A comparison of time series models for forecasting GDP growth and inflation," Bocconi University, accessed July 20, 2018 at https://www.researchgate.net/publication/228650389_A_comparison_of_time_series_models_for_forecasting_GDP_growth_and_inflation.

Massoumi, R.L. and S. Koduri (2015), "Adverse effects of political sanctions on the health care system in Iran," *Journal of Global Health*, **5**(2), 020302.

Mohammed, A. (2012), "Exclusive: Of diapers and drugs, Iran's trouble paying bills," *Reuters*, March 20, accessed July 20, 2018 at https://www.reuters.com/article/us-iran-usa-sanctions/exclusive-of-diapers-and-drugs-irans-trouble-paying-bills-idUSBRE82J18Z20120320.

Moret, E.S. (2015), "Humanitarian impacts of economic sanctions on Iran and Syria," *European Security*, **24**(1), 120–40.

Nasseri, L. and G. Motevalli (2015), "Iran's middle class plans for life after a deal," *Bloomberg Businessweek*, No. 4422, April 13, 14–15.

Normand, R. (1996), "Iraqi sanctions, human rights and humanitarian law," *Middle East Report*, **26**, 40–43.

Obama, B. (2010), "Statement on signing the Comprehensive Iran Sanctions, Accountability, and Divestment Act of 2010," July 1, accessed July 20, 2018 at www.presidency.ucsb.edu/ws/index.php?pid=88145.

Reuters (2017), "Russia's banking system has SWIFT alternative ready," March 23, accessed July 20, 2018 at https://www.rt.com/business/382017-russia-swift-central-bank/.

Rogin, J. (2012), "Senate begins another Iran sanctions push, targets Ahmadinejad and Khamenei," *Foreign Policy*, February 1.

Sahimi, M. (2010), "New sanctions miss the target," *Pbs.org*, January 20, accessed July 20, 2018 at www.pbs.org/wgbh/pages/frontline/tehranbureau/2010/01/misguided-sanctions.html.

Scott, S.V. and M. Zachariadis (2014), *The Society for Worldwide Interbank Financial Telecommunication (SWIFT): Cooperative Governance for Network Innovation, Standards, and Community*, London: Routledge.

Setayesh, S. and T.K. Mackey (2016), "Addressing the impact of economic sanctions on Iranian drug shortages in the joint comprehensive plan of action: Promoting access to medicines and health diplomacy," *Globalization and Health*, **12**(1), 31.

Shagabutdinova, E. and J. Berejikian (2007), "Deploying sanctions while protecting human rights: Are humanitarian 'smart' sanctions effective?," *Journal of Human Rights*, **6**(1), 59–74.

Sitt, B., M. Asada and M. Eriksson et al. (2010), *Sanctions and Weapons of Mass Destruction in International Relations*, Geneva: Geneva Centre for Security Policy.

Stock, J.H. and M.W. Watson (2012), *Introduction to Econometrics*, Boston, MA: Pearson Education.

SWIFT (2016a), "SWIFT offers secure financial messaging services to CIPS," March 25, accessed July 20, 2018 at https://www.swift.com/insights/press-releases/swift-and-cips-co_sign-memorandum-of-understanding-on-cross-border-interbank-payment-system-cooperation.

SWIFT (2016b), *Annual Review 2016*, accessed July 20, 2018 at www.swift.com/about-us/financials.

The White House (2010), "Fact sheet on the new UN Security Council Sanctions on Iran," June 9, Congress Office of the Press Secretary, accessed July 20, 2018 at https://obamawhitehouse.archives.gov/the-press-office/fact-sheet-new-un-security-council-sanctions-iran.

The White House (2015), *National Security Strategy*, accessed July 20, 2018 at nssarchive.us/wp-content/uploads/2015/02/2015.pdf.

US Department of the Treasury (2014), "Remarks of Under Secretary for Terrorism and Financial Intelligence David S. Cohen at The Practicing Law Institute's 'Coping with US Export Controls and Sanctions' Seminar, 'The Evolution of US Financial Power'," December 11, accessed July 20, 2018 at www.treasury.gov/press-center/press-releases/Pages/jl9716.aspx.

US Department of the Treasury, Financial Crimes Enforcement Network (2006), "Feasibility of a cross-border electronic funds transfer reporting system under the Bank Secrecy Act," Appendix D, pp. 55–69.

Valadkhani, A. (2003), "The causes of unemployment in Iran," *International Journal of Applied Business and Economic Research*, **1**(1), 21–33.

Wang, T. (2016), "Forecast of economic growth by time series and scenario planning method," *Modern Economy*, **7**, 212–22.

Warrick, J. and J. Ball (2012), "Food prices, inflation rise sharply in Iran," *The Washington Post*, October 5.

Xin, L., J. Xie and C. Li (2008), "The statistical forecast model on the GDP of Guangxi and its application," *Mathematics in Economics*, **3**, 289–93.

10. Changing rules of the game of global finance: Glimpses from Argentina's sovereign debt restructuring*

Mohit Arora

INTRODUCTION

Sovereign debt restructuring refers to debt workout procedures for sovereigns that involve rescheduling of the debt and/or reduction in the face of unsustainable debt burdens of a country. A restructuring of debt is done through an exchange of outstanding sovereign debt instruments, such as loans or bonds, for new debt instruments or cash through a legal process. As far as corporations are concerned, the idea that the unsustainable debt burden of the corporations may require restructuring is not new. Corporations in the United States do have access to Chapter 11 of the US Bankruptcy Code if they want to restructure their debts. They can also liquidate their firms by utilizing Chapter 7 in the same code (Arora, 2016b). However, when it comes to sovereigns, the international financial architecture lacks any legal mechanism to restructure their debt burdens, although the idea of an international law for governing sovereign debt is centuries old: "When it becomes necessary for a state to declare itself bankrupt, in the same manner as when it becomes necessary for an individual to do so, a fair, open and avowed bankruptcy is always the measure that is both least dishonourable to the debtor, and least hurtful to the creditor" (Smith, 1776 [1950]).

The theoretical literature on sovereign debt makes a key distinction between private and sovereign debt. Unlike private debt, sovereign debt cannot be enforced in a court of law. This has been the hallmark of this literature since the days of the Third World debt crisis in the 1980s and it continues to be so. A paper by Eaton, Gersovitz and Stiglitz claims that "[c]reditors do not have the means to seize the assets of a borrower in default" and Aguiar and Amador similarly claim that "[t]he defining feature of sovereign debt is the limited mechanisms for enforcement" (Eaton,

Gersovitz and Stiglitz, 1986, p. 391; Aguiar and Amador, 2013, p. 1). The lack of an exogenous enforcement mechanism is tackled by use of endogenous enforcement to protect the credit contracts. These enforcements can take several forms: trade embargoes, refusal to provide future loans to the defaulting borrower, and military interventions. An endogenous enforcement mechanism has severe implications for developing countries' access to external finance. Although there is a drop in transaction costs through the opening of global markets to finance, there is not a corresponding drop in enforcement costs (Epstein and Gintis, 1995). The lenders are reluctant to lend because they are not sure whether they will get their money back, while the borrowers are reluctant to borrow because of the threat of penalty in the case of non-repayment of their debts. This leads to massive credit rationing in the sense that those developing countries in genuine need of finance are not able to secure it. A logical conclusion that one would draw is that a solution to the problem of such pervasive credit rationing is instituting exogenous enforceability of sovereign debt contracts in a court of law. This would reduce the enforcement costs together with the transaction costs and allow countries' unmet needs for finance to be met. The chapter looks at the Argentinian debt restructuring story to understand how an exogenous enforcement mechanism may have perverse outcomes. This provides a cautionary tale for future attempts to implement this type of enforcement in international creditor–debtor disputes.

Some major institutional changes in the international financial and legal architecture in the previous decades created the conditions for difficulty in the restructuring of Argentina's sovereign debt. First, a process of financial disintermediation was in place after the advent of Brady bonds[1] from the early 1990s onwards whereby countries moved from bank to bond finance as their preferred source. This increased the volatility in bond markets in Argentina too since the structure of the bond markets became so dispersed that it became difficult to identify the actual lender. It should be noted that Argentina issued bonds under the Fiscal Agency Agreement (FAA) in 1994, which were bought by the hedge funds and contained the infamous "*pari passu*" clause, a topic that will be explored in greater detail in this chapter. Second, from the 1990s onwards, developing countries including Argentina also saw a surge in capital inflows that was unrelated to their current needs of trade and investment. Third, there were changes in the sovereign immunity laws in the United States and United Kingdom in the late 1970s. The sovereigns did not enjoy absolute immunity from litigation attempts by their commercial creditors in the United States as they had earlier. Hedge funds, which had deep pockets, strategically used the above changes in the landscape of sovereign debt to further their own interests and made huge gains by dragging Argentina into US courts.

Although they succeeded in making sovereign debt enforceable, it was at the cost of relinquishing what was in the best interest of Argentina and other creditors who had acted in good faith.

This chapter proceeds as follows. The next section looks at Argentina's attempts to restructure its debt after an external default in 2001. The third section focuses on the judicial interpretation of the infamous "*pari passu*" clause that sounded the death knell for a successful debt restructuring in Argentina. The fourth section examines the history of Argentina in the late nineteenth century to see how sovereign debt crises were resolved historically and tries to answer the following question: can history guide us towards a "good faith" and orderly debt workout? This section also explores the inter-war period when the United States had taken over as the new centre of international money and finance after the demise of the gold standard era. This episode gives a counter-example to the conventional understanding in the literature of the role of "reputation" in sustaining sovereign lending. The fifth section concludes.

ARGENTINA'S ATTEMPTS AT DEBT RESTRUCTURING

Argentina resorted to a hard currency peg (a currency board arrangement) in 1991 to solve its inflation problem. The currency board arrangement was an extreme form of fixed exchange rate regime wherein the country adopted "an explicit legislative commitment" to fix the nominal exchange rate at certain parity with the US dollar (1 peso = 1 US dollar). The central bank of the country was permitted to issue the domestic currency only on the condition that it was backed by an equivalent purchase of US dollars (Frenkel and Rapetti, 2010). The name "convertibility" was earned because pesos could be exchanged for dollars on a one-to-one basis with the backing of the legislature. The idea was that such a hard currency peg would reduce the future inflationary expectations of agents in the economy and would make the actions of the government sound more credible. What the convertibility programme did in effect was to make the imbalances in the balance of payments adjust through output and employment changes rather than through changes in prices. This was because any addition to the foreign exchange reserves had to be balanced by an equal expansion of the monetary base of the economy that led to an increase in output and employment. Similarly, any contraction of the foreign exchange reserves had to be balanced by an equal contraction of the monetary base that led to a reduction in the output and employment in the economy (ibid.).

The convertibility programme was able to instil confidence among market participants and, as a result, inflationary expectations in the economy went down. This led to a drastic decline in the inflation rate in the economy in the 1990s. The country attracted huge inflows of capital after the convertibility programme was implemented and this swelled its foreign exchange reserves. There were three important reasons for this surge in the capital inflows into the country – a decrease in the interest rates in the United States in the early 1990s; the increase in price stability in the country after the adoption of the convertibility programme; and the incentives given to the private investors by the large-scale deregulation of the economy under the convertibility programme. The increase in capital inflows led to a surge of liquidity in the economy, which subsequently caused a reduction in interest rates, which led to a rise in aggregate demand and employment in the economy. The expansion of aggregate demand led to an increase in the prices of non-tradables, which caused real exchange rate appreciation. The real exchange rate might also have appreciated due to the presence of inertial inflation. The inertia in inflation arose due to the indexation of wage contracts and the indexation of many non-tradables like housing rents, school fees and mortgage payments (Frenkel and Rapetti, 2010; Arora, 2016a, 2016b). These led to the worsening of the current account balance, which, in turn, increased the need for external financing, which further boosted the accumulation of debts in the economy in the latter half of the 1990s.

The rise in external indebtedness significantly increased the fragility of the economy. This led to a weakening of the credibility in the economy's management of the exchange rate system. The risk premium rose with the increase in the probability of an exchange rate devaluation causing a rise in the domestic interest rate. The economy thus became vulnerable to speculative attacks against its currency and faced a banking and currency crisis after two exogenous shocks in the late 1990s – the Asian and the Russian financial crises. The country eventually defaulted on its external debt in 2001. The period of "euphoria" had added significantly to the debt burden of Argentina and most of that debt was held in the hands of the public sector.

To most observers, there was no doubt that such a large debt burden was unsustainable and that it would eventually require restructuring. Unfortunately, the restructuring exercise could not take place preemptively. This debt stock was later restructured in 2005 and 2010 after Argentina defaulted on payments that were due to its private foreign creditors. The Kirchner government that came to power in 2003 decided to save the resources of the country from being wasted on servicing debt and utilize the savings on increased social sector spending. The restructuring

Table 10.1   Region-wise distribution of non-performing debt

Region	Percentage of Debt Held
Argentina	46.9
Europe	34.6
United States	12.3
Asia	3.7
Other Latin American countries	2.5

Source: Hornbeck (2004).

of debt in Argentina was not a simple exercise, for two important reasons. First, because the government had issued 152 bonds denominated in seven currencies and governed by multiple jurisdictions by the time of the default (Hornbeck, 2004) the negotiation process was extremely difficult. Second, domestic banks in Argentina were holding a lot of government-issued bonds as their assets. Any decline in the face value of such bonds could destroy the intermediation channels in Argentina. The region-wise distribution of non-performing debt that was to be restructured in 2005 is shown in Table 10.1 and the details of the restructuring are shown in Box 10.1.

The majority of the debt that was to be restructured in 2005 and later on in 2010 was held by domestic creditors (Table 10.1). This consisted of the ordinary citizens of Argentina, the pension fund holders, and other retail investors who had invested their life savings in buying their country's bonds, which are considered to be the most risk-free asset in any country. The next big group of bondholders consisted of European (mostly Italian)

BOX 10.1   DETAILS OF THE 2005 DEBT RESTRUCTURING EXERCISE

Post-default restructuring	US$66 and Argentine peso-denominated bonds exchanged for US$5 and Argentine peso-denominated bonds
Total duration	42 months
Haircut	76.8 per cent
Participation rate	76 per cent (others were holdouts who litigated)
Creditor structure	Dispersed

Source: Trebesch, Papaioannou and Das (2012).

retail investors who, again, were investors with marginal savings. It is interesting to note here that the major threat to this restructuring exercise came eventually from a minority of the bondholders (holdouts from the United States). The attempt at restructuring both in 2005 and 2010 were aimed at bilaterally negotiating with the private creditors in "good faith" in the hope that there would not be any holdouts, but this was not to happen.

The debt swap agreement of the 2005 restructuring contained many novel features. The debt restructuring that was being done under the Peronist government of Nestor Kirchner heavily penalized the practice of capitalizing past-due interest and increasing the overall debt burden. So, the deal included the provision that Argentina would not recognize the past-due interest for the period between December 2001 and December 2003 (Sturzenegger and Zettelmeyer, 2006). The other interesting part of the deal was that the newly restructured bonds were gross domestic product (GDP) linked, which means interest payments on these bonds would be conditional on the growth of the economy. The conditions were as follows: "GDP had to be higher than the stipulated trend; growth in the previous year had to be larger than 3 percent; and the total payments made by the facility could never be larger than 48 cents on the dollar" (Sturzenegger and Zettelmeyer, 2006, p. 190). The agreement also encompassed a *stick*: the Kirchner government passed a new law – the Ley Cerrojo (The "Lock Law") – which forbade the government from reopening any additional exchanges in the future for the bondholders who refused to abide by the 2005 terms of exchange. This was also the first debt restructuring exercise in Argentina that had made use of the collective action clauses (CACs).[2] The use of CACs in US law was permitted after 2003, when they were initially used by Mexico. After the restructuring exercise in 2005, the Argentine government took another historic step by making the debt renegotiation process completely bilateral – it cleared all its IMF dues and made its restructuring deal free from IMF surveillance. The IMF programme was suspended in August 2004 and full payment was made on IMF obligations in 2006.

The 2010 debt restructuring exercise was an attempt by the Cristina Kirchner government to carry forward the process of honouring the sovereign debtor's payment commitments that was started in 2005. The Cristina Kirchner government had to repeal the Lock Law, which had been enacted in 2005, to enable another debt swap in 2010. The main reason behind opening another debt swap was that the government wanted to rope in the holdouts, those creditors who were refusing to go along with the terms of the agreement, to avoid litigation that had started emerging after 2005 in courts across the globe against Argentina. The terms of agreement that were offered in the 2010 debt swap were almost the same as those in

2005. This was due to a law that the Argentine government had passed in 2009 – the RUFO clause. The RUFO (Rights upon Future Offers) clause barred the government from giving bondholders who had filed lawsuits any more favourable treatment than what was offered to those who had not done so. This law was to have important implications later for Argentina in 2014. The result of the debt swap was encouraging since it did rope in some holdouts and the participation rate for both 2005 and 2010 exchange combined was 91.3 per cent.

The minority creditors who still did not agree to abide by the terms of the agreement were majorly hedge funds who had deep pockets and could fight cases against what they called the "rogue debtor". The hedge funds who owned $4.4 billion of Argentine bonds were the major non-participants in the 2010 debt swap. A group of hedge funds in America had formed an organization in the early 2000s to advance their interests. This group was known as the American Task Force Argentina (ATFA). NML, a Cayman Islands-based subsidiary of Elliot Funds Limited, was a major force behind this grouping. US businessman Paul Singer owns Elliot Funds and, using his political clout among the Republicans in the United States, the ATFA spent around US$6.7 million in lobbying from 2007 to June 2015.[3] Various coercive measures were deployed against Argentina by these hedge funds throughout the restructuring period and even after that – ranging from seizing Argentinian assets in the central bank, capturing a ship on foreign soil, and attempting to capture the President's plane. Indeed, these actions are reminiscent of "gunboat diplomacy".

THE LITIGATION AND THE "*PARI PASSU*" CLAUSE

NML Capital Ltd. took the lead in litigating against Argentina in US courts. The example it set was then followed by other creditors, so much so that the debt restructuring exercise became what is called in the literature a "rush to the courthouse" (Sturzenegger and Zettelmeyer, 2006). NML's case was heard in the United States District Court (Southern District of New York) by Judge Thomas Griesa. Judge Griesa gave a series of judgments on matters related to the debt restructuring exercise of Argentina, but the most remarkable was the one given in November, 2012 when Judge Griesa very creatively used the "*pari passu*" (a Latin phrase meaning "on equal footing") clause (which was present in the agreement of the bonds issued to the holdout creditors) to aid the plaintiffs. This judgment was a landmark judgment that thwarted all the work that had gone into gaining international support for a sovereign bankruptcy regime. In what follows, the judicial interpretation of this clause is examined in greater detail.

In 1994, the bonds were issued by the Fiscal Agency Agreement (FAA) in Argentina, with the agreement containing this clause. The agreement read:

> [t]he Securities will constitute. . .direct, unconditional, unsecured and unsub-ordinated obligations of the Republic and shall at all times rank *pari passu* and without any preference among themselves. *The payment obligations of the Republic under the Securities shall at all times rank at least equally with all its other present and future unsecured and unsubordinated External Indebtedness.* (*NML Capital, Ltd.* v. *Republic of Argentina*, pp. 4–5, No. 12-105 (L) (2d Cir. 2012); original emphasis)

The initial ruling by Judge Griesa's court was upheld by the Court of Appeals for the Second Circuit. The Court of Appeals observed:

> The combination of Argentina's executive declarations and legislative enact-ments have ensured that plaintiffs' beneficial interests do *not* remain direct, unconditional, unsecured and unsubordinated obligations of the Republic and that any claims that may arise from the Republic's restructured debt *do* have priority in Argentinian courts over claims arising out of the Republic's unstruc-tured debt. Thus, we have little difficulty concluding that Argentina breached the *Pari Passu* Clause of the FAA. (*NML Capital, Ltd.* v. *Republic of Argentina*, p. 20, No. 12-105 (2d Cir. 2012); original emphasis)

This ruling certainly overlooked the facts of the matter in the case because the restructured bondholders had applied deep haircuts[4] to get "priority" over claims compared to other unstructured creditors. There was no men-tion of this fact in the judgment of the Court of Appeals.

After getting approval from the Court of Appeals regarding the breach of the *pari passu* clause, the task was left for Judge Griesa's court to decide appropriate punishment for the rogue debtor and also to explain the terms of payments to the bondholders. Judge Griesa awarded an injunction to the Republic of Argentina in the case and ruled that "The Republic accordingly is permanently ORDERED to specifically perform its obliga-tions to NML under Paragraph 1(c) of the FAA as follows:

> a. Whenever the Republic pays any amount due under terms of the bonds or other obligations issued pursuant to the Republic's 2005 or 2010 Exchange Offers, or any subsequent exchange of or substitution for the 2005 and 2010 Exchange Offers that may occur in the future (collectively, the "Exchange Bonds"), the Republic shall concurrently or in advance make a "Ratable Payment" (as defined below) to NML. (*NML Capital, Ltd.* v. *Republic of Argentina*, pp. 2–3, United States District Court, Southern District of New York, 2012)

The court explained the idea of "Ratable Payment" as follows: "if 100% of what is *currently due* to the exchange bondholders *is paid*, then 100% of what is currently due to plaintiffs must also be paid" (*NML Capital, Ltd.* v. *Republic of Argentina*, p. 7, United States District Court, Southern District of New York, 2012; original emphasis).

Although the breach of the *pari passu* clause does not merit an injunction, Judge Griesa had his own reasons for ordering an injunction:

> In accepting the exchange offers of thirty cents on the dollar, the exchange bondholders bargained for certainty and the avoidance of the burden and risk of litigating their rights on the FAA Bonds. However, they knew full well that other owners of FAA Bonds were seeking to obtain *full payment* of the amounts due on such bonds through persisting in the litigation. Indeed, the exchange bondholders were able to watch year after year while plaintiffs in the litigation pursued methods of recovery against Argentina which were largely unsuccessful. However, decisions have now been handed down by the District Court and the Court of Appeals based on the *Pari Passu* Clause, which give promise of providing plaintiffs with full recovery of the amounts due to them on their FAA Bonds. This is hardly an injustice. The exchange bondholders made the choice not to pursue the route which plaintiffs have pursued. (*NML Capital, Ltd.* v. *Republic of Argentina*, p. 8, United States District Court, Southern District of New York, 2012; original emphasis)

This is a very narrow reading of the contract given the fact that the exchange bondholders did not choose the route of litigation because they did not have deep pockets like the hedge fund NML. The restructured bondholders, as has already been shown earlier, consisted of ordinary citizens like the Argentine pension holders and the small retail investors in Italy who did not have the financial wherewithal to pursue litigation in US courts. Although this judgment might sound like a narrow reading of the contract, it does fit in well within the established principles of jurisprudence under the New York Law. In an earlier case arguing about the interpretation of the acceleration clause in FAA bonds in 2004, the Court of Appeals had observed that, "[i]n New York, a bond is a contract. . . Thus, the parties' dispute over the meaning of the Equal Treatment Provision presents a 'simple question of contract interpretation'" (*EM Ltd.* v. *Republic of Argentina*, 382 F.3d 291, 292 (2d Cir. 2004), quoted on p. 16 of *NML Capital, Ltd.* v. *Republic of Argentina*, No. 12-105 (2d Cir. 2012)).

This order also had the power to impair the system of financial intermediation since the third parties were prohibited to make payments to the restructured bondholders on behalf of Argentina. Initially, only those third parties who were making payments to restructured bondholders with bonds issued under New York Law jurisdiction were included. Even after the Bank of New York Mellon (which was the indenture trustee for making payments to the US bondholders who had agreed to the restructuring) was barred from making payments to Argentina's US creditors, the government of Argentina held its fort and decided to focus on other sources of finance. The country started issuing more bonds under the Argentine jurisdiction so as to have a less volatile source of financing at hand. This attempt by the Argentine government to avoid making payments to the holdouts, those who were refusing to sign on to the agreement, and still keep itself current on its payment commitments to the restructured bondholders, received a death blow after it lost its case in the US Supreme Court in June 2014.

The US Supreme Court denied a writ of certiorari[5] and denied Argentina's claim that the judgment transgressed sovereign immunity. FSIA (Foreign Sovereign Immunities Act) 1976 had already weakened such immunity. There are two kinds of sovereign immunity: "jurisdictional" and "execution". The court held that:

> [t]he first, jurisdictional immunity was waived here. The second, execution immunity, generally shields "property in the United States of a foreign state" from attachment, arrest and execution. The Act [FSIA, 1976] has no third provision forbidding or limiting discovery in aid of execution of a foreign-sovereign judgement debtor's assets. (*Republic of Argentina* v. *NML Capital, Ltd.*, pp. 1–2, Certiorari to the United States Court of Appeals for the Second Circuit, Supreme Court of the United States, 2014)

The judgment by the Supreme Court vindicated the stand of the US District Court and it was now ready to cross every jurisdiction to make sure that its orders were held. Since Argentina was adamant that it would not pay the holdouts, Citibank – which is into the custody business for dollar-denominated bonds issued under the Argentine jurisdiction – was asked to stop making payments to the restructured bondholders. This led Argentina to another default on payments due on 30 July, 2014. Citibank appealed again in the District Court, requesting that it be allowed to resume its duties (that of an intermediary), citing sanction by the Argentine government as the reason. To this, Judge Griesa replied in another judgment on 12 March, 2015:

> By observing the injunction, Citibank asserts that it risks sanction in Argentina. However, if Citibank processes payments on exchange bonds, it violates the injunction issued by this court. Neither option is appealing. But if Citibank's predicament is a matter of comity, it is only because the Republic has refused to observe the judgements of the court to whose jurisdiction it acceded. Comity does not suggest abrogating those judgements, or creating exceptions to the Injunction designed to enforce them. Rather, comity suggests that the Republic not penalize third parties, like Citibank, who *must* observe the orders of United States courts. (*Various Plaintiffs* v. *The Republic of Argentina*, p. 13, United States District Court, Southern District of New York, 2015; original emphasis)

Argentina had explored the possibility of issuing bonds to its restructured bondholders in its own jurisdiction but the original sin[6] problem had played its role. Although the bonds were issued under the Argentine jurisdiction, the currency denomination of most of the bonds remained US dollars and the US court decision made full use of this lacuna to hold Argentina accountable in this case. Between June and October 2015, Judge Griesa granted the "ME TOO" injunctions to 49 more plaintiffs so that even they could seek legal aid under the *pari passu* clause (Rule 62.1 Indicative Ruling, United States District Court, Southern District of New York, February 2016). The change of government in Argentina in December 2015 vindicated the stand of the US courts even further because the new government under the stewardship of Mauricio Macri settled with the holdouts. Judge Griesa removed the injunction that was applied in 2012 and Argentina became free to pay for everybody including the holdouts. In the first round, Argentina agreed to settle with four of the holdouts who represented almost 66 per cent of the total claims of the plaintiffs for the sums shown in Table 10.2 (Shearman and Sterling LLP, 2016). The important point here is that these holdouts had not even bought these securities at their original face values. They had hedged and bought the securities at deep discounts. NML, for example, had bought the bonds at around $177 million and were now asking for full face value, full past-due interest and also legal fees that they had to incur during the litigation process. Table 10.2 shows the compensation on principal that the four holdouts with whom the Republic of Argentina had agreed to settle would receive.

Argentina's settlement with these "vulture" hedge funds, who had bought Argentina's debt at heavily discounted prices and were later paid

Table 10.2   Argentina's settlement with its four major holdout creditors

	Original Principal Amount Contained in Claims (US$ million)	Compensation on Principal Contained in Claims (US$ million)
NML	617	2422
Blue Angel	177	330
Aurelius	299	759
Bracebridge	120	1146

Note: Data filed in the court on 29 February 2016 by the Under Secretary of Finance, Argentina.

Source: Shearman and Sterling LLP (2016).

the face value in full, called into question the very idea of sovereign debt restructuring in good faith. It set a dangerous precedent for restructuring attempts in the future. This settlement will likely make it more difficult to make a binding agreement with those creditors who were ready before this episode to renegotiate their contracts in "good faith" with the sovereign debtor, unlike the holdouts that include hedge funds who buy emerging market debt for speculative purposes. The idea of CACs will take a beating in the future. The most important fallout of this deal in Argentina for the economic theory of sovereign debt is that sovereign debt might not remain *unenforceable* anymore in US jurisdiction (Arora, 2016a, 2016b). However, enforceability rather than aiding the developing country debtor has enabled the creditors to be able to force a sovereign debtor to pay off its debts at least in this instance. Given the fact that past decisions of courts are often cited as precedent in future cases, this is a real threat.

LOOKING BACK: WAS THE PAST ANY BETTER?

It is instructive to look back at history and see if it has some lessons to offer. This chapter looks at the terms under which Argentine debt was restructured after the Barings crisis of 1890. This way of looking at history is not entirely novel. Economists have drawn an analogy between the Barings crisis and the tequila crisis of 1995 (Eichengreen, 1999). Some have also looked at quantitative easing in the United States through the "prism of the Barings crisis" (Vasudevan, 2014). But the comparison of the debt restructuring "then" and "now" for Argentina has hitherto remained unexplored, although the Barings episode in general has been looked at in the past (Fishlow, 1989). Latin American countries in general have had a long association with international capital markets, dating back to the Gold Standard era of the nineteenth century when capital markets thrived as they did in the 1990s. Argentina saw a similar wave of incoming liquidity in the 1880s as it did in the 1990s and, in fact, there are a number of striking similarities between the two inflows. There were low interest rates prevailing in the core[7] in the 1880s and the early 1990s, which facilitated huge capital inflows into Argentina (in the periphery). During both these decades, the Argentinian economy was working on a more or less fixed exchange rate system (the gold standard from the early 1880s and the convertibility programme from 1991) and the "euphoria" (Kindleberger, 1978) in both was succeeded by a "sudden stop" (Dornbusch, Goldfajn and Valdes, 1995).

The Baring Brothers (the richest merchant bankers in Britain at the time) had invested heavily in Argentina in the 1880s and the shock was delivered in 1888 when the Barings failed to float a bond (a Buenos Aires Drainage and Waterworks Company bond). Argentina was unable to pay and its GDP fell by 11 per cent between 1890 and 1891. Like the Lehman Brothers case, the "too big to fail" theory was put forth to save the Baring Brothers. This was unusual since governments in the Gold Standard era had an ambivalent attitude towards intervention in creditor–debtor negotiations. Some past economists have argued that less intervention by governments and national banks was the reason for the default clusters in the late nineteenth century (Eichengreen and Portes, 1989). Although intervention to save Baring Brothers was an exception rather than a rule in those times, the case itself is interesting to explore for its ramifications. The liquidation of the Baring Brothers required that its assets be in a "marketable" state and since most of its assets were Argentine securities, the panacea to the Barings crisis was a recovery of the Argentine economy so that repayment on its debt could start again. A committee was set up under Lord Rothschild, who was also a merchant banker in England, to suggest solutions for Argentina's debt overhang. The committee came up with three solutions:

1. Argentina should go for structural reforms and no finance should be extended till the time serious reforms have started.
2. Argentina should be pressurized to clear its dues towards its creditors but at the same time, some sources of external finance should be kept open for the country.
3. A funding loan commensurate to Argentina's needs should be advanced to the country and the policy reforms should be pushed in the long term (Fishlow, 1989).

In hindsight, the first two solutions seem to be two variants of austerity. The first solution cited above is the harsher version of austerity, while the second is more like the lending-in-arrears policy of the IMF that envisages structural reforms in the future as the cost of emergency funding. It is heartening to note that the committee chose the third option and Argentina was lent money without being coaxed into immediate reforms in exchange.

What followed next is even more surprising given the generally assumed antagonistic nature of the relationship between the debtor and the creditor. The loan that was approved by the Rothschild Committee failed to improve the situation very much since the amount extended could cover only about a third of foreign exchange requirements for full debt service. Due to the failure of the above plan, a debt restructuring deal (the Arreglo Romero) was devised in 1893, and included the following suggestions: (1)

for five years until 1898, interest payments were to be reduced by an average of 30 per cent; and (2) amortization was to be suspended until the beginning of 1901 (Fishlow, 1989, p. 90).[8] Creditors acceded to this demand and the Argentine economy saw a large influx of capital post-restructuring: between 1901 and 1915, 47 per cent of gross fixed investment was foreign financed (Diaz-Alejandro, quoted in Fishlow, 1989, p. 91).

The focus of the chapter now shifts to the inter-war period when major geopolitical and institutional changes pertaining to sovereign debt renegotiations had taken place. After World War I, the United States became the new centre of global finance after achieving a net creditor status. The role of the United States in deciding the direction of global capital flows became entrenched by the end of World War II. The United States had used "gunboat diplomacy" to establish its supremacy at the dawn of the twentieth century; by the time of the Great Depression, it turned to the *carrot* policy of "dollar diplomacy". The major institutional change that had taken place is that creditor country governments now started intervening in the creditor–debtor relationship on behalf of their creditors, though the extent was still small as compared to their current actions. Argentina was a poster child for good debtor behaviour during the inter-war period since it remained current on its repayment obligations while other sovereign debtors in its neighbourhood like Bolivia, Colombia, Chile and Peru had reneged on their payment commitments to their creditors. This can be seen clearly from the historical record (Figure 10.1).

The present value ratio is the ratio of repayments to borrowings and, as can be seen from Figure 10.1, Argentina was the only country that was a faithful debtor in the region since its ratio of repayments to borrowings was greater than that in the inter-war period. All other countries considered here were defaulters during the inter-war period since their present value ratio was less than one. According to the standard models on sovereign debt, one of the major incentives for sovereign debtors to repay was fear of loss of reputation (Eaton et al., 1986). The evidence from Argentina after the inter-war period poses a serious threat to the assumption of reputation incentive in the models. Although Argentina was a faithful debtor and conducted its negotiations in good faith with its creditors, it did not receive any prizes for preserving its reputation (Figure 10.2).

Figure 10.2 shows 15-year averages of the ratio of external finance (flowing through various sectors shown on the graph) to the exports of the countries for the period 1950–64. It explains the fact that after the effects of the Great Depression had started waning and international lending picked up post-World War II, Argentina performed worse in attracting capital inflows compared to countries in its neighbourhood that were serial defaulters in the inter-war period. In fact, as far as inflows through

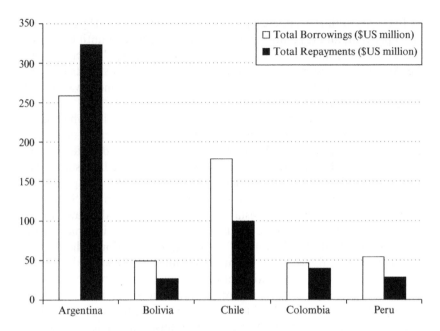

Note: The above figures are for the inter-war period and are discounted for 1920 year-end.

Source: Jorgenson and Sachs (1989).

Figure 10.1   Sovereign borrowings and repayments during the inter-war period

government and official transfers in the post-war period are concerned, Argentina was the worst performer; all countries in the region considered here were shown more generosity by official lenders. So, the defaulters had a higher ratio of government and official transfers to their exports than Argentina.

The lesson one learns from the historical experiences cited above is quite clear: though there can be no denial of the fact that the relationship between the debtor and the creditor is always antagonistic, there *were* possibilities by which the debt negotiation solution could be made amicable. During the Gold Standard era, the intervention by the Bank of England on behalf of the Baring Brothers was a rare instance of official creditor intervention. Creditor country governments did not resort to such an intervention on behalf of their creditors on a routine basis. And, arguably, even after the Bank of England intervention in the Barings case, the solution was in the interests of both the sovereign debtor and creditor.

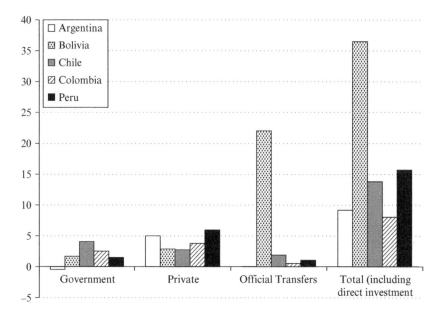

Source: Jorgenson and Sachs (1989).

Figure 10.2   *Fifteen-year averages of the ratio of external finance to
               exports 1950–64*

Such resolutions in the interests of the debtor became rarer in the dollar
diplomacy days of the inter-war period when interventions in the private
creditor and sovereign–debtor relation became contingent on the foreign
policy interests of the United States, the world's major creditor nation
and the new linchpin of global finance. But even those days look brighter
from the vantage point of Argentina's debt restructuring, when courts have
crossed their respective jurisdictions to protect hedge funds in their fight
against a sovereign debtor. The worsening possibilities for a successful
negotiation between the sovereign debtor and its creditors can have serious
repercussions.

CONCLUSION

The story of Argentina offers some new insights to the prevailing literature
on sovereign debt. First, it is a standard feature of almost all theoretical
literature on sovereign debt to mention that a creditor only has limited
means to enforce repayment because the debtor here in question is not

an individual but rather a country. However, reality is not so simple. The story of Argentina shows that there are attempts being made by powerful interests in this age of finance to challenge that key feature and make sovereign debt exogenously enforceable in a court of law. Although one can say that Argentina is a special case and this story would not necessarily be repeated in all contexts, one should be aware that US courts generally work on past precedents and New York is the most common jurisdiction for international bond issuance. Given the fact that there are several debt restructuring exercises around the globe, the Argentina story might be an example of a rush to the courthouse.

Even more intriguing is the second insight from this chapter. The general assumption was that if a sovereign debt contract were secured by an exogenous enforcement mechanism, it would allow finance to play its productive role of intermediation so that developing countries could access international capital markets. However, creeping exogenous enforcement in the context of Argentina suggests the opposite. If anything, judicial intervention has wreaked havoc in the context of Argentina. Rather than taking the side of the 91 per cent of bondholders who had agreed on deep haircuts in earlier restructurings, the court ruled in favour of the hedge funds that made a huge gain on their bets. This would give a fillip to speculation in the sovereign debt markets across the globe. Hedge funds would learn from this episode that it is easy to buy bonds cheaply and then litigate against a developing country borrower in a developed country jurisdiction. This would become an easy recipe for gaining manifold compensation on the principal amount contained in the original claims. In a world where global foreign exchange transactions are many times greater than GDP or the actual needs of the countries for trade (Epstein and Habbard, 2013), developing country bonds are soft targets. As the historical evidence presented in this chapter shows, the global financial architecture has gradually worsened over time as far as the treatment of debtors in any sovereign debt contract is concerned.

NOTES

*   The author would to thank Professor Gerald Epstein for his valuable comments on the first draft of this chapter.
1. Brady bonds were created in March 1989 to convert bank loans to mostly Latin American countries into a variety of new bonds after many of those countries defaulted on their debt in the 1980s.
2. These are clauses that are added in a debt contract. In the event of a need for a debt restructuring, these clauses kick in as follows: if 75 per cent of the creditors have agreed for a restructuring of the debt burden of the sovereign debtor, the minority creditors are also roped in irrespective of their wishes.

3. Source: Embassy of Argentina in the United States.
4. In a debt restructuring context, haircuts refer to the loss suffered by creditors due to a reduction in the amount that is repaid to them. To be more precise, a haircut is a loss in the present value of creditor claims due to a reduction in the face value of the old debt instruments.
5. A writ seeking judicial review.
6. The original sin problem was the "inability of countries to borrow abroad in their own currencies" (Eichengreen, Hausmann and Panizza, 2003, p. 3).
7. Britain constituted the core in the 1880s while the fulcrum shifted to the United States after the Great Depression.
8. Repayment of principal loan.

REFERENCES

Aguiar, M. and M. Amador (2013), "Sovereign debt: A review", *NBER Working Paper No. 19388.*

Arora, M. (2016a), "Sovereign debt restructuring: A study of some selected episodes", *Jawaharlal Nehru University*, unpublished MPhil dissertation.

Arora, M. (2016b), "Changing rules of the game of global finance: Glimpses from a sovereign debt restructuring episode", *MPRA*, 18 August, mpra.ub.uni-muenchen.de/73181/.

Dornbusch, R., I. Goldfajn and R.I. Valdes (1995), "Currency crises and collapses", *Brookings Papers on Economic Activity*, **26**(2), 219–94.

Eaton, J., M. Gersovitz and J.E. Stiglitz (1986), "The pure theory of country risk", *NBER Working Paper No. 1894.*

Eichengreen, B. (1999), "The Baring crisis in a Mexican mirror", *International Political Science Review*, **20**(3), 249–70.

Eichengreen, B. and R. Portes (1989), "After the deluge: Default, negotiation and readjustment during the inter-war years", in B. Eichengreen and P. Lindert (eds), *The International Debt Crisis in Historical Perspective*, Cambridge, MA: MIT Press, pp. 12–47.

Eichengreen, B., R. Hausmann and U. Panizza (2003), "Currency mismatches, debt intolerance and original sin: Why they are not the same and why it matters", *NBER Working Paper No. 10036.*

Embassy of Argentina in the United States (n.d) [website], accessed 24 April 2016 at www.eeeuu.mrecic.gov.ar.

Epstein, G. and H. Gintis (1995), "International capital markets and national economic policy", *Review of International Political Economy*, **2**(4), 693–718.

Epstein, G.A. and P. Habbard (2013), "Speculation and sovereign debt: An insidious interaction", in M.H. Wolfson and G.A. Epstein (eds), *The Handbook of the Political Economy of Financial Crises*, Oxford: Oxford University Press, pp. 326–56.

Fishlow, A. (1989)."Conditionality and willingness to pay: Some parallels from the 1890s", in B. Eichengreen and P. Lindert (eds), *The International Debt Crisis in Historical Perspective*, Cambridge, MA: MIT Press, pp. 86–105.

Frenkel, R. and M. Rapetti (2010), "A concise history of exchange rate regimes in Latin America", *University of Massachusetts Amherst Working Papers*, accessed 20 July 2018 at scholarworks.umass.edu/cgi/viewcontent.cgi?referer=https://www.google.com/&httpsredir=1&article=1096&context=econ_workingpaper.

Hornbeck, J.F. (2004), "Argentina's sovereign debt restructuring", *Congressional Research Service Report for Congress, No. RL32637.*

Jorgenson, E. and J. Sachs (1989), "Default and renegotiation of Latin American foreign bonds in the interwar period", in B. Eichengreen and P. Lindert (eds), *The International Debt Crisis in Historical Perspective*, Cambridge, MA: MIT Press, pp. 48–85.

Kindleberger, C.P. (1978), *Manias, Panics, and Crashes: A History of Financial Crises*, New York: Basic Books.

Shearman and Sterling LLP (2016), "Supplemental materials on behalf of Argentina in support of motion to vacate ratable payment injunction, including memo of law and declarations", accessed 20 July 2018 at https://argentine.shearman.com/Supplemental-materials-to-vacate-Ratable-Payment-Injunction.

Smith, A. (1776 [1950]), *An Inquiry Into the Nature and Causes of the Wealth of Nations*, London: Methuen.

Sturzenegger, F. and J. Zettelmeyer (2006), *Debt Defaults and Lessons from a Decade of Crises*, Cambridge, MA: MIT Press.

Supreme Court of the United States (n.d.) [website], accessed 24 April 2016 at www.supremecourt.gov/.

Trebesch, C., M.G. Papaioannou and U.S. Das (2012), "Sovereign debt restructurings 1950–2010: Literature survey, data, and stylized facts", *IMF Working Paper No. 12/203.*

United States Court of Appeals for the Second Circuit (n.d.) [website], accessed 24 April 2016 at www.ca2.uscourts.gov/.

United States District Court Southern District of New York (n.d.) [website], accessed 24 April 2016 at www.nysd.uscourts.gov/.

Vasudevan, R. (2014), "Quantitative easing through the prism of the Barings crisis in 1890: Central banks and the international money market", *Journal of Post Keynesian Economics*, 37(1), 91–114.

11. Solidarity vs similarity: The political economy of currency unions

Francisco Perez

INTRODUCTION

The fate of monetary unions depends on whether the wealthier members are willing to subsidize the poorer ones. Neoliberal economists and policy-makers emphasize similarity – defined as high levels of trade, synchronized business cycles and labor mobility – between countries as the main criterion for membership in a currency union. They argue that any payments imbalances between countries can be resolved by internal devaluation – provided governments commit to limits on fiscal spending and to weakening labor protections. They also assume that free markets in goods, services, capital and labor will lead to higher growth in the poorer countries, and therefore convergence of incomes to those of the richer regions. Yet, the sovereign debt and banking crises of 2010 and growing divergence in the Eurozone reveal the pitfalls of the neoliberal approach to monetary and economic integration. Instead, history suggests that "solidarity" criteria – political mechanisms to facilitate fiscal transfers from surplus to deficit regions or countries – are essential to the survival of monetary unions, while similarity between regions is a secondary concern.

The biggest political obstacle is persuading governments in surplus countries to agree to bear the burden of adjustment during crises, and not simply impose it on weaker, deficit countries. The optimal case is for economic integration to correspond with political integration, for monetary[1] unions to have common fiscal *and* monetary policies. Political integration makes progressive and redistributive fiscal policy possible; such large and automatic transfer payments from surplus to deficit regions are vital for containing centrifugal forces within currency unions. Without formal political/fiscal integration, however, a "hegemonic power" will have to establish and sustain a "political surplus recycling mechanism" to avoid economic divergence and political discontent. Ironically, the original optimum currency area theorists understood the need for fiscal integration and the undeniably political nature of dealing with imbalances within a currency union, yet those insights were lost in the design of the Eurozone and the reform of the CFA franc zone in the 1990s (Krugman, 2013).

This chapter examines three historical case studies – the euro, the CFA franc and the East African shilling – to illustrate how the existence of a political surplus recycling mechanism determines the success of currency unions. The next section compares the similarity and solidarity criteria for currency union membership and argues that a political surplus recycling mechanism is necessary for the success and longevity of a currency union. It also describes how neoclassical growth theory overlooks the possibility of divergence between countries, while heterodox traditions have devoted more attention to processes of uneven development. The third section explains how the German government's failure to act like a "good" hegemon has led to divergence within the Eurozone and threatens its future. The fourth section argues that the old colonial franc – the CFA – has survived nearly 60 years after independence because the French government has been a good hegemon, providing substantial foreign aid to CFA zone countries to ease adjustment during the debt crises of the 1980s and 1990s. The fifth section describes how the unwillingness of the United Kingdom and Kenya to establish themselves as hegemons in East Africa led to the collapse of the East African Currency Board shortly after independence in the 1960s. Section six discusses the implications of this analysis for the future of the Eurozone, the CFA zone, and the proposed revival of the East African shilling zone.

SIMILARITY AND SOLIDARITY CRITERIA

Similarity Criteria

The similarity criteria are built on the theory of optimum currency areas (OCA). Robert Mundell (1961), Ronald McKinnon (1963) and Peter Kenen (1969) examine what factors delineate an OCA, and how to address imbalances within currency areas. Mundell (1961) emphasizes that regions that are most similar in their response to external shocks are an OCA, and that factor mobility is necessary for fast adjustment. If a shock – for instance, an increase in the price of a key import – affects the entire region in a similar way, then a common monetary policy is effective. But, if one region is experiencing an economic boom while another is in a deep recession, the monetary policy that is appropriate for one region may not be optimal for the other. In that case, it is more efficient for each region to maintain its own flexible exchange rate with the others.

When confronted with asymmetric shocks, Mundell (1961) stresses the importance of factor – especially labor – mobility across the currency area.

For adjustment to happen smoothly, workers should be able to move easily from areas of high unemployment to low unemployment, capital from depressed areas to booming ones, and goods to regions where prices are lower to those where they are higher. Factor mobility should determine currency borders; ideally, labor is mobile within currency areas and immobile across them.

Imbalances between regions, however, are the norm; no large economic area is ever homogeneous. More importantly, imbalances may be structural. Regions or countries with higher labor productivity and income levels often have persistent trade surpluses with regions with lower relative productivity and incomes. Large current account surpluses and deficits are not self-correcting in the short to medium run, even with floating exchange rates. Keynes, aware of these persistent imbalances in international trade and finance, proposed a tax on trade surpluses at Bretton Woods but the US delegation refused to give up control over the United States' surpluses to the Europeans (Eichengreen, 2012; Varoufakis, 2016). This historical episode underscores the fundamental asymmetry in international finance: while deficit regions are forced to reduce their payments deficits at some point, there is little pressure for surplus regions to do the same.

According to neoliberal economists, deficit regions should regain competitiveness by lowering their wages and prices relative to surplus regions, allowing them to eventually achieve external balance. With currency devaluation no longer an option, governments in currency unions should facilitate internal devaluation, especially employers' ability to reduce wages by making it easier to hire and fire workers (Stiglitz, 2016; Varoufakis, 2016).

But neoliberal economists and policymakers disregard the lessons from the classic OCA literature about the political nature of managing imbalances within a currency union. Mundell (1961) explains that a common central bank can achieve full employment across the currency area through expansionary monetary policy but reducing unemployment in deficit regions comes at the expense of higher inflation in the surplus regions. The choice to "inflate away" these surpluses – or not to do so – is a political decision. If surplus regions resist price and wage inflation, then they are imposing lower incomes and employment on deficit regions. A currency union then behaves like the gold standard, ensuring the transmission of deflationary conditions via the foreign trade multiplier.

Peter Kenen (1969), in contrast, stresses the importance of fiscal integration for adjustment. He agrees that labor mobility is important but notes that labor is never perfectly mobile; production in different regions may be more or less labor intensive and labor is rarely homogeneous – especially skilled labor. Labor mobility alone may not be sufficient to substitute for independent monetary and exchange rate policies. A common fiscal policy is indispensable in dealing with persistent imbalances. Large-scale transfer payments are an important adjustment mechanism since "fiscal systems are interregional, not just interpersonal, and the rules which regulate many of those transfer payments relate to the labor market" (Kenen, 1969, p. 47). Fiscal transfers are a more effective way to achieve full employment in a currency area facing asymmetric shocks than inflationary monetary policy or factor mobility. The Eurozone's recent woes prove, as Paul Krugman (2013) quips, that "Kenen has turned out to dominate Mundell" (p. 445).

Political Surplus Recycling Mechanism and Hegemony

Therefore, the most important determinant for the success of a currency union – for common prosperity and longevity – is the existence of a "political surplus recycling mechanism" (Varoufakis, 2016). The "similarity criteria," the typical focus of most economists, are secondary. Instead, political mechanisms to redistribute income from surplus to deficit regions, or "solidarity criteria," are essential. The most successful currency unions are also political and fiscal unions – like the United States. Automatic and countercyclical fiscal transfers serve to mitigate regional imbalances and promote economic convergence.

Without the corresponding formal political union, the "second-best" political solution is for the most powerful member of a currency union to emerge as a responsible "hegemon." A "good" or responsible hegemon is willing and able to act as lender and buyer of last resort for deficit regions especially during economic crises (Kindleberger, 1973). It provides for countercyclical fiscal transfers to deficit or peripheral regions to make adjustment smoother. In contrast, a "bad" or irresponsible hegemon is a government unwilling (or unable) to share the burden of adjustment with deficit regions. In refusing to redistribute some of its surpluses, the bad hegemon ensures a divergent dynamic within the monetary union that is likely to stoke political discontent in deficit regions.

The Politics of Convergence and Divergence

The history of the Eurozone shows how economic integration without political integration can lead to divergent growth paths among members and create social pressures that may tear apart currency unions. Neoclassical growth models, starting with Solow (1956), predict convergence in international income and productivity levels. Instead, over the last two centuries, income inequality between countries has grown spectacularly (Pritchett, 1997).

In contrast, heterodox models frequently assume increasing returns to scale in production (IRS), which result in multiple equilibria and potentially divergent growth paths. The virtuous and vicious cycles created by IRS exist in dialectical tension with other social and political forces. Heterodox growth models have three key features: first, path dependency; second, destabilizing (or positive) feedback effects that are cumulative; and third, growth is constrained not by exogenously given technology and production possibility sets but by social and institutional factors. Instead of countries each arriving at a unique, predetermined, stable equilibrium growth rate, economic growth can be explosive or implosive and depends on initial conditions. Moreover, the heterodox tradition suggests that eventually, "divergent growth paths will provoke institutional change" (Skott and Auerbach, 1995, p. 386). The response to such divergence is impossible to predict, but political authorities are certain to intervene when faced with an economic collapse or long-term stagnation.

The productivity gains essential to IRS may be lost through international trade and finance, with some countries unable to take advantage of the possibilities for growth offered by IRS and instead ending up in a low-growth, long-run equilibrium. The classical development economics of Raúl Prebisch (1962), Hans Singer (1950), and W. Arthur Lewis (1954, 1978), and the Marxist dependency analyses of Arrighi Emmanuel (1977), Samir Amin (1976), and André Gunder Frank (1979), assert that free trade with "core" (or surplus) regions leads to divergence in the "periphery" (or deficit regions). These theories of unequal exchange describe how structural asymmetries in international labor, product and capital markets ensure that productivity gains lead to higher incomes in the core, but not in the periphery. For example, if the periphery exports products with a low income elasticity of demand, while importing products with a higher income elasticity of demand and/or if workers in the core have greater bargaining power than workers in the periphery, then productivity gains in the periphery may be captured by capitalists and workers in the core (Bacha, 1978). The dynamic interaction of IRS, unequal exchange, and political intervention drives uneven development across space and time – with some countries climbing up the global income ladder as others fall further behind. A political surplus recycling mechanism is necessary to counter these tendencies towards divergence between regions in a currency union.

Generalized IRS both helps explain divergence between members and provides a justification for the formation and expansion of currency unions. Monetary systems have significant network externalities – a form of increasing returns to scale. The value of using a currency grows exponentially with the number of users. Several countries in proposed or existing African currency unions – like Guinea-Bissau, Togo, Benin,

Equatorial Guinea, Niger, Burkina Faso, the Central African Republic, and Burundi – have populations under 10 million inhabitants and/or are among the dozen poorest countries in the world. Economic growth in these countries is constrained by the small size of domestic markets. Hence, currency unions may lead to greater intraregional trade, and higher labor and capital mobility by expanding the relevant economic unit; the similarity criteria may, therefore, be met ex-post. Although controversial, there is some evidence that joining a currency union boosts trade among members, including the CFA zone (Tsangarides and Qureshi, 2008).

GERMANY AS BAD HEGEMON IN THE EUROZONE

The Eurozone was built on the premise that monetary integration would compel political integration. Instead, Germany – the largest surplus country – has refused to be a good hegemon, threatening the Eurozone's future. Neoliberal policymakers and academics stress fiscal spending limits to lessen asymmetric shocks and "flexible" labor markets to make internal devaluation possible. But instead of convergence, the "convergence criteria" outlined in the Maastricht Treaty – limiting annual government deficits to 3 percent and overall debt to 60 percent of GDP – have promoted austerity and reinforced centrifugal forces. Internal devaluation and austerity are long and torturous processes with enormous social costs borne by the most vulnerable sections of the population in the form of lower wages, higher unemployment and reduced public services.

By focusing on fiscal deficits instead of trade deficits, policymakers ignored the real source of imbalances in the Eurozone. Fiscal surpluses in Ireland and Spain, for example, did not protect those governments during the financial storm of 2010 (Varoufakis, 2016). Since 2001, Germany has had a merchandise trade surplus with the rest of the Eurozone, and consistent surpluses with all Eurozone members except for Belgium, the Netherlands and Ireland (Figure 11.1). The imbalances in the Eurozone are rooted in the productivity differentials of its members' human and physical capital stocks not in government balance sheets.

The free mobility of capital within the Eurozone did encourage private capital flows "downhill" from the surplus to the deficit countries before the crisis, but since then flows have reversed. German banks, for example, were happy to lend to Irish and Spanish banks during the real estate boom of the 2000s, but as soon as there is a crisis "vendor-financed trade will always go into sudden, violent spasm." Therefore, "[b]ankers in this sense are fair-weather surplus recyclers" (Varoufakis, 2016, pp. 10–11). Such pro-cyclical private capital flows intensify financial crises. Consequently, the

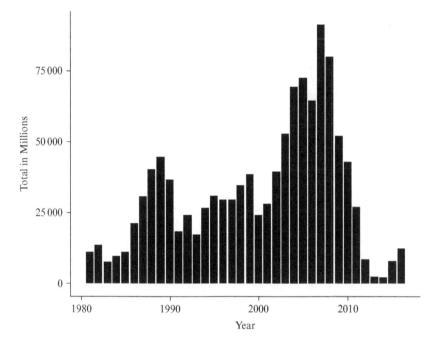

Source: IMF Direction of Trade Statistics.

Figure 11.1 *German trade surplus with the Eurozone (1980–2016) (US dollars)*

Eurozone has been growing more unequal; German GDP went from 10.4 times that of Greece in 2007 to 15 times that of Greece in 2015 (Stiglitz, 2016). Skilled labor is typically more mobile than unskilled labor, causing a brain drain from peripheral regions. Instead of uniting a prosperous and democratic Europe, the euro has fueled economic divergence, stagnation, and political turmoil.

The German government has stated repeatedly that the Eurozone is not a "transfer union," and has refused to share the burden of adjustment for the Eurozone's imbalances, placing it entirely on the periphery. The German government could promote expansionary fiscal and wage policies in Germany to increase inflation and consumption with regard to the peripheral countries and eliminate its surpluses with them. It could write off Greek debt and allow the Greek government to pursue similarly expansionary fiscal policies to end the depression of the Greek economy. It could, in other words, act like a "good" hegemon. Better yet, it could advocate more formal fiscal integration. Instead, the EU budget is miniscule, about 1 percent of EU GDP compared to a US federal budget of over 15 percent of GDP. Feyrer and Sacerdote (2013) estimate that if the EU had the same level of fiscal integration as the United States, Greece would have received additional transfers equal to 4 percent of its GDP. This would have mitigated the massive social costs of the depression in Greece. In short, "one of the reasons for the failure of the Eurozone is that economic integration has outpaced political integration" (Stiglitz, 2016, p. 35).

In contrast, in the United States, the institutions of the New Deal formed the basis for an effective political recycling mechanism. According to Varoufakis (2016), three adjustment mechanisms make the United States successful as a monetary union. First, as Mundell (1961) suggests, is labor mobility. Americans (mostly) speak the same language and share a common culture, which makes it easier for unemployed workers to move. Second, the United States also has a national banking system, with a *Federal* Deposit Insurance Corporation and the *Federal* Reserve as lender of last resort. Third and most important, the United States is a fiscal union, where some states like Connecticut and Minnesota pay more in federal taxes than they receive in spending, subsidizing others like Mississippi and West Virginia that receive more in spending than they generate in revenue. In addition, federally funded safety net programs work as automatic stabilizers by increasing federal spending in the hardest hit areas during recessions.

Such fiscal transfers need not be entirely altruistic, however. When other states subsidized federal transfers to Nevada after the real estate bubble there burst in 2007, "[i]t was not just an act of solidarity to the state of Nevada by the rest of the US. It was rather an automated mechanism that kicked in so as to stop the Nevadan malaise from spreading further afield" (Varoufakis, 2016, p. 13). Sharing the burden of adjustment is in the interest of surplus regions as well. The German government's refusal to act like a good hegemon may prove short-sighted.

FRANCE AS GOOD HEGEMON IN THE CFA FRANC ZONE

The CFA Zone

The best example of French support for the CFA was the period during the late 1980s and early 1990s when the regional central banks had a negative balance on their operations accounts for the only time in the currency union's history. Since independence in 1960, the French government has provided direct budgetary support to the CFA zone governments. France

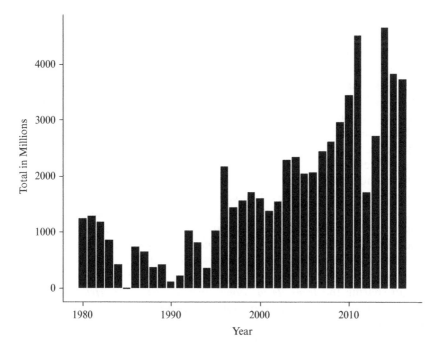

Source: IMF Direction of Trade Statistics.

Figure 11.2   French trade surplus with the CFA zone (1980–2016) (US dollars)

has had a small but consistent trade surplus with the CFA zone (Figure 11.2). French governments have recycled some of these surpluses to the region, especially in times of need. In the 1980s, French policy softened the balance of payments constraint for its African client regimes, while other African economies were undergoing rapid neoliberal restructuring. French leaders prioritized the political stability of their allies in francophone Africa and were able to delay devaluation and ease austerity in the CFA zone.

The French government created the *franc de colonies françaises d'Afrique* or CFA franc in December 1945, to spare their colonies a post-World War II devaluation of the French franc (FF). Like their British counterparts, the French colonial authorities also set up currency boards for their colonies grouped by region, but they operated differently. The British East African Currency Board (EACB), for example, could only issue East African shillings fully backed by British pounds.[2] The French government, on the other hand, offered its colonial currency boards an overdraft facility on their operations accounts with the Treasury. Colonial governments received interest on their reserves and had to pay interest on overdrawn balances – but, in principle, colonial governments could borrow FF in unlimited amounts from the Treasury to make up for any balance of payments deficit. The French government offered to maintain the convertibility guarantee for the CFA, and the promise of monetary stability was one of the incentives for the governments of former French colonies to keep the CFA after independence (Stasavage, 2003; Gulde and Tsangarides, 2008).

Upon independence in 1960 the former colonies of French West Africa – Benin, Burkina Faso, Côte d'Ivoire, Mali, Mauritania, Niger, Senegal and Togo – became members of the *Banque centrale des Etats de l'Afrique de l'ouest* (Central Bank of West African States or BCEAO), which began issuing the *franc de la communauté financière d'Afrique* (African Financial Community franc). The former members of French Central Africa – Chad, Congo-Brazzaville, Central African Republic, Cameroon, and Gabon – began sharing the *franc de la cooperation financière en Afrique centrale* (Central African Financial Cooperation franc) issued by the *Banque centrale de l'Afrique centrale* (Central Bank of Central Africa or BEAC). The two CFA francs have a fixed exchange rate to one another and to the FF, therefore analysts typically treat the CFA as a single currency area.[3] In the early 1970s, the regional central banks were moved from Paris to Dakar, Senegal and Yaoundé, Cameroon and the number of French governors on the boards reduced, although the French Treasury retained veto power over monetary policy.

The decision to maintain colonial currency arrangements after nominal independence, reflects the extraordinarily close links between French and African political elites. The French government had promoted a policy of assimilation of colonial African elites, emphasizing the adoption of French culture and language, and providing limited voting rights. As a result, in France, unlike Britain, Portugal or Belgium, African deputies served in parliament and several were ministers in governments during the Fourth Republic (1946–58). In most of the French colonies, nationalist sentiment among elites was relatively low, and the French handed power to friendly regimes typically headed by men like Léopold Sédhar Senghor of Senegal and Félix Houphouët-Boigny of Côte d'Ivoire who had close personal ties to leading French politicians and bureaucrats. Nearly all the newly independent governments also signed secret defense agreements, and the French maintained their influence through the large number of technical assistants working in African governments, military advisors, businesspeople and other expats playing major roles in West and Central

Africa long after independence (Wallerstein, 1961, 1965, 1967; Manning, 1998; Stasavage, 2003; Le Vine, 2004).

French Hegemony in Action

During the 1980s' debt crisis, African governments were reluctant to accept IMF prescriptions to liberalize trade, cut government spending and devalue their currencies (Van de Walle, 2001). Most succumbed quickly to IMF pressure, but the French government under President François Mitterrand decided to accommodate governments in the CFA zone. Although the CFA countries were not entirely spared "the rigors of adjustment, membership in the franc zone has conferred on the indebted francophone states, with respect to the medicines of the IMF and World Bank, a margin for maneuver that makes their situation sweeter than that of nations like Zambia or Ghana"[4] (Vallée, 1989, p. 24). French foreign aid (an intergovernmental fiscal transfer) loosened the balance of payments constraint for its African client regimes.

The overall net foreign asset position of the BCEAO – the West African regional bank – began to decline steadily in 1979. The French Treasury used the positive balance generated by oil exports in Central Africa – out of Cameroon, Gabon and Equatorial Guinea – to finance West Africa's deficits. The BCEAO had a negative balance on its operations account from 1979 to 1985, peaking at over 5 billion FF, then another small dip from 1988 to 1991. The BEAC's account held up better due to oil export revenues, but it fell into negative balance from 1987 to 1990 and again from 1993 to 1995, although it never reached one billion FF. After the accounts for both central banks were overdrawn in 1988, the French Treasury became alarmed and started pressuring Mitterrand for a devaluation of the CFA to close the CFA zone's balance of payments deficit (Stasavage, 2003).

The French Treasury preferred to extend grants and loans directly to African government instead of indirectly through the operations account. For example, "Even in 1988, when the French Treasury was required to advance 2.3 billion French francs to fund operations accounts overdrafts for UEMOA [West African Economic and Monetary Union] and CEMAC [Central African Economic and Monetary Community], this was still only equivalent to about a quarter of French bilateral aid to the CFA states" (Stasavage, 2003, p. 40). France heavily subsidized the budgets of governments in the CFA zone from 1986 to 1993. In addition, from 1989 to 1991, the Paris Club of creditors – historically led by the French Treasury – restructured the CFA countries' debts.

The French government was, perhaps, a more willing hegemon because its hegemony in Africa has been rather cheap. Despite the Treasury's fears, the costs of maintaining the convertibility guarantee have always been small. "Given the size of France compared to the CFA franc zone," IMF researchers state that "the resources available are sufficient to defend a parity if France is willing to do so, and the 1994 devaluation was only necessary because France had decided that the real exchange rate was severely out of line" (Masson and Pattillo, 2005, p. 168).

Repeating European Mistakes?

The climactic devaluation of 1994 – to this day the only time the CFA's fixed rate to the FF/euro has ever been changed – spurred a third round of reforms of the economic accords governing the CFA zone. CFA zone governments signed on to convergence criteria like those of the Maastricht Treaty of 1992 that created the euro. For the primary criteria, governments promise to achieve a balanced primary fiscal budget, zero budget arrears, a debt-to-GDP ratio lower than 70 percent and an inflation rate of less than 3 percent. The secondary criteria consist of the following targets: a public-sector wage bill less than 35 percent of fiscal revenue, tax revenue of at least 17 percent of GDP, domestically financed public investment of at least 20 percent of receipts, and current account deficits of less than 3 percent of GDP (Gulde and Tsangarides, 2008). Predictably, governments have had a difficult time meeting the convergence criteria by the agreed timeline. IMF researchers decry the lack of reliable and comparable data, and the absence of sanctions for non-compliance (Masson and Pattillo, 2005).

   Like the Eurozone, the rules of the CFA zone have failed to promote economic convergence or political integration. Most observers agree that CFA zone is not an OCA: it does not meet the similarity criteria (Tsangarides and Qureshi, 2008). Intraregional trade in the UEMOA from 1990 to 2005 was about 10 percent of imports compared to over 60 percent in the EU, and 12 percent of exports, compared to nearly 70 percent for the EU. For CEMAC it was 5 and 2 percent respectively (Tsangarides and Martijn, 2007). Tsangarides and van den Boogaerde (2005) find no evidence of convergence within the CFA zone or of better economic performance compared to the rest of Sub-Saharan Africa. Despite these poor results, the CFA zone is likely to survive as long as the French government is willing and able to maintain its hegemony in the region.

Who Would Replace France?

So far, regional political integration in West and Central Africa has been replaced with political integration with France. In the late 1950s, once decolonization seemed inevitable, the French government pushed for political disintegration but continued monetary union of its colonies. Instead of granting independence to the two existing regional federations – French West Africa and French Central Africa – Charles de Gaulle's administration preferred to hand power to the smaller territorial governments. French authorities believed that "12 small nations would be more likely to stay close to France than two large ones" (Manning, 1998, p. 146).

Moreover, the first President of Côte d'Ivoire – the wealthiest colony – opposed federation since it meant his government would have to subsidize the countries of the landlocked periphery (where Côte d'Ivoire obtained much of its labor). Radical nationalists like Modibo Keïta of Mali were pan-Africanists and advocated for continued political federation of the former colonies. President Senghor wanted to keep French West Africa together since Dakar was the capital, and Senegal – the only colony with an industrial sector – depended on markets in the periphery. A group of conservative African leaders led by Houphouët-Boigny worked with French diplomats and intelligence services to undermine the pan-Africanists' attempts at political unification, like the short-lived Federation of Mali between Senegal and the French Sudan (which then kept the name Mali) and the Union of African States (comprising Mali, Guinea and Ghana) (Wallerstein, 1961, 1967).

Without French support, the CFA zone would face challenges similar to the Eurozone: lack of political integration or a willing hegemon. The CFA zone is also riddled with structural trade imbalances. The coastal countries have permanent trade surpluses with those in the interior. For example, both Senegal and Côte d'Ivoire have never had a trade deficit with Mali. Likewise, Côte d'Ivoire has only ever posted trade surpluses with Burkina Faso (Figure 11.3). The governments of the three largest and most developed economies – Côte d'Ivoire, Cameroon and Senegal – have demonstrated little enthusiasm for fiscal and political integration, and the transfer of resources to the rest of the CFA zone that this would imply (Amuwo, 1999). Indeed, many of the political and economic divisions between surplus and deficit regions that contributed to the demise of the regional federations in the late colonial and early post-independence period are still in place.

HEGEMONY IN EAST AFRICA

Unlike the CFA franc zone, the attempt by British East Africa – Uganda, Tanzania, and Kenya – to maintain its colonial currency union failed a few years after independence. East Africa was – and remains – closer to

(a) Senegal trade surplus with Mali (1980–2016)

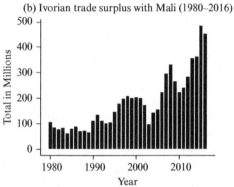

(b) Ivorian trade surplus with Mali (1980–2016)

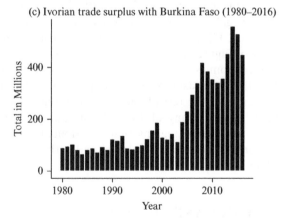

(c) Ivorian trade surplus with Burkina Faso (1980–2016)

Source: IMF Direction of Trade Statistics.

Figure 11.3a–c   Trade surpluses in the CFA zone (US dollars)

an OCA than the CFA zone, with a high degree of intraregional trade and labor mobility (Masson and Pattillo, 2005). Yet, neither the colonial nor the regional hegemon was able to establish a political surplus recycling mechanism, leading the East African Currency Board to collapse in 1966. The most important factor in the failure of the currency union was the British government's decision to withdraw from the direct management of the currency board in 1960. When the task of keeping the EACB alive fell to the Kenyan government, it proved unwilling to redistribute its surpluses to its poorer neighbors, condemning the EACB to death.

The British Colonial Office established the EACB in 1919 to issue notes in Kenya and Uganda.[5] As a strict currency board, the EACB's sole function was to issue East African shillings upon receipt of sterling and redeem shilling for sterling at the official rate (for a small fee). Hence, the EACB had no independent monetary or credit policies until it was authorized to buy East African government bonds in 1955. It was not allowed to finance short-term Treasury bills until 1959. In 1960, the EACB was moved to Nairobi and its board filled with representatives from each local government as it assumed more of the functions of a central bank (Kratz, 1966).

Unlike the French, British authorities did not offer a convertibility guarantee or any other incentive to keep their former colonies in the sterling zone (Masson and Pattillo, 2005). As a result, the number of countries fixing their exchange rate to sterling decreased steeply in the 1960s and 1970s (Ilzetzki, Reinhart and Rogoff, 2017). Guillaume and Stasavage (2000) contend that the British government could have afforded to guarantee convertibility of the East African shilling to sterling but chose not to, even though East African trade surpluses would have helped the balance of payments position of the sterling zone. Britain's post-war economic difficulties and the devaluation of the pound in 1967 suggest that the British government may have been more unable than unwilling to maintain its hegemony in East Africa. In either case, unlike the French, the British did not play the role of external guarantor willing to provide liquidity in an international reserve currency to favored governments in Africa.

Without British support, Kenya, the regional power, would have needed to create a political surplus recycling mechanism. Instead, Ugandan and Tanzanian leaders felt that Kenya – the larger, more industrialized partner – benefitted disproportionately from the union and did not do enough to recycle its surpluses to them. Indeed, Kenya has consistently posted trade surpluses with its East African neighbors since independence (Figure 11.4). The Tanzanian and Ugandan governments wanted direct subsidies and infant industry protection as compensation from Kenya for their membership in the EACB. The Kenyan government of Jomo Kenyatta, however, had a more orthodox economic policy and resisted

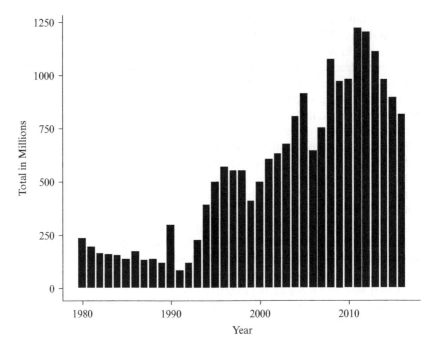

Source: IMF Direction of Trade Statistics.

Figure 11.4   Kenyan trade surplus with the EACB (1980–2016) (US dollars)

attempts by Uganda and Tanzania to ease the limits on the monetization of fiscal deficits. Tanzania's President Julius Nyerere had an ambitious program for socialist development that required more activist credit, fiscal and industrial policies than Kenyatta's conservative government would allow. Already by the spring of 1964 there were rumors that the Tanzanian government would create its own currency (Guillaume and Stasavage, 2000). The failure of the Kenyan government to subsidize the poorer members of the EACB led to the latter's rapid demise.

CONCLUSION

Most researchers assessing the viability of proposed currency unions are still focused – mistakenly – on the level of similarity between possible members. Using a variety of statistical methodologies, empirical studies on the desirability of expanded currency unions in West, East, and South Africa yield mixed results (Asongu, Nwachukwu and Tchamyou, 2017). These studies, however, downplay the most important factor determining the viability of a currency union: the existence of a political surplus recycling mechanism. Post-colonial African economic history "underscores the importance of political forces in leading to" the dissolution of currency unions "or, in the case of the French involvement with the CFA franc zone, in encouraging their continued existence. Either a strong shared commitment to regional integration in its various dimensions or a hegemonic power willing to support other members seem to be essential for the durable success of a monetary union" (Masson and Pattillo, 2005, p. 32).

The failure of the EACB should serve as a powerful lesson to current policymakers in East Africa that economic integration without political integration is unsustainable. When they created the East African Community in 2000, the governments of Tanzania, Uganda, and Kenya – now joined by Rwanda, South Sudan, and Burundi – also agreed to resuscitate the East African shilling. More importantly, they agreed to move towards political union, committing to an eventual East African Federation. The success of the reborn East African shilling will hinge not on whether growth and inflation in Burundi and Kenya are correlated, but on Kenya's willingness to redistribute some of its surpluses to Burundi.

The Eurozone will remain politically unstable unless the German government reverses its policies and supports further fiscal integration. In September 2017, the recently elected French President, Emmanuel Macron, proposed a shared Eurozone budget and finance minister (Erlanger, 2017). The future of the Eurozone may well hinge on whether such proposals lead to greater solidarity as some intend and not more effective enforcement of punitive fiscal rules as others would prefer.

The CFA zone is unlikely to survive if the French government ever withdraws its support. In November 2017, Macron stated (Reuters, 2017) that he was open to reforming the CFA – a topic long taboo among French and African political leaders – raising the possibility of a CFA zone without the French Treasury's convertibility guarantee to the euro. Its members would have to move towards political union or have a successful regional hegemon emerge if the CFA zone cuts its ties with France. Despite decades of monetary union, the CFA zone countries seem no closer to political integration. The obstacles to political federation remain as formidable as they were immediately after independence.

The experience of the Eurozone and CFA zone provides an "important lesson for the rest of the world: be careful of anyone who suggests that political integration will naturally follow from economic integration. And be especially skeptical of anyone who proposes a monetary union in the absence of adequate political integration" (Stiglitz, 2016, p. 322). Successful regional economic integration must be built on a politics of international solidarity, where wealthier nations agree to support their poorer neighbors.

NOTES

1. The terms monetary union and currency union are used interchangeably.
2. Although the EACB only achieved 100 percent backing in 1950. The cover was as low as 10 percent in 1932. See Kratz (1966).
3. France's North African colonies, Tunisia, Algeria and Morocco, adopted their own currencies upon independence. Guinea-Conakry was famously the only Sub-Saharan colony that opted for immediate political – and monetary – independence after the referendum on the French Community of 1958. Mali abandoned the CFA zone in 1962 but rejoined the zone in 1984. Mauritania left the CFA zone in 1973. Madagascar also cut its peg to the FF in 1973. Equatorial Guinea, a small, oil-rich former Spanish colony, joined the Central African CFA in 1984, and Guinea-Bissau, a small, poor, unstable former Portuguese colony, joined the West African CFA in 1997.
4. Author's translation.
5. The EACB later included Tanganyika, Zanzibar, Eritrea, British and Italian Somaliland, and Aden. All adopted their own currencies or joined other countries with their own currencies, leaving Kenya, Uganda, and Tanzania (Tanganyika and Zanzibar after their merger) as the remaining three members in 1965.

REFERENCES

Amin, S. (1976), *Unequal Development: An Essay on the Social Formations of Peripheral Capitalism*, New York: Monthly Review Press.

Amuwo, K. (1999), "France and the economic integration project in Francophone Africa," *African Journal of Political Science*, 4(1), 1–20.

Asongu, S., J. Nwachukwu and V. Tchamyou (2017), "A literature survey on proposed African monetary unions," *Journal of Economic Surveys*, 31(3), 878–902.

Bacha, E.L. (1978), "An interpretation of unequal exchange from Prebisch-Singer to Emmanuel," *Journal of Development Economics*, 5(4), 319–30.

Eichengreen, B.J. (2012), *Exorbitant Privilege: The Rise and Fall of the Dollar and the Future of the International Monetary System*, Oxford: Oxford University Press.

Emmanuel, A. (1977), *Unequal Exchange: A Study of the Imperialism of Trade*, New York: Monthly Review Press.

Erlanger, S. (2017), "Emanuel Macron's lofty vision for Europe gets mixed reviews," *New York Times*, September 28, accessed July 21, 2018 at www.nytimes.com/2017/09/28/world/europe/france-macron-european-union-reforms.html.

Feyrer, J. and B. Sacerdote (2013), "How much would US style fiscal integration buffer European unemployment and income shocks?," *American Economic Review*, 103(3), 125–8.

Frank, A.G. (1979), *Dependent Accumulation and Underdevelopment*, New York: Monthly Review Press.

Guillaume, D. and D. Stasavage (2000), "Improving policy credibility: Is there a case for African monetary unions?," *World Development*, **28**(8), 391–407.

Gulde, A.-M. and C.G. Tsangarides (2008), *The CFA Franc Zone: Common Currency, Uncommon Challenges*, Washington, DC: International Monetary Fund.

Ilzetzki, E., C.M. Reinhart and K.S. Rogoff (2017), "Exchange arrangements entering the 21st century: Which anchor will hold?," *NBER Working Paper No. 23134*.

Lewis, W.A. (1954), "Economic development with unlimited supplies of labour," *The Manchester School*, **22**(2), 139–91.

Lewis, W.A. (1978), *The Evolution of the International Economic Order*, Princeton, NJ: Princeton University Press.

Kenen, P. (1969), "The theory of optimum currency areas: An eclectic view," in R. Mundell and A. Swoboda (eds), *Monetary Problems of the International Economy*, Chicago, IL: University of Chicago Press, pp. 41–60.

Kindleberger, C. (1973), *The World in Depression, 1929–1939*, Berkeley, CA: University of California Press.

Kratz, J.W. (1966), "The East African Currency Board," *Staff Papers – International Monetary Fund*, **13**(2), 229–55.

Krugman, P. (2013), "Revenge of the optimum currency area," *NBER Macroeconomics Annual*, **27**(1), 439–48.

Le Vine, V.T. (2004), *Politics in Francophone Africa*, Boulder, CO: Lynne Rienner Publishers.

Manning, P. (1998), *Francophone Sub-Saharan Africa, 1880–1995*, Cambridge, UK: Cambridge University Press.

Masson, P.R. and C.A. Pattillo (2005), *The Monetary Geography of Africa*, Washington, DC: Brookings Institution Press.

McKinnon, R.I. (1963), "Optimum currency areas," *The American Economic Review*, **53**(4), 717–25.

Mundell, R.A. (1961), "A theory of optimum currency areas," *The American Economic Review*, **51**(4), 657–65.

Prebisch, R. (1962), *The Economic Development of Latin America and Its Principal Problems*, New York: United Nations.

Pritchett, L. (1997), "Divergence, big time," *Journal of Economic Perspectives*, **11**(3), 3–17.

Reuters (2017), "CFA France is a matter for Africans, France open to changes, Macron says," accessed July 21, 2018 at uk.reuters.com/article/uk-africa-france-macron-franc/cfa-franc-is-a-matter-for-africans-france-open-to-changes-macron-says-idUKKBN1DS1U6.

Singer, H. (1950), "The distribution of gains between investing and borrowing countries," *American Economic Review*, **40**, 377–82.

Skott, P. and P. Auerbach (1995), "Cumulative causation and the 'new' theories of economic growth," *Journal of Post Keynesian Economics*, **17**(3), 381–402.

Solow, R.M. (1956), "A contribution to the theory of economic growth," *The Quarterly Journal of Economics*, **70**(1), 65–94.

Stasavage, D. (2003), *The Political Economy of a Common Currency: The CFA Franc Zone Since 1945*, Aldershot, UK: Ashgate.

Stiglitz, J.E. (2016), *The Euro: How a Common Currency Threatens the Future of Europe*, New York: W.W. Norton & Co.

Tsangarides, C.G. and J.K. Martijn (2007), *Trade Reform in the CEMAC*, Washington, DC: International Monetary Fund.

Tsangarides, C.G. and M.S. Qureshi (2008), "Monetary union membership in West Africa: A cluster analysis," *World Development Oxford*, **36**(7), 1261–79.

Tsangarides, C. and P. van den Boogaerde (2005), "Ten years after the CFA franc devaluation: Progress toward regional integration in the WAEMU," *IMF Working Paper No. WP/05/145*.

Vallée, O. (1989), *Le prix de l'argent CFA: Heurs et malheurs de la zone franc*, Paris: Karthala.

Van de Walle, N. (2001), *African Economies and the Politics of Permanent Crisis, 1979–1999*, Cambridge, UK: Cambridge University Press.

Varoufakis, Y. (2016), *And the Weak Suffer What They Must?: Europe's Crisis and America's Economic Future*, New York: Nation Press.

Wallerstein, I. (1961), *Africa, the Politics of Independence: An Interpretation of Modern African History*, New York: Vintage Books.

Wallerstein, I. (1965), "Elites in French-speaking West Africa: The social basis of ideas," *The Journal of Modern African Studies*, **3**(1), 1–33.

Wallerstein, I. (1967), *Africa, the Politics of Unity: An Analysis of a Contemporary Social Movement*, New York: Vintage Books.

12. International financial flows and the future of EU–Turkey relations*

Hasan Cömert

INTRODUCTION

After the 1970s, with the collapse of the Bretton Woods system and increasing liberalization, the size and the importance of the financial sector and financial flows increased all around the world. Some researchers conceptualize this process as the financialization of the world economy (Epstein, 2005). Turkey followed these steps very closely. Domestic and external liberalization policies were put into practice after the 1980s. Since then, financial flows have gradually gained ground and many important macroeconomic variables have become very sensitive to financial flows in Turkey.

This chapter focuses on the role of financial flows in future EU–Turkey relations. However, given the fact that financial flows emanating from Turkey have not been very significant for Europe, how financial flows drive EU–Turkey relations will be explored mostly from the Turkish perspective.

Because the direction and magnitude of financial flows is affected by future developments in relations, financial flows can be considered one of the major factors significantly influencing the possible path of EU–Turkey relations. Therefore, the decisions of Turkish policymakers on EU–Turkey relations are conditional upon the sensitivity of financial flows to their policies regarding EU–Turkey. Given the dependence of Turkey on financial flows and assuming that the EU would stabilize its internal problems, Turkish policymakers cannot afford conflict scenarios for a long time. As a result, EU–Turkey relations are expected to evolve into the forms of either convergence or cooperation. If Turkish policymakers find ways to decrease the vulnerability of the economy to financial flows, this may increase their ability to maneuver in the negotiation process.

The outline of the chapter is as follows. First, utilizing descriptive statistics, the historical trends in financial flows to the Turkish economy will be studied. Second, the relative influence of financial flows on the economy will be explored. Third, the implications of EU–Turkey relations for financial flows to the Turkish economy will be investigated, as well as how financial flows can drive the future of EU–Turkey relations in light of previous discussions and considering the scenarios of conflict, cooperation, and convergence.

HISTORICAL TRENDS IN FINANCIAL FLOWS IN THE TURKISH ECONOMY

Financial flows are composed of portfolio flows, other flows,[1] and foreign direct investment (FDI). As will be elaborated on in the following sections, different financial flows categories may have different implications for a country. Therefore, in this section, to be able to locate financial flows in the Turkish economy properly, trends in the main categories of financial flows will be explained in detail. Although net flows can reveal some clues on the overall picture of financial flows, it is important to investigate gross flows as much as possible as well (Borio and Disyatat, 2011). However, it is not an easy task to obtain data on gross flows. Therefore, our gross flows analysis will be based on the assets and liabilities components of portfolio flows, other flows and FDI reported by the Central Bank Republic of Turkey balance of payments statistics (CBRT BOP Statistics).[2] In Turkey, in line with the common practices in the world, before the 1980s there were heavy restrictions on financial flows. Although domestic financial liberalization steps were taken as early as 1981, considerable external financial liberalization steps began in late 1983. In this vein, Decree 28 and Decree 29, which were put into practice in December 1983, introduced significant financial liberalization policies.[3] Turkey completed its capital account liberalization before many other relatively advanced countries in 1989. As a result of full financial liberalization both Turkish citizens and foreigners were allowed to make financial transactions without any restrictions. The importance of financial flows has increased along with rising integration between EU and Turkey.

The difference between purchases and sales of foreign assets by residents is called net financial outflows (hereafter referred to as financial outflows). The magnitude of financial outflows has never reached significant levels in Turkey (Figure 12.1). The average amount of financial outflows from Turkey was only about $230 million during the entire period 1975–89 (Table 12.1). This figure reached only $5 billion in the period from 2010 to 2016 (Table 12.1). In total, this implies about $33 billion worth of net purchases of foreign assets by Turkish citizens in this period.[4,5]

Apart from the last period, Turkish financial outflows have been mostly in the form of lending and portfolio investments. However, Turkish

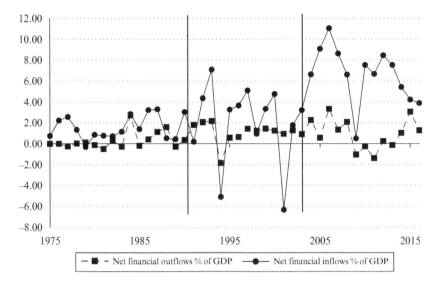

Note: Vertical lines demonstrate three distinct periods of financial flows. These periods are discussed briefly in the text.

Source: CBRT BOP Statistics and World Bank Development Indicators.

Figure 12.1   Financial inflows and outflows (% of GDP)

investors made more purchases of foreign firms (or share of foreign firms) and/or open new plants outside Turkey relative to their lending and portfolio investment activities in the last period. In other words, it seems that Turkish firms' genuine internationalization attempt regarding FDI activities started slowly after 2010. Turkish investors made $26.8 billion worth of FDI from 2010 to 2016, whereas this figure was only $1.6 million and $9 billion in the periods 1987–99 and 2000–09, respectively (CBRT BOP Statistics).

It is difficult to trace the sources of financial flows by looking at balance of payments statistics. However, it is relatively easy to trace the sources of FDI into a country. Therefore, although it is not possible to understand the importance of Europe in other components of financial flows, the importance of European investors in FDI to Turkey and the size of Turkish FDI in European countries can be assessed.

Europe in general and EU countries specifically have been the most important destinations for Turkish FDI. Turkish investors made about $5.7 billion worth of FDI in EU countries in eight years during the period 2002–09. In the next seven years (2010–16), this figure, in total, reached

Table 12.1 *The average amounts of financial flows (millions $)*

	Other Investment Inflows	Portfolio Investment Inflows	Direct Investment Inflows	Net Financial Inflows	Other Investment Outflows	Direct Investment Outflows	Portfolio Investment Outflows	Net Financial Outflows	Net Financial Account
1975–1989	646.07	205.47	129.53	981.07	223.27	0.60	6.00	229.87	751.20
1990–1999	2888.10	1425.90	771.70	5085.70	1162.60	162.50	666.60	1991.70	3094.00
2000–2009	12880.80	4067.30	9060.20	26008.30	3156.90	1096.60	1718.40	5971.90	20036.40
2010–2016	23856.29	16849.71	13498.57	54204.57	404.57	3838.71	567.71	4811.00	49393.57
1990–2001	2198.23	1050.00	1010.23	4258.46	1158.00	241.15	771.69	2170.85	2087.62
2002–2016	21150.43	11373.57	12834.00	45358.00	2212.36	2594.79	1270.86	6078.00	39280.00

Source: CBRT BOP Statistics.

approximately $13.7 billion. As can be seen from Table 12.2, among EU countries, the Netherlands, with $10 billion from 2002 to 2016, was the most important country for Turkish FDI. Germany, UK, Malta, and Luxembourg followed the Netherlands with $2, $1.9, $1.2 and $1.1 billion during the same period, respectively.

The difference between purchases and sales of domestic financial assets by foreigners is called net financial inflows (hereafter referred to as financial inflows). Although financial outflows have been relatively shallow in Turkey, along with financial liberalization of the 1980s, the amounts of financial inflows have gradually increased (see Figure 12.1). While the average amounts of total financial inflows to Turkey was only about $981 million for the period 1975–89, on average, $54 billion in financial flows entered Turkey in the period 2010–16 (Table 12.1). This means that Turkey attracted about $380 billion dollars of foreign capital in the form of borrowings, portfolio investments, and FDI in the last seven years.[6]

Other investments (composed of the international financial transactions of central banks, general government, banks and other sectors in the forms of loans, trade credits, currency, and deposits) have been the dominant components of financial inflows to Turkey. Turkey attracted about $128 and $167 billion of other flows in the periods 2000–09 and 2010–16, respectively. In general, the transactions of other sectors (i.e., the non-financial sector) have been the most important type of flows in other investment accounts. Turkish non-financial private firms obtained an enormous amount of credits ($96.8 billion) for their operations from 2002 to 2008. The borrowings of the Turkish banks have been another significant component of other flows. The financial liberalization process has provided Turkish banks and other firms with ample opportunities to borrow at a lower cost from the international financial markets. Turkish banks attracted $37.4 billion and $119.5 billion dollars of finance from financial markets in the periods 2000–09 and 2010–16, respectively. As a result of the striking borrowing levels of banks and non-financial firms, the indebtedness of Turkish private banks and firms reached unprecedented levels in Turkey after 2002, though official foreign debt decreased to relatively low levels.

The importance of FDI in financial inflows increased significantly through time. Although, in total, Turkey attracted only about $2 billion worth of FDI during the period 1975–89, the accumulated amounts of FDI reached about $90.6 billion and $94.4 billion in the periods 2000–09 and 2010–16, respectively. The surge of FDI into Turkish financial markets after 2001 was mostly related to the privatization of major public companies in this period. After fundamental changes in the legal framework, a significant portion of public companies were sold to foreign investors. In

Table 12.2 The destination for and sources of FDI

FDI Outflows (million dollars)

	2002–09	2010–16	2002–16
TOTAL WORLD	11213	25512	36725
EUROPE	6816	15911	22727
EU	5782	13725	19507
Netherlands	1919	8102	10021
Azerbaijan	2433	3765	6198
USA	887	3090	3977
Germany	1029	1019	2048
United Kingdom	212	1771	1983
Malta	1077	180	1257
Luxembourg	528	631	1159
Russia	258	587	845
Switzerland	421	339	760
Ireland	241	501	742
Kazakhstan	175	283	458
Austria	46	395	441
Iraq	44	324	368
Italy	141	219	360
Romania	137	193	330
UA Emirates	65	251	316
Belgium	240	72	312
Croatia	15	228	243
Belarus	100	130	230
Tunisia	212	13	225
India	42	174	216
Bosnia and Herzegovina	55	154	209

FDI Inflows (million dollars)

	2002–09	2010–16	2002–16
TOTAL WORLD	68782	70647	140176
EUROPE	52893	50629	103833
EU	50162	44962	95200
Netherlands	13645	8370	21760
USA	6366	4832	11145
Austria	3093	6661	10036
United Kingdom	3457	6081	9756
Luxembourg	4522	4463	9021
Germany	3737	5120	8989
Belgium	5739	2470	8027
Spain	1693	5943	7955
France	4386	2464	6752
Greece	6058	809	6546
Russia	1803	3379	5311
Azerbaijan	105	4794	5235
UA Emirates	3511	652	3990
Italy	1774	1186	2934
Switzerland	753	1688	2515
Japan	176	2023	2333
Saudi Arabia	1385	564	1903
Kuwait	661	918	1603
Qatar	126	1350	1565
Lebanon	136	1149	1359
Malaysia	33	838	929
China	7	801	865

Source: CBRT BOP Statistics.

addition to this, Turkey allowed foreigners to buy real estate and land in Turkey after 2003. Therefore, FDI inflows data reported in the balance of payments statistics also include real estate purchases by foreigners in Turkey after 2003.

The purchases of Turkish real estate by foreigners has become a very important source of foreign exchanges for the country after 2003. This also enabled the real estate market to have a lucrative source of demand, especially for luxury houses in big cities and touristic areas. The accumulated amount of real estate purchases by foreigners in Turkey were approximately $17 billion and $22 billion during the periods 2003–09 and 2010–16, respectively. In other words, real estate investments of foreigners made up about one-fourth of the total FDI inflows in the last period. Excluding real estate investments of foreigners, Turkey, in total, attracted about $69 and $71 billion of FDI from all over the world during the periods 2002–09 and 2010–16, respectively.[7] About $50 billion and $45 billion of this originated in EU countries during the periods 2002–09 and 2010–16, respectively. From 2002 to 2016 the Netherlands, Austria, UK, Luxembourg, Germany, Belgium, Spain, France and Greece with $21.7, $10, $9.7, $9, $8.9, $8, $7.9, $6.7 and $6.5 billion dollars, respectively, contributed most to FDI entering Turkey from EU countries.

The EU share of total FDI into Turkey has gradually declined. However, on average, FDI coming from the EU still makes up more than 65 percent and 75 percent of total FDI in the periods 2010–16 and 2002–09, respectively. In the same period, there was an increasing trend in the share of Asia in the FDI. Among the Asian countries the role of Near and Middle East countries gained importance (CBRT BOP Statistics).[8] However, political and geopolitical uncertainty surrounding Near and Middle East countries may make these countries somewhat unreliable alternatives to FDI originating in Europe.

Although FDI inflows have gained importance throughout time and have become the second most important component of financial inflows in the period 2000–09, portfolio inflows are usually more important than FDI inflows. About $100 billion worth of portfolio flows entered Turkey from 2010 to 2016. In general, increasing global liquidity and decreasing interest rates in major developed countries have been external driving forces behind the surge of other and portfolio flows to Turkey from 2002 onward.

As a result of an increase in financial inflows and relatively low financial outflows, the Turkish economy has generally enjoyed positive net financial flows in absolute and relative terms. Net financial flows can be very important for those countries that cannot pay their debt with their own currency

(Cömert and Düzçay, 2015). In the literature this phenomenon is known as *original sin* or the *hierarchy of money* (Eichengreen, Hausmann and Panizza, 2003; Mehrling, 2012). Those countries with accumulated debt should find necessary foreign currencies by either giving current account surpluses, depleting their existing foreign exchange reserves, and/or being able to continue rolling over their accumulated debt. For those developing countries resorting to the second and third options for a long time, crisis is inevitable. If net financial flows are positive, this will contribute to the much-needed supply of foreign currency in the country, which can be used to cover current account deficits, to roll over accumulated external debt or/ and to accumulate foreign exchange reserves. Due mainly to restrictions on financial flows, Turkey ended up attracting only about $11 billion in net financial flows from 1975 to 1989. This figure reached $30.9 billion in the 1990s. Then, after the 2000s, there was a spectacular growth in net financial flows to Turkish economy. The accumulated amounts of net financial flows skyrocketed and reached $200 billion during the period 2000–09. In the next seven years, accumulated net financial flows broke another record by reaching $345 billion.[9]

Nominal values may be misleading in an environment in which the size of the overall economy grows steadily. However, when one considers net financial flows relative to GDP, the striking picture does not change. While the average amount of net financial flows was 1.14 percent of GDP ($751 million) during the period 1975–89, it was 5.71 percent of GDP (about $49 billion) in the period 2010–16 (CBRT BOP Statistics).

As can be seen from our discussions and Figure 12.1, three structurally different periods seem to have existed in the movements of the financial flows in Turkey. When one investigates financial inflows and outflows separately, these periods are much more apparent. As expected, due mainly to restrictions, financial inflows and outflows were negligible until the 1990s. The importance of financial inflows increased in the 1990s while financial outflows remained unimportant in the same period. The period after the crisis of 2002 seems to be a structurally different period than the earlier periods. In this sense, the surge of financial inflows (and net flows) to the Turkish economy after 2002 was unprecedented, which was also the case for many developing countries. There was a sudden stop in net financial flows during the recent crisis. However, financial flows reached their pre-crisis levels in a very short time after 2010.[10]

One of the key characteristics of these three different periods of financial flows to the Turkish economy is high volatility of flows. Figure 12.2 shows the volatility of financial flows based on a ten-year moving average of the standard deviations of the different components of financial inflows.

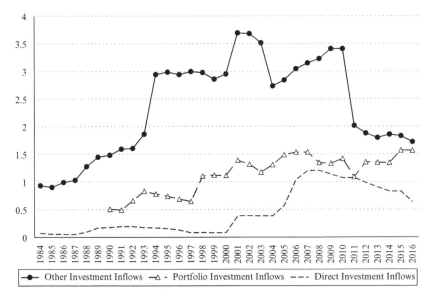

Source: Calculation based on CBRT BOP Statistics and World Bank World Development Indicators.

Figure 12.2   The volatility of the different components of financial inflows

Accordingly, the volatility of financial flows increased along with the completion of financial liberalization. A high volatility of financial flows means high uncertainty in the supply of foreign exchanges in developing countries, which can be easily translated into exchange and/or financial crises. When one investigates the volatility of different components of financial flows, net other flows are the most volatile components, whereas FDI demonstrates relatively more stability, as we might expect (Figure 12.2). After 2010, there seems to be a relative decline in the volatility of other investment inflows and direct investment inflows, whereas portfolio inflows became much more volatile.

Overall, as a result of very high financial flows, the Turkish economy was able to cover its chronic current account deficits, did not face a debt repayment problem, and started to accumulate considerable amounts of foreign currency reserves too. However, when the Turkish economy encountered a sudden stop or financial reversal, it could not avoid significant declines in its GDP growth. The crises of 1994, 2001, and (partially) 2009 were directly or indirectly caused by a reversal/stop of financial flows (Akyüz and Boratav, 2003; Özatay, 2009; Cömert and Yeldan, 2018).

THE GENERAL MACROECONOMIC IMPLICATIONS OF FINANCIAL FLOWS IN TURKEY

As in the case of many developing countries, financial flows have had many crucial implications for the Turkish economy. There are various transmission channels linking main macroeconomic variables to financial flows. Here, we will shortly explain these mechanisms under the broad headings of credit and asset price channels. An obvious direct mechanism works through credit creation capacity of financial flows. This mechanism can be simply labeled as a credit channel. There are three strands of a credit channel. First, some of the big, non-financial sector firms can directly borrow from international financial markets, which can contribute to the investment capacity of the firms and GDP growth. As mentioned above, thanks to massive liquidity and low interest rates, Turkish private firms obtained an enormous amount of credit ($96.8 billion) for their operations from global financial markets from 2002 to 2008 (CBRT BOP Statistics). The second strand of the mechanism works through the banking system. Financial flows in the form of borrowings of domestically operated banks can increase the capacity of the banks to give more credit to domestic consumers and firms. Those banks with access to cheap credit from international financial markets can generate more credit domestically (Igan and Tan, 2017). In this way, Turkish banks borrowed $37.4 and $119.5 billion from international financial markets in the periods 2000–09 and 2010–17, respectively (CBRT BOP Statistics). These borrowings were partially responsible for very high credit growth in Turkey. Third, as elaborated on below, net high positive financial flows can cause improvements in the balance sheets of banks/other firms. As a result, on the one hand, banks would be eager to give more credit; on the other hand, due to strong balance sheets, non-financial firms would be more eligible to borrow. This link is known as the *balance sheet effect* within the credit channel.[11] Signaling prospects for a healthy economy, high GDP growth may also ease credit constraints on domestic firms to borrow from the rest of the world. Therefore, in general, high financial flows and high GDP growth can create a virtuous credit circle and feed each other until an external or endogenously driven shock hits the economy. The scatter diagram (Figure 12.3) shows a high positive correlation between financial flows and credit growth, which seems to support this observation in Turkey.

The second channel works through domestic asset prices. Financial flows may exert pressure on the prices of domestic assets by altering supply and demand conditions in financial markets. The asset prices channel can be broadly further divided into interest rates, stock prices, and exchange rate channels. With regard to the interest rates channel and in relation to

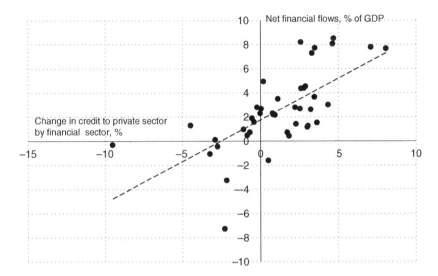

Source: CBRT BOP Statistics and World Bank World Development Indicators.

Figure 12.3   Credit growth and net financial flows

high net positive financial flows, a high demand for domestic bonds can increase the price of domestic assets. Indeed, there was only $13.2 billion worth of demand for Turkish debt securities such as bonds by foreigners from 1989 to 1999. Turkish investors were able to sell $21.6 billion worth of securities from 2000 to 2009. There was an unprecedented increase in the demand for Turkish debt securities in the next seven years. Foreigners demanded the equivalent of $107.3 billion in securities in this period (2010–16) (CBRT BOP Statistics).

Although, to the best of our knowledge, there is no study investigating the exact amounts of the influence of foreigners on the price of Turkish securities, such large amounts of purchases of domestic securities by foreigners might have contributed to a big decrease in the interest rates on these assets by driving up their price. In general, these securities were almost entirely issued by the general government for the first two periods. After 2010, non-governmental sectors were also able to issue significant amounts of bonds. However, the net demand for general government securities was still massive, with $60 billion from 2010 to 2016. Partially owing to this trend, the Turkish general government sector has been able to obtain access to relatively cheap borrowing. Furthermore, if domestically operated banks find cheap funding from international financial markets, they can decrease their lending rates at home without jeopardizing their overall profits. This may imply a decline in overall interest rates, which may induce demand for credit and, in turn, consumption and investment expenditures. Financial flows may exert some influence on an economy through stock prices too. Portfolio flows include the purchase of domestic stocks by foreigners. The demand for Turkish stocks exchanged in Borsa Istanbul (the Turkish domestic stock exchange market) by foreigners can be seen under the heading of equity liabilities reported in the balance of payments statistics. In times of high portfolio inflows in the forms of stock exchange purchases, the stock prices increase. For Turkish equities (broadly referring to shares/stocks issued by Turkish firms), there was about \$2.4, \$19, and \$10.5 billion net foreign demand in the periods 1989–99, 2000–09 and 2010–16, respectively. Given the fact that the share of foreigners in the Turkish stock market has been more than 65 percent, their operations can easily shape stock prices in Borsa Istanbul.[12] In addition to this, if, due to high financial flows, there is an overall decrease in interest rates in the economy, domestic stock markets may also attract domestic investors, which can cause a further increase in stock prices. This may generate a lucrative funding source for the firms issuing stocks at the domestic stock exchange markets. As a result, investment expenditures of these firms may expand. In the countries where there is widespread public participation in stock exchange markets, high stock prices may also cause a *wealth effect*: economic entities holding high amounts of domestic stocks may feel richer, thereby making them inclined to spend more during times of high stock prices.

In developing countries, exchange rates are among the most important asset prices. In Turkey, an increase in the supply of foreign currencies resulting from higher net financial flows brings about nominal appreciation of Turkish lira (TL) against major foreign currencies. There is a vast literature on the role of exchange rates in developing countries (Calvo and Végh, 1994; Eichengreen and Hausmann, 1999). Changes in exchange rates can have impacts on an economy through balance sheets, inflation, and the current account.[13] If the agents operating in an economy have different foreign assets and foreign liabilities structures, any significant movement in exchange rates may either deteriorate or improve the balance sheets of the agents considerably. For example, if the majority of firms have more liabilities denominated in foreign currencies relative to their assets, a considerable appreciation of the domestic currency resulting from high net financial flows may improve the balance sheet by decreasing the value of the liabilities in terms of domestic currency. In other words, this process leads to an increase in net worth (the difference between assets and liabilities). As discussed in the balance sheet effect as a part of the credit channel, an increase in net worth can induce more investment by either easing credit constraints and/or creating extra available funds.[14] Nominal appreciation of TL in the periods after 2002 might have induced more credit and investment in Turkey. As opposed to the case of appreciation, as documented by the third-generation crisis literature, a significant depreciation of domestic currency resulting from financial reversals (or from abrupt, large slowdowns) may generate a balance sheet crisis (Krugman, 1999). In the Turkish case, the severity of the crisis of 2001 can be partially explained by the balance sheet effect resulting from a sudden and big depreciation of TL (Özatay, 2009). Changes in exchange rates can also directly influence inflation through its impact on imported intermediate goods. Since financial flows directly affect both the price of imported goods and credit conditions in the Turkish economy, CBRT may not easily determine inflation by using conventional monetary policy instruments. Therefore, even under the inflation-targeting regime, CBRT might benefit from the nominal appreciation of TL or the slowdown in the depreciation of TL to bring inflation under control (Benlialper and Cömert, 2015). Indeed, in the Turkish case, inflation shows a considerable declining trend during the periods of abundance of financial flows, causing domestic currency to appreciate relative to other currencies (ibid.).

Apart from very rare cases that are mostly related to adverse developments in inflation expectations, the appreciation of domestic currency is mostly translated into real appreciation. The appreciation of the real exchange rates mostly related to financial flows makes Turkish exports more expensive and imports prices lower, which might have been one of the reasons behind the aforementioned current account deficit.[15] Besides this, whenever Turkish economy grows fast, current account deficits reach record levels. Therefore, financial flows may also widen current account deficits by suddenly easing credit conditions, leading to a demand boom partially boosting imported goods expenditures. Overall, as detailed above, financial flows exert a substantial influence on the Turkish economy through many different channels such as asset prices and credit channels. As a result, GDP growth, inflation, and the current account balance have been exposed to boom–bust cycles of financial flows.[16] Indeed, during the boom periods, the Turkish economy experiences relatively high growth while the growth either becomes negative or slows down considerably during the bust periods.

Considering the relationship between the components of financial inflows and GDP growth, although FDI and GDP growth seem to have had a weak connection, GDP growth has a very strong link with other flows (Figure 12.4a, b, c, and d). This indicates that, for the Turkish case, investors in FDI are not significantly sensitive to the short-term fluctuations of GDP growth; these investors seem to have a longer planning

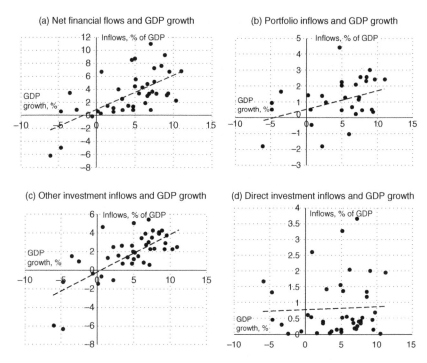

Note: a. Except for portfolio inflows and GDP growth graph (b), the relevant period for all the graphs is 1975–2016. For the portfolio inflows and GDP, the data set covers the period 1986–2016.

Source: CBRT BOP Statistics and World Bank World Development Indicators.

Figure 12.4   GDP growth and components of financial flows[a]

horizon.[17] Low volatility in FDI data shown earlier also implies less sensitivity to the short-term fluctuations.

More empirical research is necessary to verify these observations. Nevertheless, these findings are supported by simple correlation statistics as well. The simple correlation between net financial flows and growth is 0.67 and 0.71 in the periods 1975–89 and 1990–2016, respectively. For FDI, the correlation is –0.157 and 0.03, respectively, for the same periods.

Given the indisputable role and volatile nature of financial flows, policymakers must pay careful attention to the developments in flows and try to protect their respective economies from their adverse impacts. The first line of defense is to accumulate huge foreign exchange reserves. In this way, even though the CBRT officially implements a flexible exchange rate regime (as the majority of central banks in developing countries do), it has also built up some foreign exchange reserves for insurance purposes, especially since the crisis of 2001. As of July 2017, the CBRT has about $86.5 billion worth of gross foreign currency reserves (excluding gold reserves). Banks keep the equivalent of $48 billion in foreign currency reserves at the CBRT to meet their required reserve obligations.[18] In other words, the CBRT has only $38 billion of net foreign currency reserves. At the same time, the Turkish economy either has to roll over or pay about $170 billion worth of debt (short-term) denominated in foreign currency that will mature in a year (CBRT BOP Statistics). Furthermore, the Turkish reserve position relative to its liabilities cannot be considered high among comparable countries (Benlialper, Cömert and Düzçay, 2016). Although these statistics cannot be considered very alarming, it is not clear how the accumulated reserves would immunize the Turkish economy from a big external shock wave that can be intensified by an increasing, insatiable thirst among domestic players for foreign exchange, which would be the most likely rational response of domestic players.[19]

EU–TURKEY RELATIONS AND FINANCIAL FLOWS

As highlighted, Turkey, with its enormous amount of accumulated liabilities and chronic current account deficit, is obliged to attract a huge amount of financial flows each year. Any significant reversal/stop in financial flows to Turkey may have very important impacts on the Turkish economy through various channels. This phenomenon can be one of the important determinants of the future of EU–Turkey relations in many ways.

Many external and internal factors can affect financial flows. However, there is an increasing consensus regarding the existence of global cycles of financial flows to developing countries (Rey, 2015). In general, the increased risk appetite of investors along with low interest rates and high liquidity in advanced countries triggers a boom period of financial flows to many developing countries (ibid.).[20] These countries with relatively improved fundamentals, positive prospects, and relatively high interest rates attract more flows than others. However, when the risk appetite of the investors declines, the majority of developing countries either experience a slowdown or a financial reversal. Countries with high political and economic risk find themselves in a more problematic situation. Countries such as Turkey may not influence global cycles. However, they can still have some influence on the size and direction of financial flows by improving fundamentals, sustaining a well-respected institutional structure within the global capitalist structure, and having anchors such as the EU. The customs union agreement and succeeding integration steps between the

EU and Turkey coincided with the increasing role of financial flows in Turkey. The EU might act as an anchor in implementing some reforms in Turkish financial markets (Öniş and Bakır, 2007). Furthermore, as FDI data demonstrate, European investors made very considerable investments in Turkey. As a result, EU–Turkish integration processes might have contributed directly and indirectly to the rising role of financial flows (Başçı, Özel and Sarıkaya, 2008).[21]

One of the mechanisms through which EU–Turkey relations may influence financial flows is how rating agencies or international investors factor EU–Turkey relations in their decision-making process. Rating agencies affect the magnitude of financial flows by signaling the riskiness of countries through their ratings. In many cases in the past, international rating agencies mentioned the developments in EU–Turkey relations in their rating of Turkey (Öniş and Bakır, 2007). For example, during the heyday of the EU–Turkey integration process (2002–07), rating agencies partially justified increases in the ratings of Turkish assets based on positive developments in EU–Turkey relations. The choices of Turkey in the EU–Turkey integration process may therefore send signals to rating agencies. Furthermore, the future of FDI investments in Turkey by EU countries can be relatively conditioned on political stability and dependent upon institutional structures immune from direct political influence. This means that any positive or negative developments in the EU–Turkey integration process may directly and indirectly have an impact on the size and direction of financial flows to Turkey. Given the importance of financial flows to the Turkish economy and the possible influence of EU–Turkey relations on the size and direction of flows, any rational policymaker cannot avoid taking into account the influence of changes in EU–Turkey relations on financial flows when deciding the future of EU–Turkey relations.[22]

At present, the future path of EU–Turkey relations is very uncertain. There are many possibilities leading to significantly different outcomes for both parties. Each trajectory may have different implications for financial flows. It is not possible to go through all likely trajectories individually. However, as Table 12.3 demonstrates, we will consider three scenarios to investigate how financial flows can be affected, which in turn shapes the possible policies to be put into practice by Turkish authorities. These scenarios are convergence, cooperation, and conflict.[23]

The convergence scenario implies a full membership or a very similar arrangement. The cooperation scenario refers to an improvement in the current level of integration in different forms without reaching a full membership status. Under the conflict assumption, the recent tension between Turkey and EU can lead to a significant deterioration in the relations. We will shortly discuss the possible connection between these

Table 12.3 Different scenarios

Assumptions / Scenarios	Conflict	Co-operation	Convergence
High global liquidity with uncertainty about a financial reversal shock	Possible reversal, costly	Increase in financial flows, not costly	Increase in financial flows, improvement in the composition of the flows (more FDI from Europe), beneficial
Adverse global liquidity conditions	Reversal of flows, very costly	Reversal can be less sharp, not very costly	EU support mechanisms, less costly
Dominance of political concerns (or non-rational actors)	Financial flows can be less relevant for the future of EU–Turkey relations unless materialized cost is too high to put political projects under threat		
Significant EU social and economic problems	No more EU anchor; EU is less relevant for financial flows		

scenarios and financial flows under four different assumptions regarding liquidity, EU domestic problems and political concerns. As discussed above, global cycles may be very influential determinants of financial flows to developing countries including Turkey. In an environment where interest rates are relatively low and there is high liquidity for a foreseeable future in advanced economies, EU–Turkey relations would be less relevant for the direction and size of financial flows. In this atmosphere, highly positive prospects for EU–Turkey relations may even cause a flood of financial flows to the economy, which can increase the amplitude of financial boom–bust cycles. However, there is always a risk of evaporation of global liquidity. The recent speculations about higher interest rates in the United States have started to disrupt financial markets in developing countries. In this sense, if global risk appetite decreases abruptly, leading to the evaporation of liquidity and high interest rates in advanced countries, an increase in the convergence or cooperation between the parties may ease the tension in financial flows to Turkey. As a result, in these cases, Turkey may be less affected by global cycles due to an EU anchor. Investors may consider Turkey less risky and in possession of a more predictable path due to the EU anchor. Since the cost of the conflict in the case of a possible shock is very high, Turkish policymakers may avoid the conflict option even if operating under a positive global outlook. In times of declining global liquidity, if the parties choose the conflict option, this can exacerbate the possible adverse movements in financial flows, which can be very costly for Turkey. In the extreme case, the increasing tone of the conflict may reach a point where financial or other sanctions may be implemented or hinted at by EU countries. Although this option does not seem to be realistic, the recent disagreements with German politicians led to a point where the latter started to imply that there may be economic consequences of this escalation. Supposing that policymakers in both Turkey and Europe are rational, EU leverage can be relatively high over Turkish counterparts in times of decreasing global appetite towards developing countries. Given the high dependence of the Turkish economy on financial flows, a rational response by Turkish policymakers will be to find ways to lower the tone of the conflict to ease the negative influence of financial flows on the economy. This requires resorting to either convergence or mutually beneficial cooperation processes. There is a possibility of less reversal of financial flows in the case of an increasing cooperation process between the parties, while the convergence scenario may result in extra EU financial support mechanisms to mitigate the consequences of reversals.

There are two other possibilities that can significantly affect the future of EU–Turkey relations. First, the EU may find itself in a prolonged existential crisis. The doubt within Europe (EU-skepticism) about the future of the EU and its possible economic/social problems may put the EU project in danger. In this case, the EU project may be a less relevant factor, relatively speaking, for financial flows to Turkey. In this case, the cost of conflict in terms of financial flows may not be very high for Turkey. Even a rational Turkish policymaker may decide to escalate the conflict especially in a domestic environment where the conflict may be utilized as an instrument to consolidate a large support base. Interestingly enough, without being constrained by financial flows, this can increase the leverage of Turkey over Europe in an environment where the Middle East and immigration problems are part of the European existential crisis.

Second, the Turkish side of the conflict may be less concerned with the economic consequences of financial flows due to personal, ideological or other reasons. From an economic perspective, this situation may be labeled as the dominance of non-rational actors and/or the dominance of political over economic concerns. In this case too, financial flows may lose their role as a constraint on policymakers. Therefore, the trajectory of the relations may be investigated without giving much attention to developments in financial flows. However, even an actor who may ignore some economic imperatives in the short run and medium run may be forced to change their attitude if the difficulties stemming from possible changes in financial flows cause severe economic and social hardships that also may endanger the political survival of the actor. Given the fact that in the medium run, important elections are approaching in Turkey, we believe that under current conditions, Turkish policy makers cannot sustain a long-lasting conflict scenario.[24]

Overall, as Table 12.3 demonstrates, financial flows would be less relevant in the case of both the dominance of non-rational actors and the long-lasting existential problems in Europe. Under normal circumstances (i.e., assuming the existence of a viable, functioning EU project and rational actors from an economic perspective), EU–Turkey relations can be expected to evolve into either convergence or cooperation due to the possibly high cost of conflict in the world of very high financial dependence on global markets.

CONCLUSION

Financial flows, which may influence an economy through many different channels, have gradually reached unprecedented levels in the Turkish economy. As discussed in this chapter, the main macroeconomic variables have been very sensitive to financial flows in Turkey. Furthermore, the Turkish private sector has accumulated an enormous amount of liabilities denominated in foreign currencies. A positive high net financial account balance is required for covering the liabilities and not causing a huge slowdown in the economy (given relatively high current account deficits).[25] Although the Turkish central bank has accumulated some foreign exchange reserves, it may not possess enough relative to accumulated liabilities in the case of large changes in global liquidity conditions. Financial flows have been very volatile and affected by many internal and external forces. As a result, the Turkish economy is very vulnerable to changes in the direction of financial flows. In the past, the integration process between Turkey and Europe might have had some impacts on the increasing role of financial flows in Turkey. Different future paths in EU–Turkey relations can have some significant implications for the directions and the size of financial flows. Especially in the case of increasing conflict between the EU and Turkey, when global liquidity evaporates, financial flows to Turkey may slow down more than those of other developing countries. Given the vulnerability of the Turkish economy to financial reversals, in the presence of rational actors this trend may increase the leverage of Europe over Turkey and force Turkish policymakers to resort to the cooperation option. However, if serious, prolonged social and economic problems of the EU continue to exist in the near/medium-term future, the EU may become relatively less relevant for financial flows to Turkey. As a result, Turkish policymakers may not be constrained by the threat of financial flows. Apart from the case where the EU project is in serious, long-lasting trouble, EU–Turkey relations are expected to take the form of cooperation/convergence. If Turkish policymakers implement policies to decrease the vulnerability of the Turkish economy to flows, Turkey may have more room to maneuver in the negotiation process.

NOTES

*   This chapter is a part of the FEUTURE project funded by the European Union's Horizon 2020 research and innovation program under Grant Agreement No. 692976. I am very grateful to Semih Akçomak, Gerald Epstein, Erkan Erdil, Mariam Majd and Oktar Türel for their very helpful comments and suggestions. All remaining errors are mine.

1.   Other flows consist of the transactions of central banks, general government, banks, and other sectors (non-financial private sector) in the forms of loans, trade credits, currency, and deposits.

2.   The acquisition of financial assets by domestic players increases the accumulated foreign assets of a country. This implies a capital outflow from the country too. The acquisition of domestic financial assets by foreigners means an increase in the accumulated liabilities of the country, which is equivalent to a hike in foreign financial flows into the country.

3.   Therefore, the balance of payments data before 1984 include only FDI inflows and other (mainly official) transactions. No FDI outflows were recorded till 1987. Other investment outflows data start from 1977. But till 1984, the composition of other investments was not reported. The first portfolio inflows (outflows) registration in the BOP account took place in 1986 (1987).

4.   The years 2009, 2010, 2011, 2012, and 2013 in particular were exceptional years for the outflows. Turkish citizens seem to have brought some of their wealth back to the country in these years. In the BOP Statistics this appears as a negative financial outflows record (the sale of foreign assets by the residents). Other outflows and portfolio outflows were either negative or very small most of the time in these years. As a result, although FDI by Turkish residents was positive in these years, net financial outflows were negative (or very small) during the period. This episode may require a more detailed investigation.

5.   When one considers financial outflows relative to GDP, this picture does not change much. In this vein, the average amounts of financial outflows was 0.31, 0.98, 1.29 and 0.54 percent of GDP in the periods of 1977–89, 1990–99, 2000–09 and 2010–16 respectively (CBRT BOP Statistics and World Bank Development Indicators).

6.   The increase in the absolute size of financial inflows has been accompanied by a gradual increase in the relative importance of financial inflows as well. The average amounts of financial inflows were 1.45 and 2.59 percent of GDP in the periods 1975–89 and 1990–90 respectively. This figure considerably increased and reached 4.59 and 5.25 percent of GDP in the periods 2000–09 and 2010–16 respectively (CBRT BOP Statistics and World Bank World Development Indicators).

7.   Turkish data on the origins of FDI to Turkey and the destination of Turkish FDI start from 2002.

8.   In the data set, Iran, Israel, Bahrain, Qatar, Kuwait, Saudi Arabia, Azerbaijan, Georgia, Lebanon, Syria, and Jordan are considered as Near and Middle East countries. In the recent years, in this group of countries, Azerbaijan and Qatar have been distinct in terms of their contribution to the total FDI. For example, Azerbaijan is solely responsible for 8.1, 10.2, 6.9, and 9.45 percent of the total FDI in Turkey in the years 2013, 2014,

2015, and 2016 respectively (CBRT BOP Statistics). Furthermore, although the share of Qatar is very erratic, it is responsible for 5.4 percent of the total in 2016 (CBRT BOP Statistics).

9. Indeed, on a yearly base, the absolute amounts of total net financial flows broke a record with £72 billion in 2013. When one considers financial flows relative to Turkish GDP, this record was broken, with 8.5 percent of GDP in 2005.

10. There has been a slowdown in financial flows to Turkish economy in the last couple of years due to mainly global cycles and domestic and regional problems. We need to wait for a while to see if Turkey entered into a new period of slow financial flows.

11. For a different exposition purpose, this mechanism can be also explained as part of the exchange rate channel. Changes in exchange rates influence balance sheets. And, improvements/deteriorations of balance sheets alter credit capacity or/and eligibility of firms in the economy. We mention the balance sheet mechanism in the exchange rate channel within the broad asset prices channel as well.

12. TCMA (2017), *Turkish Capital Markets*, accessed July 20, 2018 at https://www.tspb.org.tr/wp-content/uploads/2015/07/Turkish-Capital-Markets-2017-07-ENG.pdf.

13. Changes in exchange rates can also influence expectations significantly. However, here, a separate expectation link for the exchange rate channel is not investigated. The discussions on the components of credit and asset price channels indirectly include expectations as well.

14. Cömert (2013) explores subjective and objective balance sheet constraints in detail.

15. The importance of exchange rates for the trade balance has been a contested topic for a long time. There has not been a consensus on the magnitude and even on the sign of the impacts. However, a long period of a significant depreciation/appreciation of a currency can sooner or later impact on the trade.

16. Since financial flows may exert a great influence on GDP growth, the flows can significantly affect employment too.

17. The literature is full of studies praising the benefits of FDI. Although FDI may have direct and indirect contributions to an economy, in some cases, especially huge profit transfers of foreign firms, it can be a source of drainage from the economy. In this vein, primary income transfers from Turkey regarding FDI upsurged from about $10 billion in the period 2002–09 to $18 billion in the period 2010–16. Therefore, there is a need for a careful investigation of the impacts of the profit transfers by foreign investors from Turkey.

18. CBRT allowed the banking system to keep some part of their required reserve obligations in the form of foreign currency and gold. This mechanism is known as the reserve option mechanism (ROM).

19. Some may argue that the performance of the Turkish economy during the recent crisis would be an indication of an increasing resilience of the economy to the shocks related to the increasing financial integration. However, this would be a misleading observation. It is apparent from Figure 12.1 that the magnitude of the financial shock that hit the Turkish economy during the recent crisis would not be considered very high relative to the shocks of the 1994 and 2001. Net financial flows were –2.5 percent and –7.5 percent of GDP in 1994 and 2001 respectively; it was only 1.64 percent in 2009.

20. Indeed, according to many researchers, the VIX, an index considered a proxy for investors' risk appetite, is very decisive in affecting the direction of financial flows (Rey, 2015).

21. The former head of the CBRT and his co-authors (Başçı et al. 2008) explicitly make the following observations about the impacts of the EU–Turkey integration process: "The progress in financial integration, as well as in the European Union (EU) accession process, emerges as the major cause of changing dynamics of monetary transmission" and "the EU convergence process not only provides an additional anchor to shape expectations, but also bears fruit by attracting more long-term capital to the economy" (p. 375). Furthermore, they state that "expectations regarding Turkey's accession to the

EU attracted sizeable portfolio and FDI flows to Turkey, which created an appreciation pressure on the local currency" (p. 485).

22. From a game-theoretical point of view, each decision of cooperation, convergence, and conflict will lead to different outcomes in terms of financial flows, which will lead to different outcomes for the whole economy. In our set-up, at time t, a rational actor formulating policies about the future of EU–Turkey relations is supposed to make decisions by comparing the impact of that decision on possible final outcomes.

23. Türel (2005) made a similar categorization in his game-theoretical framework. Different dimensions of these scenarios can be found in many online papers published as part of the FEUTURE project at http://www.feuture.eu/.

24. When this sentence was written, the presidential election had not yet taken place. On June 24, 2018, the Turkish presidential election was held. Although the ruling party lost its majority in the parliament, Erdogan won the election, granting him another five years with extensive new powers. Since, under normal conditions, local elections will be held in March 2019 and many economic indicators such as exchange rates directly related to financial flows, have deteriorated significantly, I believe that overall assessment of the chapter is still valid even after the presidential election.

25. Turkey can easily solve its current account deficit problem if policymakers are ready to accept a very low or negative growth rate. Imported goods are necessary for meeting the requirements of the growing economy that depends on high volumes of intermediate goods. If the economy grows very slowly, lower demand will automatically curb imports. However, politically, this may not be a desirable option.

REFERENCES

Akyüz, Y. and K. Boratav (2003), "The making of the Turkish financial crisis," *World Development*, **31**(9), 1549–66.

Başçı, E., Ö. Özel and Ç. Sarıkaya (2008), "The monetary transmission mechanism in Turkey: New developments," *BIS Working Paper No. 35*.

Benlialper, A. and H. Cömert (2015), "Implicit asymmetric exchange rate peg under inflation targeting regimes: The case of Turkey," *Cambridge Journal of Economics*, **40**(6), 1553–80.

Benlialper, A., H. Cömert and G. Düzçay (2016), "2002 Sonrasi Türkiye Ekonomisinin Performansi: Karsilastirmali Bir Analiz" [Post-2002 performance of Turkey's economy: A comparative analysis], *METU Studies in Development*, **43**(1), 65–110.

Borio, C. and P. Disyatat (2011), "Global imbalances and the financial crisis: Link or no link?," *BIS Working Papers, No. 346*.

Calvo, G.A. and C.A. Végh (1994), "Inflation stabilization and nominal anchors," *Contemporary Economic Policy*, **12**(2), 35–45.

Cömert, H. (2013), *Central Banks and Financial Markets: The Declining Power of US Monetary Policy*, Cheltenham, UK and Northampton, MA, USA: Edward Elgar Publishing.

Cömert, H. and G. Düzçay (2015), "Understanding developments in current accounts and financial flows in light of discussions on global imbalances and recent crises," *Ekonomik Yaklasim*, **26**(96), 59–90.

Cömert, H. and E. Yeldan (2018), "A tale of three crises made in Turkey: 1994, 2001 and 2008–09," in G. Yalman, T. Marois and A.R. Güngen (eds), *The Political Economy of Financial Transformation in Turkey*, London: Routledge, Forthcoming.

Eichengreen, B. and R. Hausmann (1999), "Exchange rates and financial fragility," *NBER Working Paper, No. 7418*.

Eichengreen, B., R. Hausmann and U. Panizza (2003), "The pain of original sin," in R. Hausmann and B. Eichengreen (eds), *Other People's Money: Debt Denomination and Financial Instability in Emerging Market Economies*, Chicago, IL: University of Chicago Press.

Epstein, G.A. (ed.) (2005), *Financialization and the World Economy*, Cheltenham, UK and Northampton, MA, USA: Edward Elgar Publishing.

Igan, D. and Z. Tan (2017), "Capital inflows, credit growth, and financial systems," *Emerging Markets Finance and Trade*, **53**(2), 2649–71.

Krugman, P. (1999), "Balance sheets, the transfer problem, and financial crises," *International Tax and Public Finance*, **6**(4), 459–72.

Mehrling, P. (2012), "The inherent hierarchy of money," paper prepared for Duncan Foley festschrift volume, and conference April, 20–21, 2012, accessed November 16, 2014 at http://ieor.columbia.edu/files/seasdepts/industrial-engineering-operations-research/pdffiles/Mehrling_P_FESeminar_Sp12-02.pdf.

Öniş, Z. and C. Bakır (2007), "Turkey's political economy in the age of financial globalization: The significance of the EU anchor," *South European Society and Politics*, **12**(2), 147–64.

Özatay, F. (2009), *Finansal Krizler ve Türkiye* [Financial Crisis and Turkey], Istanbul: Doğan Kitap.

Rey, H. (2015), "Dilemma not trilemma: The global financial cycle and monetary policy independence," *NBER Working Papers, No. 21162*.

Türel, O. (2005), "Oyunlar Teorisi Çerçevesinde Türkiye-AB İlişkilerine Bakış" [Game theory framework of the EU–Turkey relations overview], *Mülkiye Dergisi*, **29**(248), 3–21.

Index

Printed and bound by CPI Group (UK) Ltd, Croydon, CR0 4YY

23/04/2025

14660986-0005